U.S. SPECIAL OPERATIONS FORCES

U.S. SPECIAL OPERATIONS FORCES

Benjamin F. Schemmer
Editor-in-Chief

Colonel John T. Carney, Jr., USAF (Ret)
Managing Editor

SPECIAL OPERATIONS WARRIOR FOUNDATION
HUGH LAUTER LEVIN ASSOCIATES, INC.

The Special Operations Warrior Foundation

The Special Operations Warrior Foundation (SOWF) began in 1980 as the Col. Arthur D. "Bull" Simons Scholarship Fund to provide college educations for the seventeen children surviving the nine men killed or incapacitated at Desert One, the Iranian hostage rescue attempt. It was named in honor of the legendary Army Green Beret, Bull Simons, who repeatedly risked his life on rescue missions.

Following creation of the United States Special Operations Command, and as casualties mounted from actions such as Operations "Urgent Fury" (Grenada), "Just Cause" (Panama), "Desert Storm" (Kuwait and Iraq), and "Restore Hope" (Somalia), the Bull Simons Fund gradually expanded its outreach program to encompass all Special Operations Forces. Thus, in 1995 the Family Liaison Action Group (established to support the families of the fifty-three Iranian hostages) and the Spectre (Air Force gunship) Association Scholarship Fund merged to form the Special Operations Warrior Foundation. In 1998 the Foundation extended the scholarship and financial aid counseling to also include training fatalities since the inception of the Foundation in 1980. This action immediately added 205 children who were now eligible for college funding. The Foundation mission is devoted to providing a college education to every child who has lost a parent while serving in the Special Operations Command during an operational or training mission. The Foundation is currently committed to providing scholarship grants to more than 400 children. These children survive over 380 Special Operations personnel who gave their lives in patriotic service to their country. Since 1980, the Warrior Foundation has provided $675,576 in grants and financial aid counseling. To date, forty-six children of fallen special operations warriors have graduated from college. Children from all military services have received or have been offered Warrior Foundation scholarships, including: 223 Army, 131 Air Force, twenty-six Navy and three from the Marine Corps. The Warrior Foundation is a 501 (c) (3) tax-exempt non-profit organization.

The Special Operations Warrior Foundation
2909 West Bay-To-Bay Drive, Suite 404
Tampa, Florida 33690
http://www.specialops.org/
e-mail: warrior@specialops.org

Published by Hugh Lauter Levin Associates, Inc.
© 2003 Special Operations Warrior Foundation

Design: Lori S. Malkin
Project Editor: James O. Muschett

ISBN 0-88363-105-9
Printed in Hong Kong
Distributed by Publishers Group West
http://www.HLLA.com

Contents

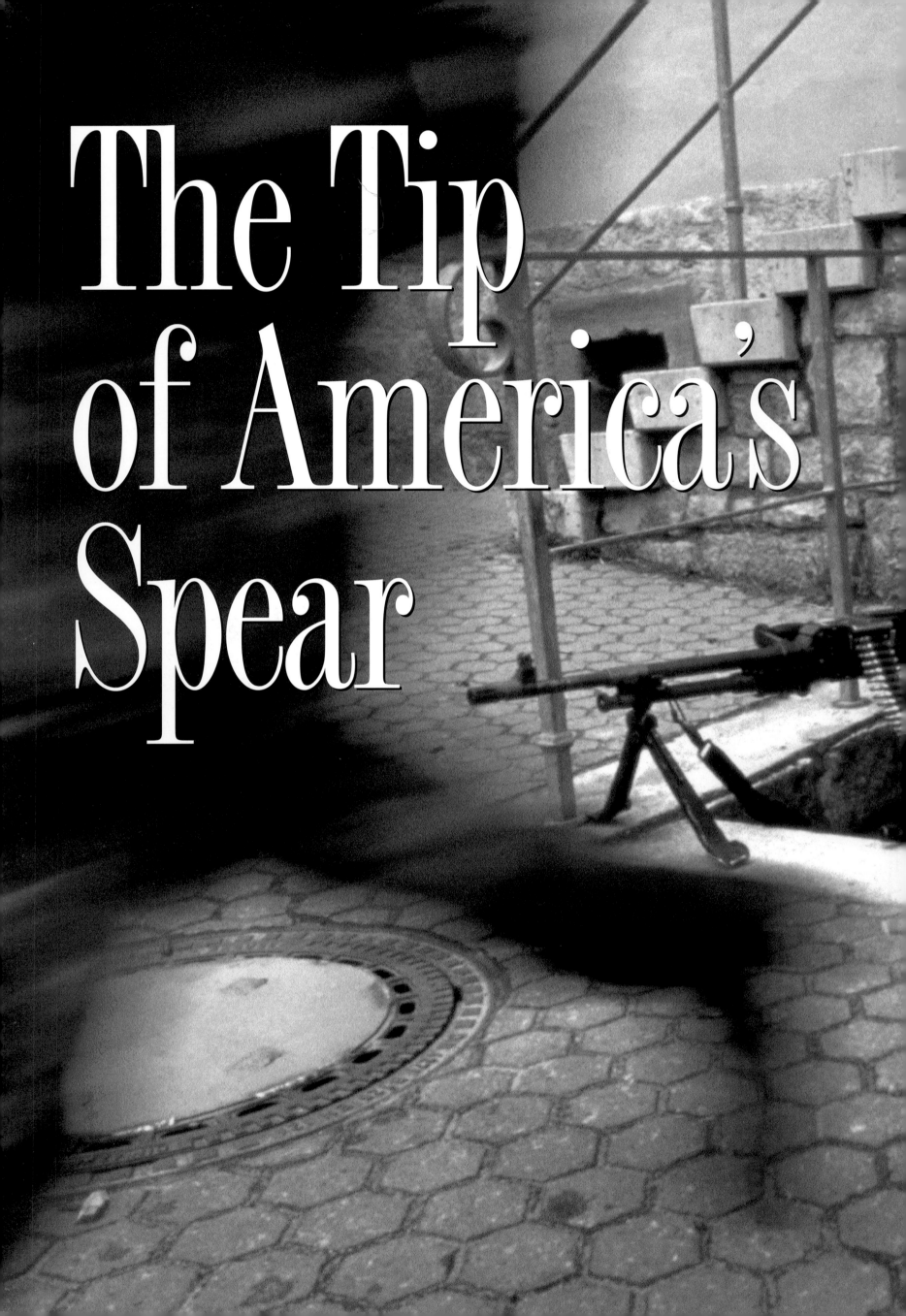

The Tip
of America's
Spear

The Tip of America's Spear

General Peter J. Schoomaker, USA (Ret)

America has the most capable special operations forces in the world, but they are a miniscule component of the United States military establishment—fewer than three-and-one-half percent of all the men and women who wear this country's uniform, and funded with less than two of every hundred dollars this nation spends on its defense. But their contributions to our national safety and to the security of our allies and oppressed peoples everywhere far outweigh their small numbers and budget.

In the short sixteen years that the U.S. Special Operations Command has existed, its forces have become the instrument of choice for U.S. ambassadors and our regional or war-fighting commanders worldwide. These regionally-oriented, language-trained, culturally-sensitive units have proven the ideal solution for crisis avoidance and crisis management on countless occasions; indeed, they have played key roles in the 97 percent of the forty-six contingencies in which U.S. military force has had to be used abroad since the Vietnam War, and they have helped the nation avoid the use of force on many more occasions.

This book details an inspiring success story, the evolution and revitalization of America's now famous but for once unknown, and continually underappreciated, underfunded, and undermanned Special Operations Forces—often just called "SOF," the tip of America's spear.

Having served in and commanded both conventional military and special operations units, I am proud to introduce to you the "Quiet Professionals"—SOF members who conducted the 1980 Desert One mission trying to rescue hostages from our embassy in Iran; who led the 1983

Above: Army Special Forces personnel jump into a river from an MH-533 Pave Low III helicopter of the 20th Special Operations Squadron during a joint Army-Air Force exercise conducted by the U.S. Special Operations Command. (U.S. Special Operations Command)

Pages 6–7: Rangers from the 3rd Ranger Battalion, 75th Ranger Regiment, stationed at Ft. Benning, Georgia, conduct assault training as an M-240G machine gun team provides security while the assault element moves across the street to clear buildings in an urban environment exercise conducted in the Federal Republic of Germany. (Russ Bryant)

Opposite: U.S. Navy SEALs participate in the non-combatant evacuation exercise Desert Rescue IX. Desert Rescue is the premiere Search And Rescue (SAR) training exercise involving Army, Navy, Air Force, and Marine personnel. It is conducted at the ranges of Fallon Naval Air Station, Nevada. (U.S. Special Operations Command)

assault on Grenada to rescue six hundred medical students in peril there; who from 1981 to 1994 worked patiently with their counterparts in El Salvador to forge peace from a brutal civil war; who were sent to the Mediterranean in 1985 trying to resolve the TWA 847 and *Achille Lauro* hijackings; who led the invasion that restored democracy to Panama in 1989; who played key but little-known roles in winning the 1991 Persian Gulf War that liberated Kuwait and decimated Iraq's Republican Guard; whose humanitarian relief work saved the lives of thousands of Kurd refugees whom Saddam Hussein had oppressed and evicted from northern Iraq and who were fleeing in harsh weather and mountainous terrain to Turkey; who fought valiantly in Mogadishu in 1993 to wrest control of Somalia from brutal tribal factions; who liberated Haiti from decades of dictatorship in 1995; whose 1996, 1997, and 1998 noncombatant evacuation operations in Liberia, Albania, Sierra Leone, the Congo, and again in Liberia rescued thousands of Americans and third-country nationals from peril during civil wars there; who fought behind the scenes to help stop ethnic cleansing in the Balkans in 1998 and 1989; and whose men in late 2001 led "the first cavalry charge of the twenty-first century" in Afghanistan (while its women sometimes navigated the side-firing AC-130 gun ships) to begin winning what this volume's managing editor, retired Air Force Colonel John T. Carney, Jr., has rightfully labeled "America's First Special Operations War." Interspersed with these major

Top: *A photographic portrait of valor and gritty determination is depicted on the face of this SEAL during an operation in the Mekong Delta in 1967. (Robert Bruce)*

Above: *75th Rangers perform a hut by hut search of a Vietnamese village in 1968. (U.S. Army Military History Institute)*

Opposite, bottom: *A SEAL team works through an urban assault/counterterrorist training exercise. The intense training and team building methods of Naval Special Warfare Command are an absolute necessity in creating the cohesive operational units that carry out real-world missions. (U.S. Special Operations Command)*

events were smaller, clandestine, and often highly successful special operations, some details of which remain classified today.

This, above all, is a story of dramatic human dimensions about brave and consummately professional warriors who serve in harm's way every day in a largely unsung manner all over the globe, so ubiquitous that we now refer to them as America's "global scouts."

SOF work involves the highest operational tempos of any element within America's military establishment, and its members have paid a disproportionate price in casualties compared to their relatively few numbers. Theirs is dangerous work: since the 1980 Desert One rescue attempt, our special operations forces have suffered over nineteen times the combat fatality rate of America's conventional forces, such as the Marines and the Army's infantry, armor, and artillery units, Air Force fighter and bomber crews, and regular Navy seamen. Thirty-nine percent of all the 274 men killed in action in seven major contingencies have been special operators. In those intervening twenty-three years, special operations men have lost their lives on real world missions in twenty-four countries, and another 232 men have died while training for those missions.

Yet there are no special survivors' benefits for their spouses or children, which is why I want to thank the publishers of this work and our chapter authors for donating royalties from this book to the Special Operations Warrior Foundation, a nonprofit body that provides full college scholarships, based on need, to *all* surviving children of *all* special operators who have given their lives, or who may lose them, on real world missions or while training for them. As of 2003, the Warrior Foundation has paid for or offered such scholarships to almost 300 children. Those scholarships cover not just tuition, room, board, and books, but travel and living expenses where necessary—and they are all grants, not loans.

Because this book describes so many operations of so many elite units over such a long span of time, let me offer a thumbnail perspective of what "special operations" entail. One of the great father figures of special operations, retired Army Lieutenant General Samuel V. Wilson, one of World War II's Merrill's Marauders, put it best when he once said, "Special Operations is a three-step dance: Get there; get it done, and get back!"

Special operations encompasses every facet of unconventional warfare, usually waged by clandestine forces that operate in small groups against high-risk, high-payoff targets deep in hostile areas. These forces handle "direct action" counterterrorist missions (offensive operations) abroad, principally handled by the Army and Navy "special mission units" usually working with a small Air Force Special Tactics team composed of combat controllers skilled in airfield seizures and controlling air strikes and whose pararescuemen (or PJs, for parajumpers) care for "precious cargo," rescued hostages or wounded and injured fellow special operators.

Special operations units also work with other federal agencies on antiterrorist measures (defensive operations) within the United States and overseas; lead the way in the war on drugs in foreign countries; work to contain the spread of weapons of mass destruction; and wage psychological warfare. Since the Vietnam War, such units have led most

Above: *After fast roping onto the Merchant Marine Vessel PFC Obergon, US Navy SEALs provide cover for each other during a search and seizure exercise. The SEAL team is training with U.S. Air Force Special Operations MH-53 Pave Low helicopters in the Adriatic Sea. (U.S. Special Operations Command)*

A special operator from the Army's 19th Special Forces Group provides small arms training to Afghan soldiers from the Northern Alliance during operation Enduring Freedom. (U.S. Special Operations Command)

forced-entry military operations and have usually been the first ones deployed to quell transnational unrest in contingencies like Haiti, Panama, the Balkans, and Afghanistan.

Special Forces are Army units, long known as the Green Berets, built around 12-man A-teams in seven groups. Each group is oriented to a different region of the world with each group authorized to have fifty-four teams, but all of which fall short of that goal because so few aspirants pass the stringent Special Forces screening process and qualification courses. Most of the teams who liberated Afghanistan within forty-nine days of their first insertions in October of 2001 working with regional warlords to destroy the Al-Qaeda terrorist network and oust the oppressive Taliban regime came from the 5th Special Forces Group at Fort Campbell, Kentucky, plus some from the 3rd Special Forces Group out of Fort Bragg, North Carolina, which is oriented to Africa. The teams are versed in local cultures around the world, functionally fluent in at

U.S. Army soldiers of the 5th Special Forces Group based at Fort Campbell, Kentucky, stand by on the flight deck of the nuclear-powered aircraft carrier USS George Washington (CVN 73) during a fleet exercise. (U.S. Special Operations Command)

Opposite: US Air Force personnel from the 320th Special Tactics Squadron (STS), Kadena Air Base, Japan, practice rope ladder exfiltration with a US Air Force 31st Special Operations Squadron (SOS) MH-53J Pave Low helicopter at Taegu Air Base, Republic of Korea, during Exercise Foal Eagle 2000. (U.S. Special Operations Command)

An Army Special Forces Zodiac raft moves up a river during a Jaguar Bite joint Army-Air Force exercise conducted by the U.S. Special Operations Command at Pope Air Force Base, North Carolina. (U.S. Special Operations Command)

Two members from the 320th Special Tactics Squadron leave the landing zone at night on a small motorcycle. They provided security during an extraction mission of simulated enemy deserters. The mission was part of Exercise Foal Eagle at Taegu Air Base, South Korea. This photograph was taken with night vision equipment. (U.S. Special Operations Command)

least one of the foreign languages spoken there, and able to recruit, train, and supply indigenous personnel or military units to operate more effectively on their own or to synchronize their work with either conventional U.S. forces or U.S. Special Operations Forces.

U.S. Special Operations Forces also include: the Army's 75th Ranger Regiment, its 160th Special Operations Aviation Regiment, two

special operations signal battalions, and psychological warfare and civil affairs units.

Special Tactics units are made up of small Air Force teams of combat controllers who are experts in airfield seizure and the control of air strikes in denied areas, pararescuemen, and combat trauma medics and rescue specialists who care for "precious cargo," rescued hostages or wounded members of the special operations teams they support.

Air Force special operations units also include the 16th Special Operations Wing (known as Air Commandos) with its fixed-wing MC-130E and MC-130H Combat Talons, AC-130H and AC-130U side-firing gun ships, and MC-130P Combat Shadow refueling aircraft. The Air Force also uses long-range MH-53J/M Pave Low helicopters for deep penetrations into or rescues in denied territory, with two groups and similar squadrons abroad, as well as EC-130E/J Commando Solo aircraft in the National Guard for psychological warfare broadcasts and electronic jamming.

The Navy's Special Warfare Command has eight Sea-Air-Land (SEAL) teams, two special boat and patrol craft squadrons, and several SEAL delivery units for clandestine insertions.

I was privileged to lead some and to work with virtually all of these units throughout my active duty military service; I have continued to work with them in one fashion or another since I "retired" in 2000; and I am

A close up view of US Air Force Staff Sergeant Brian Gilliland from the Air Force Special Operations Command, as he waits to compete in the combat weapons competition at Camp Bullis, Texas, during Exercise Defender Challenge 2000. SSgt Gilliland is armed with the 5.56mm M16A2 assault rifle. (U.S. Special Operations Command)

Opposite: *Rangers from the 1st Ranger Battalion, 75th Ranger Regiment, stationed at Hunter Army Airfield, Savannah, Georgia, initiate a training exercise raid with the 84-millimeter Carl Gustav as it fires a HEAT (high explosive anti-tank) round at bunkers on an objective. The Carl Gustav replaced the once popular 90-millimeter recoilless rifle. (Russ Bryant)*

U.S. Navy Reserve Special Warfare Unit in Suisun Bay, Carguinez Straits, California, 23 August 1991 (Richard Benne, Arms Communications)

blessed to still work with them today, helping to arrange full college scholarships for the children whom these brave warriors have left behind. I am deeply honored to have served with so many of their fathers, men who often live in official anonymity and who epitomize the best of America.

There are three little known facts about the near 48,000 men and women who serve in U.S. special operations forces. First, whereas they were viewed with near disdain by the military hierarchy in the 1970s and early 1980s, they have become among the most sought-after units in the entire U.S. military establishment. Of thirty-one so-called "low-density, high-demand" units that were in such short supply in 1999 that requests to deploy or engage them far outstripped their numbers or availability, eighteen—58 percent—were from our Special Operations Forces. That force-resource mismatch is only now beginning to be corrected.

Second, SOF operational tempos have increased dramatically since the 1991 Persian Gulf War. In the five years following Desert Storm, SOF personnel deployments rose 127 percent, and the number of SOF operations increased 57 percent (while the SOF budget shrank by more than 6 percent in real spending power). As theater commanders grew to better understand SOF capabilities, special operations units became their force of choice: between 1993 and 1999, the number of SOF personnel deployed away from their home stations grew by 253 percent, from 2,036 to 5,141 personnel in any given week—more than 10 percent of all special operations soldiers, sailors, and airmen. In 2001–2002, SOF deployed to 146 countries, handled eleven crisis response operations, conducted 132 joint or combined training exercises in fifty-nine countries,

Opposite: The U.S. Army Sniper School produces the most lethal special operations snipers in the military. Camouflage techniques are taught, and snipers design their own Ghillie suits to disguise their presence in a specific environment. Ghillie suits were developed by Scottish game wardens during the 19th century to catch poachers. (Russ Bryant)

Petty Officer 2nd Class Jeremy Moore (right) with Helicopter Anti-Submarine Squadron 5 (HS5), Jacksonville, Florida, is moved to an HH-60H by Navy SEALs during a survivor retraction exercise in Desert Rescue IX at the ranges of Fallon Naval Air Station, Nevada. (U.S. Special Operations Command)

undertook 137 counterdrug operations in twenty-three countries, and conducted humanitarian demining operations in nineteen countries. By their ubiquitous presence, these versatile, agile forces facilitate U.S. access to most parts of the world and can quickly transition to combat operations and spearhead decisive engagements.

A third little-known fact about America's special operators is that, aside from their legendary, highly honed, unique combat skills for behind-the-lines, clandestine, "direct action" and hostage rescue missions, these men (and now, increasingly, women) offer some of the most important cultural and humanitarian skills found in any uniformed force in the world. About 40 percent of all Navy SEALs and one-fourth of all Army Special Forces personnel, for instance, are medically trained to the skill levels of an emergency medical technician or physician's assistant. They are able to treat trauma wounds, deliver babies, even perform emergency surgeries. *All* Army Special Forces members speak a foreign language, some of them the toughest in the world to learn. They include Urdu, Persian Farsi, Arabic, Russian, Czech, Polish, Korean, Thai, Vietnamese, Indonesian, Tagalog, and Haitian Creole. In Desert Shield and Desert Storm, Arabic-speaking teams from Army Special Forces were assigned at brigade and battalion level to 109 units for the campaign against the Iraqi forces that had invaded Kuwait in August of 1990. General H. Norman Schwarzkopf later called them "the glue that held the coalition together."

An added "unknown" about America's special operations forces is that, overcommitted as they are, even by the assessment of the Pentagon's Joint Staff, to whom special operations forces were once almost pariahs, SOF workloads are expanding dramatically. That became particularly evident with the announcement by Defense Secretary Donald Rumsfeld in early January of 2002 emphasizing much wider responsibilities for U.S. Special Operations Command as a "supported" command, not just a "supporting" command, in the war on terrorism.

It is increasingly clear that America's global challenges require options that fall somewhere between diplomatic initiatives alone and the overt use of large conventional forces. SOF allows decision makers flexibility in tailoring responses to a wide range of political, humanitarian, and military crises. Often, these small, regionally oriented teams are the best choice for action when a rapid response or a surgically precise, focused use of force is called for, and they do not entail the risk of escalation normally associated with the use of larger, more visible conventional forces. Moreover, SOF units are relatively self-sufficient, and their small footprint limits the scope of American involvement. Used early enough, they can prevent conflict, buy time, and conserve resources; yet they can perform a wide array of pre-hostility missions—signaling determination, demonstrating support to allies, gathering intelligence, or beginning the complex process of positioning U.S. forces for combat. Increasingly, SOF has become the instrument of choice in situations where asymmetric threats and "wild card" scenarios are America's biggest concern. If larger forces must be committed, SOF's economy of force operations generate strategic advantages disproportionate to the resources they represent. They can locate, seize, or destroy strategic targets; test enemy defenses; disorganize, disrupt, and demoralize troops and divert important resources, emphasizing the indirect methods of operations rather than direct confrontation. Such missions, whether prosecuted independently or in concert with conventional units, provide a *unique* force multiplier.

Four SOF truths will earmark the future of U.S. Special Operations Command, as they have in the past: "humans are more important than hardware"; "quality is better than quantity"; special operations forces cannot be mass produced; and they cannot be created after emergencies occur. In the volatile times ahead, SOF must train for certainty but educate for uncertainty, and its operators must continue to be masters of high tech, low tech, and no tech to provide America with expanded options tailored to unique tasks.

U.S. Army's Staff Sergeant Steve Love, 10th Special Forces Group (Airborne), observes a Croatian student checking for land mines using a metal detector during a practical exercise near Mostar, as part of Operation Joint Endeavor. (U.S. Special Operations Command)

Opposite, bottom left: *Soldiers of the 1st Infantry Battalion Senegal Army attend a training class on raid techniques during Operation Focus Relief II (OFR II), in Thies, Senegal. OFR II provides training on new equipment and fighting tactics by U.S. Army Special Forces to the Senegal army to improve their proficiency level for peace enforcement in Sierra Leone. (U.S. Special Operations Command)*

Opposite, bottom right: *As seen in the green glow of a night scope, members of the 16th Special Operations Wing (SOW) off-load cargo and personnel at a forward deployed location during a nighttime operational mission. The 16th SOW is deployed to the Joint Special Operations Aviation Component South in a classified location in support of Operation Enduring Freedom. (U.S. Air Force)*

21

1670–1941

1670-1941
Genesis and Unguided Growth

Colonel John M. Collins, USA (Ret)

"*Tell me where you were born, and
who your father and mother were.*"

"*Never was born; never had no
father nor mother, nor nothin'.*"

I was raised by a speculator . . ."

—HARRIET BEECHER STOWE,
UNCLE TOM'S CABIN, CHAPTER 20, "TOPSY"

Special Operations Forces (SOF) are special because they are organized, equipped, and trained to perform enduring roles and functions as well as transitory missions that others could not duplicate. Their unique capabilities open strategic, operational, and tactical opportunities limited mainly by imagination.

Colonial officials and their U.S. successors atop the politico-military totem pole unfortunately perceived such possibilities dimly and employed Special Operations Forces sparingly for the first 270 years. Raids and ambushes predominated. A sneaky-Pete-style one-man submarine briefly saw action during the American Revolution and an enterprising balloonist began to collect otherwise unobtainable intelligence for Union troops when the Civil War was barely one week old, but land power consistently occupied center stage.

Above: *The Lewis and Clark expedition of 1804–06, which investigated routes and resources between the Mississippi River and the Pacific Ocean at President Thomas Jefferson's behest, concurrently conducted special reconnaissance missions that reaped many military benefits, including the disposition of Indian tribes encountered and locations for strategically sited forts. ("Meeting the Shoshone Indians," Charles M. Russell, Drummond Gallery, Coeur d'Alene, Idaho)*

Pages 22–23: *Small, self-reliant Special Operations Forces that capitalize on stealth, surprise, and audacity often accomplish military missions that traditional troops find infeasible. Rogers' versatile Rangers, shown here in a whaleboat en route to their epic victory over Abenaki enemies at Saint François during the French and Indian War, serve as role models for modern SOF warriors. ("Rogers' Rangers," Mort Künstler)*

Opposite: *Guerrilla warfare, a SOF specialty, features hit-and-run operations by armed insurgents or resistance groups against enemy armed forces. Colonial militia, commonly called "Minutemen," put principles into practice with devastating effects when they attacked British red coats between Lexington and Concord, Massachusetts, on 19 April 1775. ("The Retreat from Lexington and Concord," A. Lassell Ripley, courtesy of UnumProvident Corporation)*

25

SOF accordingly grew like *Uncle Tom's* Topsy, generally unguided from their genesis in the seventeenth century until the onset of World War II. The record during that period nevertheless is worth reviewing because it reveals how a few innovative individuals and experimental procedures paved the way for superlative Special Operations Forces that serve the United States of America extraordinarily well at this moment.

King Philip's War (1675-1676)

Twenty-first-century Rangers can trace their lineage to prototype units that first appeared about 1670 in plenty of time to play prominent roles during King Philip's War. Captain Benjamin Church, their commanding officer throughout that bloodletting, is the great-grandfather several times removed of all U.S. Special Operations Forces whose forte is direct action.

King Philip was not a king and his real name was not Philip. He was North American Indian Chief Metacom, who defended his homeland against English settlers who had been grabbing the best land since the *Mayflower* deposited Pilgrims at Plymouth Rock on 21 November 1620. "Philip," after fifty-five frustrating years, formed a federation of Pokanoket, Wampanoag, Nipmuc, Agawam, Narragansett, and other tribes that threatened to eradicate Plymouth, Massachusetts Bay, and Connecticut Colonies. Both sides repeatedly slaughtered opponents without compunction until

Bottom, left: *Wampanoag Chief Metacom (aka King Philip) in 1675 attacked encroaching Plymouth Colony, which threatened traditional Indian lifestyles. Ten percent of all combatants on both sides reportedly became casualties. Colonists recovered, but the Wampanoag tribe did not. Happy Hunting Grounds prematurely became Philip's permanent residence. (Library of Congress)*

Bottom, right: *Benjamin Church organized, trained, and commanded the original Rangers in North America, but the U.S. Army's 75th Ranger Regiment traces its lineage to revered Captain Robert Rogers, who in the 1750s set hit-and-run light infantry standards that have remained rock solid since the French and Indian War. (Library of Congress)*

English armed forces under General Josiah Winslow, with Benjamin Church as his right-hand man, wiped out the strongest Indian war camp in late spring 1676 and Philip's coalition collapsed.

Philip and a few followers retreated to Swansea (now a suburb of Fall River, Massachusetts), where the war started. Captain Church, accompanied by Indian guides and stealthy Rangers, tracked him from hideout to hideout until they finally made contact. Bam! One shot, one kill. King Philip's War was over.

The French and Indian War (1754-1763)

The French and Indian War, which was one facet of a global conflict called the Seven Years War, essentially was a winner-take-all collision between Britain and France to determine who would control Canada plus all lands east of the Mississippi River. Those priceless prizes belonged to Britain when the shooting stopped, partly because woodsman Robert Rogers and his Rangers outwitted French regulars in the wilderness.

Captain Rogers organized the first Ranger company in 1755 at Fort William Henry near the southern tip of Lake George in what now is upper New York State, then moved to nearby Fort Edward. He refined unorthodox small unit tactics that Benjamin Church had adapted from Indian opponents eight decades earlier; conducted live-fire training exercises that contemporary British officers considered a waste of ammunition;

Robert Rogers' Fifth Standing Order read, "Don't never take a chance you don't have to." Carefully-laid ambushes like the one depicted, which decimated a careless French patrol, enabled his Rangers to defeat numerically superior foes while escaping scot-free or minimizing casualties. ("Finish Him Up," James Dietz)

Unconventional warriors on both sides hired "Indian guns" as guerrillas during the French and Indian War. Automobiles made in Detroit still honor Pontiac, an Ottawa chief in French employ, who assailed but failed to capture that British-held city. James Fennimore Cooper's Leather Stocking Tales immortalized the "Last of the Mohicans," shown here. ("In the Heat of Battle," Robert Griffing, Paramount Press, Inc.)

27

Opposite: Francis Marion and his South Carolina militia, along with William Washington and the Continental Dragoons, use flaming arrows to set fire to the Motte house, occupied by British troops. Mrs. Motte is comforted as she turns away from her home's destruction. ("The Capture of Fort Motte," Mort Künstler)

Eighteenth century muzzle-loading flintlock muskets, which fired round lead balls of .50 to .60 caliber, could hit human heads at long range in the hands of skilled marksmen, but even woodsmen like Rogers' Rangers found that their heavy weight and overall length of about five feet made them hard to handle in underbrush and other ideal ambush sites. (National Park Service)

General Horatio Gates, who scorned Francis Marion's guerrillas, lost command of his army plus most of South Carolina after British General Cornwallis decisively trounced him and dispersed survivors at Camden on 16 August 1780. Better appreciation for relationships between orthodox and unorthodox military power might have preserved both. (National Park Service)

then sallied forth in brutal winter weather while less robust troops remained in bivouac. One daring raid, which covered much more than 300 miles of enemy-infested territory in about sixty days, took Iroquois pathfinders and 200 Rangers to Saint François on the south bank of the Saint Lawrence River, where they put Abenaki Indian war parties permanently out of business. Major Rogers later spearheaded the attack that overwhelmed French-held Pontchartrain (present-day Detroit).

Robert Rogers in some respects remains a role model of almost mythological proportions. Modern Rangers admire his *28 Rules of Ranging* and can recite his *19 Standing Orders*. Twenty-first-century U.S. Navy SEALs feel close kinship with Rogers's hatchet-wielding swimmers, who eight generations ago surprised and overpowered crews aboard five French ships on the Richelieu River north of Lake Champlain. SEAL Team TWO applauds that exploit in its Standing Operating Procedures. Not many, however, recall that Rogers's dedication to the British Crown made him unacceptable to George Washington's Continental Army in 1775, that Lieutenant Colonel Rogers led the Queen's Rangers during the American Revolution, that he raised the King's Rangers that brother James commanded, or that Robert died in London, not the United States.

STANDING ORDERS ROGERS RANGERS

1. Don't forget nothing.
2. Have your musket clean as a whistle, hatchet scoured, sixty rounds powder and ball, and be ready to march at a minute's warning.
3. When you're on the march, act the way you would if you was sneaking up on a deer. See the enemy first.
4. Tell the truth about what you see and what you do. There is an army depending on us for correct information. You can lie all you please when you tell other folks about the Rangers, but don't never lie to a Ranger or officer.
5. Don't never take a chance you don't have to.
6. When we're on the march we march single file, far enough apart so one shot can't go through two men.
7. If we strike swamps, or soft ground, we spread out abreast, so it's hard to track us.
8. When we march, we keep moving till dark, so as to give the enemy the least possible chance at us.
9. When we camp, half the party stays awake while the other half sleeps.
10. If we take prisoners, we keep'em separate till we have had time to examine them, so they can't cook up a story between'em.
11. Don't ever march home the same way. Take a different route so you won't be ambushed.
12. No matter whether we travel in big parties or little ones, each party has to keep a scout 20 yards ahead, 20 yards on each flank, and 20 yards in the rear so the main body can't be surprised and wiped out.
13. Every night you'll be told where to meet if surrounded by a superior force.
14. Don't sit down to eat without posting sentries.
15. Don't sleep beyond dawn. Dawn's when the French and Indians attack.
16. Don't cross a river by a regular ford.
17. If somebody's trailing you, make a circle, come back onto your own tracks, and ambush the folks that aim to ambush you.
18. Don't stand up when the enemy's coming against you. Kneel down, lie down, hide behind a tree.
19. Let the enemy come till he's almost close enough to touch, then let him have it and jump out and finish him up with your hatchet.

The American Revolution (1775-1783)

Many military actions during the American Revolution qualified as "irregular," beginning on 19 April 1775, when stealthy Minutemen behind stone walls harassed strait-laced British formations every step of the way during their trek back to Boston after battles at Lexington and Concord. A few trailblazers who conducted special operations in every sense of those words merit special mention.

Cat and Mouse in the Carolinas

British troops and Colonial partisans played cat and mouse in the Carolinas with one unique twist: who was cat and who was mouse frequently was in question. Those contests became deadly serious after British General Henry Clinton seized Charleston on 12 May 1780. Lieutenant Colonel Francis Marion escaped capture and immediately began to assemble a small partisan band of back-country boys. On-the-job training in combat against Cherokee warriors twenty years earlier prepared him well to engage in guerrilla warfare, but Continental Army General Horatio Gates scoffed at his ragtag gang.

Marion's marauders nevertheless proved their worth in August 1780, when General Charles Cornwallis gutted Gates's army at Camden, South Carolina. First, they freed 150 American prisoners en route to a

Wily South Carolinian Francis Marion, the "Swamp Fox," was a will-o-the-wisp warrior who found British redcoats whenever he wished during the Revolutionary War, but they never found him, no matter how hard they beat the bushes. He retired as a brigadier general and later served in South Carolina's Senate. (Library of Congress)

Commander in Chief General George Washington made a happy decision in October 1780 when he gave go-getter Nathanael Greene command over all colonial troops from Delaware to Georgia, because Greene melded orthodox and unorthodox warfare in bewildering ways that Horatio Gates, his predecessor, refused to consider. ("Nathaniel Greene at Guilford," Dale Gallon)

British stockade. Marion thereafter initiated hit-and-run raids between the Pee Dee and Santee Rivers, striking at times and places of his choosing. He and his men lived off the land by dispossessing Tory civilians and confiscating supplies after they overran isolated enemy outposts. They ambushed unwary enemy formations, sabotaged key facilities, severed lines of communication, kept red coats off balance, then vanished into boggy briar patches. Frustrated British dragoon Colonel Banastre Tarleton, their principal pursuer, dubbed wily Marion "The Swamp Fox," whom William Cullen Bryant later immortalized with *The Song of Marion's Men*:

> *Our band is few, but true and tried, our leader frank and bold;*
> *The British soldier trembles when Marion's name is told.*
> *Our fortress is the good greenwood; our tent the cypress tree;*
> *We know the forest round us, as seamen know the sea.*
> *We know its walls of thorny vines, its glades of reedy grass,*
> *Its safe and silent islands within the dark morass.*

Nathanael Greene, who replaced Gates in October 1780, used Marion as his primary source of intelligence, coordinated partisan operations with those of Continental troops, and employed collective capabilities to their best advantage. He and Marion led Cornwallis on see-saw chases across both Carolinas into Virginia and back again.

The Greene-Marion syndicate lost every pitched battle, but made antagonists pay heavy prices and, in that process, won the hearts and minds of most Carolinians. Brutal British tactics, which turned neutrals against the Crown, consequently made it easy for Colonial combatants to replenish losses and maintain pressure. British armed forces abandoned all interior positions by mid-1781 and departed Charleston on 14 December the following year, after which lightly supervised pacification programs prevailed. Marion's partisans disbanded soon thereafter, but they left a legacy that U.S. unconventional warfare practitioners, knowingly or not, have exploited ever since.

Newfangled Naval Warfare

U.S. Underwater Demolition Teams and SEAL successors can trace their antecedents to Sergeant Ezra Lee, who captained and crewed the first submarine ever employed in armed combat. His mission was to lay a 250-pound mine against the hull of Admiral Richard Howe's flagship HMS *Eagle*, put that sixty-four-gun behemoth on the bottom, and perhaps thereby break the crippling British naval blockade of New York Harbor on 6 September 1776.

Patriot David Bushnell conceived, built, and tested the man-powered *Turtle* at Saybrook, Connecticut, then transported his contraption to the Battery in Manhattan, where Colonial General Israel Putnam gave permission to attack. It was an unwieldy wooden craft, seven feet high and six feet wide, caulked at every seam, bound with iron bands, covered with waterproofing pitch, and lighted internally with phosphorescent fox-fire. Lee must have combined all the best attributes of champion weightlifters and contortionists, because one hand-cranked oar propelled

Pint-sized but brawny Sergeant Ezra Lee had to be in prime physical condition when he bucked strong cross currents while propelling the man-powered prototype submarine Turtle *half of the five miles across New York Harbor from the Battery to Staten Island and all the way back, submerged for much of the 10-mile total. (Courtesy of the Connecticut River Museum)*

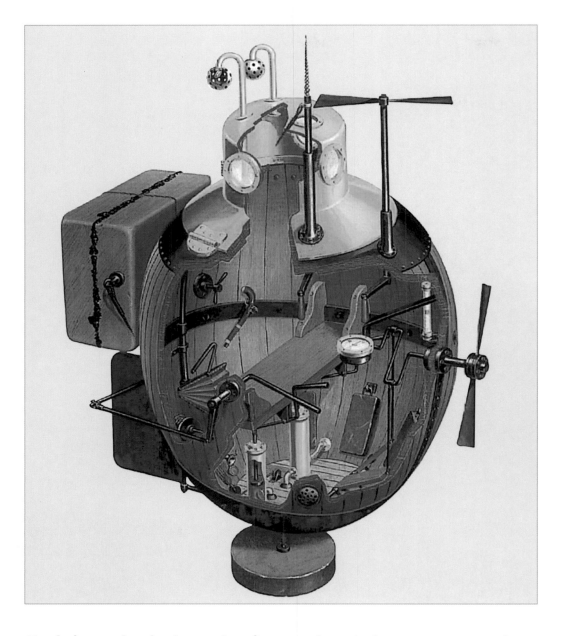

In similar daring fashion to the Turtle's failed attack on HMS Eagle in the American Revolution, the Union Navy had better results during the Civil War. The attack on CSS Albemarle by a torpedo launch was commanded by Lieutenant William B. Cushing, USN, at Plymouth, North Carolina, 27 October 1864. The torpedo boat is shown crashing over Albemarle's protective log boom to deliver its torpedo against the ironclad's hull. ("Cushings Daring and Successful Exploit," Naval Historical Center)

Turtle forward or back, another fine-tuned vertical movement up and down, while a foot pedal controlled the rudder.

A rowboat towed *Turtle* half way to *Eagle*'s anchorage at Staten Island just before midnight. Lee muscled the rest of the way against strong tides and tricky currents, submerged beneath his target, tried unsuccessfully to attach the mine, surfaced to rest and replenish air which lasted about thirty minutes, but failed again because brass plating on the keel blocked his drill. He headed home exhausted, dumped his heavy explosive near Governor's Island to pick up speed, and escaped unscathed, but not before the time-fused mine erupted with a horrendous water spout and roar. *Turtle* accordingly accomplished its basic mission, because Admiral Howe, who could not know whether rebels possessed one or several such innovative weapons, prudently moved his fleet to new locations from which it was harder to maintain a blockade.

The Civil War (1861-1865)

The Civil War spawned a swarm of new weapons, equipment, tactics, and techniques. Resourceful raiders, who diversified the purpose and scope of previously restricted repertoires, were among the most imaginative innovators. Four dissimilar cameos illustrate successful, substandard, and miscellaneous outcomes.

Engraving depicts the successful spar torpedo attack by Lieutenant William B. Cushing and his crew on the Confederate ironclad Albemarle, at Plymouth, North Carolina, 27 October 1864. ("Lieut. Cushing's Torpedo Boat Sinking the Albemarle on Roanoke River, NC," A. Stachic, Naval Historical Center)

Above and opposite, top right: *Thaddeus Lowe, well aware that who you know may outweigh what you know, enlisted support first from Union Army Commanding General George B. McClellan, then from President Abraham Lincoln. He thereby bypassed big-mouthed John LaMountain as the world's foremost military balloonist, although the latter may have been better qualified.* (National Archives)

Aerial Intelligence

Thaddeus Lowe became the forerunner of all aerial intelligence collectors in the U.S. Special Operations community when he drifted from Cincinnati, Ohio, to Unionville, South Carolina, on 20 April 1861, just eight days after secessionists bombarded Fort Sumter. That 500-mile flight afforded matchless views of Confederate bivouacs near railheads and troop trains heading north. Lowe's captors, eager to lynch or incarcerate Yankee spies, never would have released him had they known that President Lincoln would soon put him in charge of a civilian Balloon Corps.

The first American aerostat designed for military use flew from a tether early in September 1861. On the 21st of that month, at an altitude of about 1,000 feet above Arlington, Virginia, Lowe directed Federal artillery batteries against Rebel formations beyond their field of vision in Falls Church—an unparalleled feat. Secretary of War Simon Cameron immediately ordered the expeditious procurement of four more balloons.

Professor John LaMountain, at the behest of Major General Benjamin F. Butler, had already demonstrated the feasibility of intelligence collection during free flight at an altitude of 3,000 feet over Fortress Monroe. "He found the encampment of the Confederate forces [on August 13th] to be about three miles beyond Newmarket Bridge, Va.," according to *The New York Times*. "There were no traces of the rebels near Hampton. A considerable force also is encamped on the east side of the James River, some eight miles above Newport News." General George B. McClellan, who commanded the Army of the Potomac, cast his lot with tethered flight in February 1862, when rivalries between Lowe and blustering LaMountain became intolerable. Skeptics still debate the wisdom of that decision, but Lowe nevertheless registered stellar performances in Virginia during battles at Yorktown (April 1862), Fair Oaks (May–June 1862), and at Fredericksburg in April 1863, just before the collision at Chancellorsville, despite repeated attempts by Rebel gunners to shatter his gondola or burst his balloon. He concurrently introduced armed forces to aerial photography, cartography, and telegraphy, until allegations of financial impropriety prompted him to resign.

One mystified Confederate artillery commander couldn't believe it when stodgy Union generals disbanded the Balloon Corps in August 1863, well before the Civil War ended. "Even if the observers never saw anything," he mused, "they would have been worth all they cost for the annoyance and delays they caused us in trying to keep our movements out of sight."

Thaddeus Lowe. (National Archives)

Audacious Sabotage

James Andrews in April 1862 led one other civilian and twenty mufticlad military volunteers from Ohio regiments on a raid to sabotage the Western and Atlantic Railroad in Georgia. Results inspired movies that first starred Buster Keaton in *The General*, then featured Fess Parker in a remarkably accurate remake called *The Great Locomotive Chase*.

Andrews' mission was to burn major bridges, block tunnels, and uproot tracks between Atlanta and southeastern Tennessee so Confederate troops could neither reinforce nor resupply rapidly when Union General Ormsby Mitchel attacked toward Chattanooga from Huntsville, Alabama. Andrews with nineteen other raiders boarded a northbound train at Marietta early on 12 April (two more overslept), hijacked it at Big Shanty (now Kennesaw) where passengers and crew debarked for breakfast, uncoupled all but three empty boxcars behind a locomotive called *General*, and headed north. They soon severed the telegraph line that linked Atlanta with Chattanooga, then stopped at Moon's Station long enough to con gullible gandy dancers into loaning them a crowbar, which they subsequently used to pry up spikes, lift a rail, and load it into the last car.

Confederate troops quickly collared and imposed a death sentence on 33-year-old James J. Andrews, who conceived and led the raid that bears his name. He briefly eluded the noose on 2 June 1862, was recaptured the very next day, and hanged in Atlanta on 7 June 1862. Chattanooga National Cemetery has been his residence since 1887. (Colonel James G. Bogle)

William Allen Fuller, the hijacked General's *outraged conductor, badgered Andrews' raiders until they quit in April 1862, despite a series of daunting obstacles that would have deterred less dogged men. A grateful State of Georgia eighty-eight years later posthumously rewarded his exploit with a Special Gold Medal. (Colonel James G. Bogle)*

So far so good but, unbeknownst to Andrews and his co-conspirators, the first leg of a 90-mile chase had already begun in a drenching rain. William Fuller, the *General*'s conductor, engineer Jeff Cain, and passenger Anthony Murphy pursued on foot for two miles until they appropriated a hand car at Moon's Station. That intrepid trio detected the derailed section too late to stop, hurtled into a ditch, recovered quickly, put their little pole-powered vehicle back on track, and continued to Etowah, where they crossed a long bridge that Andrews left intact to avoid unveiling the raiders' true mission prematurely. They thereupon boarded the unencumbered switch engine *Yonah*, then sped 14 miles to Kingston in fifteen minutes, very nearly a world record in that day and age.

Frustrated raiders, who meanwhile waited more than an hour in Kingston while three lengthy trains lumbered south on the only through track, left a scant four minutes before the posse arrived. Sidelined freights blocked the way, so Fuller & Company abandoned the *Yonah*, sprinted through the marshalling yard, seized another locomotive by the name of *William R. Smith*, and continued pursuit in a downpour. Andrews, who could hear their whistle while his gang struggled to lever up one more rail, sidestepped the *Texas*, which towed southbound freight, and barely avoided a head-on collision with the *Catoosa* before clear shots opened.

Fuller's sharp eye spotted the uprooted rail in time for *William R. Smith* to stop. He and Murphy dismounted, then dashed three more miles on foot before they met the *Texas*, whose engineer dumped his boxcars at the first town and roared north unencumbered in reverse. Andrews cut one car loose to slow pursuit, but it barely bumped the *Texas*, which pushed the intruder back. He tried to burn another on the Oostanaula River's wooden bridge, but coals from *General's* firebox failed to ignite soaked kindling. *Texas* pushed that car too, undeterred by cross-ties that Andrews and his entourage jettisoned to impede progress, because they bounced off the tracks.

Every assigned target remained intact after Andrews's desperate raiders left a 1,477-foot tunnel untouched near the Tennessee border. One thought was paramount at that point in time: escape before the *General* ran out of fuel and water. They jumped and scattered, but Confederate troops caught all twenty-two within two weeks, hanged eight including Andrews, and imprisoned the other fourteen, of whom eight escaped. Six parolees on 25 March 1863 received the first Medals of Honor ever awarded. Their civilian leader, who laid down his life for the United States, ironically, was ineligible.

Bonus Abduction

Flamboyant John Singleton Mosby, who was a fabled guerrilla chieftain before he became a famous Confederate colonel, was the most versatile raider on either side during the Civil War. Meticulous plans characteristically underpinned his operations, but Mosby's flashiest coup occurred when he set out from Centerville, Virginia, with fewer than thirty men on 8 March 1863 to avenge a personal affront by Yankee colonel Percy Wyndham. Given last-minute information, he abducted a general instead, and thereby gained additional space in history books.

Hapless Brigadier Edwin Stoughton, the victim, hosted a party that evening for his mother and sister, who were guests at the home of Antonia Ford and her father near his Fairfax Court House headquarters. Wine, it is said, flowed freely before the Great Man retired. All was quiet until shortly after midnight, when his groggy aide with a coal-oil lamp in hand opened the unguarded door to receive late dispatches and found himself looking down a gun barrel. Mosby, resplendent in a scarlet-lined cape and plumed cap, bounded up the stairs, roused Stoughton from a sound sleep, and engaged in the following conversation:

"Have you ever heard of Mosby?"

"Of course. Have you caught him?"

"No, but he has caught you."

Whereupon, the raiders departed with the general, several lesser ranks, and fifty-eight rustled steeds. President Lincoln later lamented that he could make new generals at will, but he sure hated to lose those horses.

Antonia Ford, a known Rebel sympathizer described as a "decidedly good looking woman with pleasing, insinuating manners," immediately came under suspicion that culminated in imprisonment. The Union major

Opposite, top: *Confederate General John Hood on 1 September 1864 torched the* General, *five other engines, and eighty-one freight cars full of ammunition to keep those prizes out of Union hands when Sherman overran Atlanta, as the movie* Gone With the Wind *depicts spectacularly. The* General, *beautifully restored, remains on display in a Kennesaw, Georgia, museum. (Colonel James G. Bogle)*

Above: *Confederate Colonel John Singleton Mosby, who arguably was the Civil War's most successful guerrilla commander, had a flair for flashy uniforms that featured a scarlet plumaged chapeau and thigh-high boots. His fashion statements by no means detracted from peerless professional competence. (National Archives)*

Pages 36–37: *Traveling more than 600 miles in sixteen days, Grierson's raiders had captured 500 Confederates, killed or wounded another 100, destroyed more than 50 miles of railroad and telegraph, and thousands of dollars worth of supplies and property, in addition to tying up all of Pemberton's cavalry, one-third of his infantry and several regiments of artillery. Grierson suffered, including Hatch's losses, total casualties of thirty-six. A most unlikely warrior and music teacher turned soldier, suddenly found himself thrust into the role of a hero, writing to his wife; "I, like Byron, have had to wake up one morning and find myself famous." Grierson's picture was featured on the covers of* Harper's Weekly. *He was breveted to brigadier general and later major general of volunteers. ("Grierson's Butternut Guerillas," Mort Künstler)*

who won her release in 1864 married that "good looking woman," but her reputation among Federal officials was permanently ruined, despite Mosby's repeated assertions that she was innocent.

Hare-Brained Hijacking

The Confederate Government in 1864 established a Forward Operating Base in southwestern Ontario. Jacob Thompson, its civilian leader, lacked military skills, but concocted grandiose schemes. His most ambitious aim was to seize USS *Michigan*, use its guns to liberate 2,700 Rebel prisoners of war incarcerated on Johnson's Island near Sandusky, Ohio, then bombard U.S. ports along Lake Erie from Detroit to Buffalo, New York. Plans required glad hands aboard the *Michigan* to drug its crew with spiked champagne, so hijackers could take charge unimpeded. Inside-man Charles Cole, with his mistress Annie Brown, accordingly feted that warship's key officers for almost a month, then scheduled a splendid deck party for 19 September 1864.

Operations opened exactly as envisaged, when Confederate pirates grabbed the defenseless transport *Philo Parsons*, put passengers ashore on one of the Bass Islands near Sandusky, seized and scuttled a second steamer that arrived unexpectedly, and made a beeline for the three-masted *Michigan*. Alas, they waited in vain for a prearranged signal to confirm that the crew was sedated because a Confederate turncoat with access to their innermost circle uncovered the plot and informed Detroit's provost marshal, who sounded alarms on *Michigan* two days before Thompson said, "Go!"

Unscathed raiders beat a hasty retreat, but Federal authorities quickly captured feckless Cole, found him guilty of treason, and sentenced him to hang. Only a full confession that implicated associates kept him from the scaffold. Annie escaped to Toronto, where Thompson remained until Jefferson Davis ordered him home. Thompson chose sanctuary in England instead, and stayed there until the war was over.

Forcible Fund-Raising

Willie Sutton, a skillful safecracker, "withdrew" more than $2,000,000 from 100 repositories between the late 1920s and 1952. When asked why he robbed banks, Slick Willie allegedly replied, "Because that's where the money is." Impecunious insurgents, with that thought in mind, steal from foes to finance military operations.

The most bizarre bank robbery began on the morning of 19 October 1864 at St. Albans, Vermont, 12 miles south of the U.S.–Québec border near the eastern shore of Lake Champlain. A small advance party picked the optimum time to attack, then called forward two dozen horsemen led by Lieutenant Bennett H. Young, a Confederate cavalry officer who won his spurs riding with Brigadier General John Morgan's raiders. They sacked three banks in quick succession, tried unsuccessfully to torch the town, then made a quick getaway with $200,000 after fatally wounding unarmed Elinus J. Morrison, who tried to bar the way and thereby became the northernmost fatality of the Civil War. A telegram alerted Canadian police, who apprehended Lieutenant Young along with half of his band and

37

Jacob Thompson, the incompetent Confederate spymaster in Toronto, Canada, may not have concocted the wackiest scheme during the Civil War, but his hair-brained attempt to sedate the USS Michigan's captain and crew on Lake Erie was a serious contender. (Library of Congress)

U.S. Army commanders on the western frontier, starting about 1865, tailored Indian scouting parties to suit situations. Some contained one or two lightly armed trackers who operated alone or in tandem with uniformed units, while others featured combatants loaded for bear, depending on missions and anticipated opposition. (U.S. Army)

retrieved $50,000 at the international border. Others skirmished elsewhere before most of them evaded capture and made it to Richmond with bounteous bundles of cash.

Events took an unexpected twist during a pretrial hearing in Montréal, where Lieutenant Young contended, "Whatever was done at St. Albans was done by the order and authority of the Confederate Government. I have not violated the neutrality law of either Canada nor Great Britain." Presiding Judge Coursol announced, "This raid was an act of war, and I have no jurisdiction. . . . Therefore I order the prisoners released and the stolen money given back to them."

Most of the raiders retrieved their ill-gotten lucre and melted away before a superior court overruled Coursol's verdict the very next day. Police rearrested Young plus the few others who had failed to flee and planned to try them in Toronto, then turned loose all but one when General Robert E. Lee surrendered to Grant at Appomattox Courthouse in April 1865. Lieutenant Young, the sole exception, practiced law in England when finally released, returned to Kentucky in accord with the 1868 amnesty agreement, and terminated a distinguished career as president of Southern Railroad.

Frontier Warfare (1865-1889)

U.S. forces on the frontier included few experienced Indian fighters. Selected cavalry and infantry constabularies therefore benefited immeasurably when they integrated indigenous Indian scouts, who possessed peerless tracking, intelligence collection, and survival skills. Sixteen

received the Medal of Honor for "conspicuous gallantry and intrepidity in action at the risk of his life above and beyond the call of duty." Relatively lax criteria make some awards seem frivolous compared with current standards, but a few performed deeds that likely would merit a Medal of Honor today.

Area-oriented junior officers raised in the region put Indian scouts to best use because they were familiar with pertinent languages and cultures as well as topographic conditions for many miles in every direction. They also employed tactical techniques that foreshadowed modern Army Special Forces (Green Berets), whose branch insignia since 1987 has resembled crossed arrow emblems U.S. Indian scout predecessors wore.

Pawnee Scouts

Pawnee Scouts under savvy twenty-four-year-old Captain Frank North helped save Nebraska Territory after Sioux, Cheyenne, and Arapaho warriors began running wild in the summer of 1864. His subordinates belonged to the only Great Plains tribe that never bore arms against the United States, but conveniently bore grievances against almost every neighboring Indian nation.

The original group disbanded in January 1871, but Major North, at General Philip Sheridan's behest, reenlisted 100 Pawnee hot shots in October 1876 after Custer's dismal defeat at Little Big Horn, then hied to Wyoming Territory, where they joined General George Crook's Powder River campaign against Hunkpapa chiefs Sitting Bull and Gall plus Cheyenne chief Dull Knife. Sub-zero combat ensued in brutal terrain that hid hostile Indians—just as it later sheltered Butch Cassidy, the Sundance Kid, and other members of the notorious Hole-in-the-Wall Gang. Pawnee Scouts demobilized permanently on 19 April 1877, soon after those actions terminated, but are enshrined forever as an Oklahoma National Guard reconnaissance platoon with the 45th Infantry Brigade.

Seminole-Negro Scouts

Some escaped slaves married Seminole Indians before the United States Army in the early 1840s forced-marched them (along with Cherokees, Creeks, Choctaws, and Chickasaws) along the Trail of Tears from Florida to reservations in what now is Oklahoma. Some soon migrated to Mexico, where they fought marauding Lipan Apaches and Kickapoos.

The first group of experienced Seminole-Negro Indian fighters recrossed the Rio Grande on 16 August 1870 to enlist as scouts with the 24th Infantry Regiment at Fort Duncan, near Eagle Pass, Texas, and at Fort Clark, 45 miles farther north. They never numbered more than 100, but their tracking skills, stamina, willingness to subsist on half rations whenever required, and abilities to live off the land made them cost-effective. One contingent, for example, stalked elusive Mescalaro Apaches across frozen, waterless deserts for more than a month before they finally accomplished their mission.

Lieutenant (later Brigadier General) John Lapham Bullis took charge of Seminole-Negro mobile strike forces in 1873 and retained command for eight years. Their most widely publicized exploit took place on

Rebel Lieutenant Bennett H. Young (far right) struck fear throughout Vermont with flamboyant bank robberies in St. Albans on 19 October 1864. The Confederate Government conferred no Medals of Honor during the Civil War but, for actions on that day, he received one of forty-eight that the Sons of Confederate Veterans approved in 1977. (Civil War Journal)

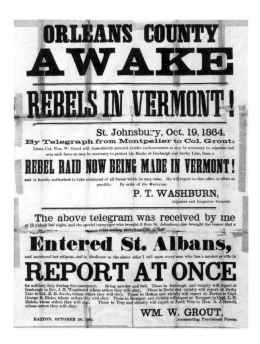

The handbill depicted appeared on 20 October 1864, before dust settled completely after Bennett Young's raid in St. Albans, Vermont, the day before. Frank Leslie's Illustrated Newspaper *subsequently printed eleven pictures that tracked his spectacular foray from start to finish. (Civil War Journal)*

39

Four Seminole-Negro Scouts received the Medal of Honor while serving with the 24th Infantry Regiment. All displayed "conspicuous gallantry and intrepidity." Three, including Private Pompey Factor, participated in "a charge against twenty-five hostiles while on a scouting patrol" at Pecos River, Texas, on 25 April 1875. His is the only photo extant. (U.S. Army)

Above: *George Crook, who commanded the Department of Arizona, resigned that office in April 1886 after President Grover Cleveland and Army Chief of Staff Philip Sheridan repudiated terms he granted Chiricahua Apaches, then imprisoned all but a handful of elusive renegades in Florida. (National Archives)*

Right and opposite, top: *With the aid of Apache and other Indian scouts, Army scouts and cavalry were successful in crushing the last remaining resistance by Native Americans in Arizona and New Mexico. ("In the Shadows" and "Apache Feet Leave No Trail," Mort Künstler)*

25 April 1875, when he and three scouts jumped roughly twenty-five Comanches near the mouth of the Pecos River. Bullis told his scouts to disengage when that uneven contest became too hot, but by that time he was surrounded, afoot instead of on horseback, and about to lose his scalp. Sergeant John Ward hollered, "We can't leave the lieutenant, boys," whereupon they dashed back. One bullet severed Ward's rifle sling and another smashed the stock before he hauled Bullis behind his saddle and all four escaped unscathed. Medals of Honor rewarded Sergeant Ward, Trooper Pompey Factor, and Trumpeter Isaac Payne for that selfless service.

Apache Scouts

Lieutenant Colonel George F. Crook enlisted Apaches to fight Apaches in the early 1870s, a practice alien to U.S. Army officers who pitted Indian scouts against tribal enemies on the Great Plains. Crook's practice worked so well from 1873 until early 1886 that "without reservation or qualification of any nature," he asserted, "these Chiricahua scouts . . . were of more value in hunting down and compelling the surrender of renegades than all other troops combined."

Brigadier General Nelson A. Miles, Crook's replacement in April 1886, distrusted Apaches, so he sent Pima, Yuma, and Mohave Scouts into Mexico's broiling Sierra Madre Mountains, where they spent several unsuccessful months trying to find elusive medicine man Geronimo. General Miles, in desperation, called on Lieutenant Charles B. Gatewood, who had long been headman at the Fort Apache Agency and knew every member of Geronimo's insurgent gang. Martine and Kieta, the only Apache Scouts who accompanied him, tracked the evasive target to his

Brigadier General George Crook, who spent most of his adult life in the frontier security business, was wise in the ways of American Indians. Here, seated second from the right in the mid-1880s, he pow wows with Geronimo, the most famous of all Apaches who resisted U.S. encroachment on their territory. (Library of Congress)

41

The ghostlike Geronimo, the last of the Indian chiefs to defy U.S. authority, finally surrendered in July 1886. With an escort of U.S. Army scouts and his Apache brethren, Geronimo is brought into custody. ("Bringing in Geronimo," Mort Künstler)

Proud Geronimo, a great Apache guerrilla, posed in an eagle plumed bonnet during his heyday, but ended ignominiously in 1886 with a command that consisted of sixteen warriors, twelve women, and six children. Apache Cemetery at Fort Sill, Oklahoma, honors his grave. (Library of Congress)

lair, made unsupervised contact at great personal peril, then called Gatewood forward for a meeting that culminated in Geronimo's ultimate capitulation and permanent captivity on 25 August 1886.

U.S. authorities rewarded Martine, Kieta, and thirteen other scouts with nominal house arrest at Fort Marion, Florida, for the next twenty-seven years simply because they were Apaches. Gatewood's frontier service totaled fifteen years, but he never wore captain's bars, despite exemplary accomplishments. General Miles belatedly endorsed a Medal of Honor recommendation that lauded him "for gallantry in going alone at the risk of his life into the hostile Apache camp of Geronimo in Sonora," but higher authorities disapproved because Gatewood engaged in no armed combat on that occasion.

Philippine Insurrections (1899-1915)

The United States acquired the Philippine Islands for $20 million in December 1898 immediately after the Spanish-American War, occupied all ceded territories, and installed a military government. Textbooks could be written on how military campaigns that used brute force to quash indigenous resistance movements have failed. Complementary pacification programs contrastingly paid rich dividends in Christian parts of that archipelago, but collapsed in Muslim territories after duplicitous U.S. administrators reneged on agreements that previously kept peace.

Filipinos who initially welcomed the United States as their savior sought to expel U.S. "invaders" as soon as annexation loomed. Armed outbreaks erupted in Manila on 4 February 1899, then spread to the provinces. U.S. adversaries easily won conventional battles, but fared less well when *insurrectos* switched to guerrilla warfare.

Both sides were insensitive. Close-quarter combat gave the U.S. .45-caliber pistol its baptism of fire against bolo-wielding sugar cane cutters as atrocities escalated. Barbarous insurgent behavior inspired the following bit of doggerel, which Secretary of State John Hay passed to President Theodore Roosevelt for his entertainment:

> *I'm only a common Soldier-man, in the blasted Philippines;*
> *They say I've got Brown Brothers here, but I dunno what it means. . . .*
> *I never had a brother who could take a wounded boy*
> *And bury him to the armpits, with a most unholy joy.*
> *Then train the Red Ants on him, like some caged Bubonic Rat.*
> *Thank God, I've got no brother who would ever stoop to that!*

The conduct of "ugly American" troops frequently was little better. Army Brigadier General "Roaring Jake" Smith's instructions to hard-bitten Marine Major L. W. T. Waller, for example, left little room for misinterpretation after guerrillas butchered a U.S. infantry company on Samar Island: "I want no prisoners, I want you to burn and kill; the more you burn and kill, the better it will please me." Waller watered down that directive, but not enough for either officer to avoid punishment by court-martial.

Future U.S. President William Howard Taft, who understood connections between Civil Affairs and pacification far better than any U.S. military officer in the Philippines, received a chilly reception from General Arthur MacArthur when he arrived as head of a potent commission in July 1901, then became Governor-General the following year. He nevertheless was well able to accomplish perceived missions because Secretary of War Elihu Root, with President McKinley's approval, issued marching orders that gave him legislative powers plus control over every penny spent in America's new colony.

Pacification Procedures

Taft gradually replaced U.S. troops with home-grown police, constabularies, and newly authorized Philippine Scouts, offered amnesty to insurgents who surrendered, promised eventual independence, drafted governing documents that showcased a Bill of Rights much like the first ten amendments to the U.S. Constitution (less trial by jury), and reformed the corrupt judiciary. He further established a civil service system, recruited 1,000 U.S. instructors and raised the salaries of indigenous teachers to give education a head start, promoted public health programs, appropriated funds to improve transportation facilities, resettled some rural populations where they could partake of benefits more consistently, and persuaded the Vatican to sell approximately 400,000 acres of prime church property, which he parceled out to peasants on low mortgage payment terms. Those positive acts in compilation made present and future prospects look brighter for the war-weary nation than insurgents could promise.

Colonel Frederick C. Funston, who fought with Cuban rebels against Spain in 1896, knew a lot about counterinsurgency before he

Top and above: *Many Moros who battled U.S. troops on Mindanao armed themselves with razor sharp, single-edged* Barongs, *which featured an 18-inch, leaf-shaped blade. Others preferred two-handed, double-pointed* Kampilans *that were wider at the tip than at the hilt, or wielded blunt, wavy-bladed, double-edged* Kris *daggers and swords. (National Archives)*

Secretary General William Howard Taft, seen here in consultation with Secretary of War Elihu Root, his guiding light, became an unexcelled pacification expert in the Philippines at the turn of the twentieth century. Few practitioners of that art have been more skillful in any theater of operations. (Library of Congress)

A U.S. soldier mingles with Filipino civilians while assisting to enroll local children in school. The concept that assistance and helpful programs to benefit local civilians would contribute to American success has proven successful over many years in many countries. It became formalized with PSYOP. (National Archives)

arrived on Luzon, where he earned a Medal of Honor on 27 April 1899. His tactics gradually eroded resistance, except for hardcore disciples of Emilio Aguinaldo, a guerrilla kingpin who proclaimed himself president of the Philippine Republic. The basic objective therefore was to put that chieftain out of business.

An incredible stroke of good luck befell Funston on 8 February 1901, when one of Aguinaldo's trusted messengers defected, pinpointed his employer's hideout near Luzon's northeastern coast, described its skimpy defenses, and turned over dispatches that directed subordinates to send reinforcements. Armed with that information, Funston planned one of the shrewdest Special Operations imaginable: eighty-some Macabebe (Little Mac) Scouts, with a few of Aguinaldo's personal acquaintances in charge, posed as requested reinforcements. Funston and four other officers simulated U.S. Army prisoners of war in tow, while a message in Aguinaldo's own code told him to anticipate their arrival.

The ruse worked precisely as planned, after a harrowing overland trek in mid-March. Aguinaldo's "friends" made contact first, received warm welcomes, and retired with him to his residence, where they told tall tales about the POWs. Little Macs soon scattered the guards, "friends" wrestled little Aguinaldo to the floor, the largest sat on him until Funston arrived, and all returned safely on 25 March. Four weeks later, Aguinaldo called for rebels to capitulate and accept U.S. sovereignty. Most did during the next fifteen months

Mishandled Moros

The United States promised not to interfere in Moro affairs when Brigadier General John C. Bates and the Sultan of Sulu signed a mutually beneficial pact on 20 August 1899. Muslims on Mindanao and throughout the Sulu Archipelago in response remained passive while U.S. Armed Forces fought Christians elsewhere in the Philippines. Those "divide and conquer" arrangements disintegrated on 4 July 1902, when President Teddy Roosevelt declared victory everywhere "except in the country inhabited by the Moro tribes, to which this proclamation does not apply."

The U.S. Military Academy at West Point rejected Frederick Funston, who flunked the entrance exam and at five feet four inches failed to meet minimum height requirements. "Shorty's" astounding exploits in Cuba and the Philippines, which reaped a Medal of Honor, nevertheless make him an admirable role model. (Library of Congress)

U.S. authorities established a Moro province the following year, replaced Islamic law with a secular legal system, introduced non-Muslim curricula in Moro schools, and outlawed slavery. John J. "Black Jack" Pershing's ensuing exploits in mortal combat propelled him directly from captain to brigadier general between February 1901 and June 1903, when promotions were exceedingly scarce. Fanatical Moros continued to fight until 1913, 1914, or 1915, depending on which disputatious cutoff date one prefers.

Even after U.S. forces defeated the Filipino Nationalist insurrection following the end of the war with Spain, many areas fell under the influence of bandits and pirate elements. Brigadier General John J. Pershing, as commander of the Moro province, Mindanao, took to the field to defeat Moros in a four-day battle in June 1913. ("Knock Out the Moros," H. Charles McBarron, Army Art Collection)

Far left: Philippine patriot Emilio Aguinaldo fought to free his country from foreign domination, first by Spain, then by the United States. He gullibly collaborated with Japanese invaders, who falsely promised independence during World War II, but became a national hero after his death in 1964. (Library of Congress)

Left: Army Captain John J. "Black Jack" Pershing bypassed 862 senior officers in 1906 when he leaped directly to brigadier general. As governor of Moro Province on Mindanao in the Philippines from 1909 until 1913, he not only embellished his own fame, but introduced enemies to the .45 caliber Colt pistol, which still possesses astounding stopping power. (Library of Congress)

45

The Banana Republics (1915-1934)

Unstable regimes in so-called Banana Republics gave the United States government heartburn after the Panama Canal opened in 1914. So did incompetent economic practices that threatened U.S. commercial interests. Theodore Roosevelt's 6 December 1904 corollary to the Monroe Doctrine accordingly declared that "chronic wrong-doing" anywhere in the Western Hemisphere "may force the United States, however reluctantly" to function as "an international police power."

Haiti

President Woodrow Wilson put Roosevelt's principle into practice on 28 July 1915, when Haiti verged on political and economic collapse. Counterguerrilla campaigns and the creation of a reasonably competent Haitian Gendarmerie that could help keep peace were important parts of one package.

A 2,000-man Marine brigade quickly pacified urban areas, but pitched battles with intractable Cacos in rural Haiti continued throughout the second half of 1915. Direct-action tactics quite unlike those that other Marines soon employed in France at Belleau Wood and the Argonne Forest featured offensive small unit engagements, surprise, agility, and economy of force. Six heroes wore a Medal of Honor for contributions above and beyond the call of duty before situations finally stabilized. Gunnery Sergeant Dan Daly, a Marine Corps icon similarly decorated during the Boxer Rebellion, received his second such award on 24 October 1915, after his thirty-five-man patrol defeated 400 Cacos under desperate conditions. Major Smedley Butler, Daly's battalion commander, picked up his second Medal of Honor at Fort Riviere three weeks later.

Marines at an early date began to reorganize, reequip, and retrain Haiti's inept Gendarmerie. Relatively generous rations and reliable pay made it easy to recruit impecunious peasants, but barely twenty literate patricians became officer candidates, and only one ever saw active duty. Marine Major Smedley Butler, seconded to the Gendarmerie as its original Commandant, gave enlisted Marines brevet commissions to fill the resultant gap. Lewis B. "Chesty" Puller occupied one such slot in 1919–1920.

Interpreters were hot properties until enough Marine "officers" learned the lingo because no Marine initially could converse in Creole and few recruits could speak English or French. Black peasants, the descendants of slaves, were suspicious of white supervisors until enlightened leaders allayed their doubts. The revitalized Gendarmerie thereafter became an invaluable source of intelligence concerning enemy strengths, arms, locations, dispositions, and movement, acted as guides, updated maps, and translated captured documents.

Charlemagne Massena Péralte encouraged Caco insurgents to initiate a second uprising near Haiti's mountainous northeastern frontier in October 1918. His announced aim was to oust despised *Yanquis*. Rebel forces, with widespread support from peasants who hated "whitey," spilled blood but gained little ground for a full year, until Gendarmerie Captain Herman Hanneken (Sergeant, USMC) and Lieutenant William Button (Corporal, USMC), given tips from informants, hit Péralte in his

Marine Corps Gunnery Sergeant Daniel Daly received his Second Medal of Honor in 1915 "for conspicuous gallantry . . . incident to the capture of Fort Riviere and Fort Dipitie" in Haiti. Daly later netted an Army Distinguished Service Cross at Belleau Wood, France, after he bellowed to his men, "Come on, you sons of bitches, do you want to live forever?" (U.S. Marine Corps)

Marine hero Smedley Butler, who as a major received his second Medal of Honor for services rendered in Haiti, resented "being a high-class muscle-man for Big Business, for Wall Street, and for the Bankers. . . . There are only two things we should fight for. One is the defense of our homes and the other is the Bill of Rights." (U.S. Marine Corps)

hideaway, carted his body to Cap Haïtien for public identification, then buried the corpse in concrete to prevent its use for voodoo purposes. Superiors decorated each Leatherneck with a Medal of Honor.

Benoit Battraville, Péralte's ham-handed successor, never made much headway. He committed a costly error on 4 April 1920 when, based on voodoo advice, he beheaded a captured Marine, then cut out, cooked, and ate his heart in a misguided attempt to increase his own prowess. A Marine patrol killed that cannibal six weeks later. The second Caco rebellion terminated in October 1920, after lesser chieftains collapsed.

The Dominican Republic

Circumstances that prompted U.S. military intervention in the Dominican Republic were similar to those in Haiti. Political instability, financial chaos, violence, and poverty were endemic. Foreign investors dominated the economy. Rumors that hostile Germany wanted a foothold fostered fears for the Panama Canal. Not all lessons learned in Haiti were transferable, but basic solutions to insurgencies otherwise were much the same.

Nicaragua

Long-standing U.S. concerns about Nicaragua became acute in May 1927 when civil war caused President Calvin Coolidge to conclude that "if the revolution continues, American investments and business interests will be very seriously affected, if not destroyed." He dispatched a U.S. Marine brigade "to ensure the adequate protection of all American interests . . . whether they be endangered by internal strife or by outside interference."

U.S. emissaries backed by Marines quickly quelled the revolution, but Augusto Sandino, a warlord with political aspirations, refused to recognize the Peace of Tipitapa, proclaimed the Republica de Nueva Segovia, and fired his opening salvo on 16 July 1927. Marines defeated him twice and twice he withdrew to foreign sanctuaries, first in Honduras (January 1928), then in Yucatan (June 1929). He returned to Nicaragua, where he formed a loose confederation that numbered about 2,000, and resumed offensive action.

Systematic civic action programs were scarce, but U.S. responses in other respects generally mirrored operations in Haiti and the Dominican Republic. Nicaragua's revitalized *Guardia Nacional* by 1930 bore the brunt of armed combat, with Marines in command down to platoon level. (Chesty Puller acquired the first two of five Navy Crosses in that capacity.) Open warfare ended shortly after the Marine expeditionary force departed in January 1933, when crafty *Guardia* chief Anastasio Somoza offered gullible Sandino an olive branch and gunned him down in Managua. President Somoza, elected by hook and crook on 29 May 1936, established a gluttonous dynasty that lasted more than forty years.

U.S. interests in Haiti, the Dominican Republic, and Nicaragua were far less than vital and the absence of a long-term political strategy made lasting benefits scarce. The price paid in lost lives and ruined property was high. The Marine Corps' *Small Wars Manual*, first published about 1935 and revised in 1940, nevertheless catalogued lessons learned that laid foundations for present-day U.S. counterinsurgency doctrine.

Nicaraguan Augusto Sandino was popular at home and a rallying point against Yanqui imperialism throughout Latin America from 1927 until his murder in 1933. He became the patron saint of left-leaning Sandinista insurgents who seized power in Nicaragua forty-six years later. (Library of Congress)

Two U.S. Marine "Banana Warriors," flanked by two Guardia Nacional NCOs, relax in 1931 between battles with Nicaraguan guerrillas. First Lieutenant Chesty Puller, sucking on a pipe, had just waltzed away with the first of his five Navy Crosses. (U.S. Marine Corps)

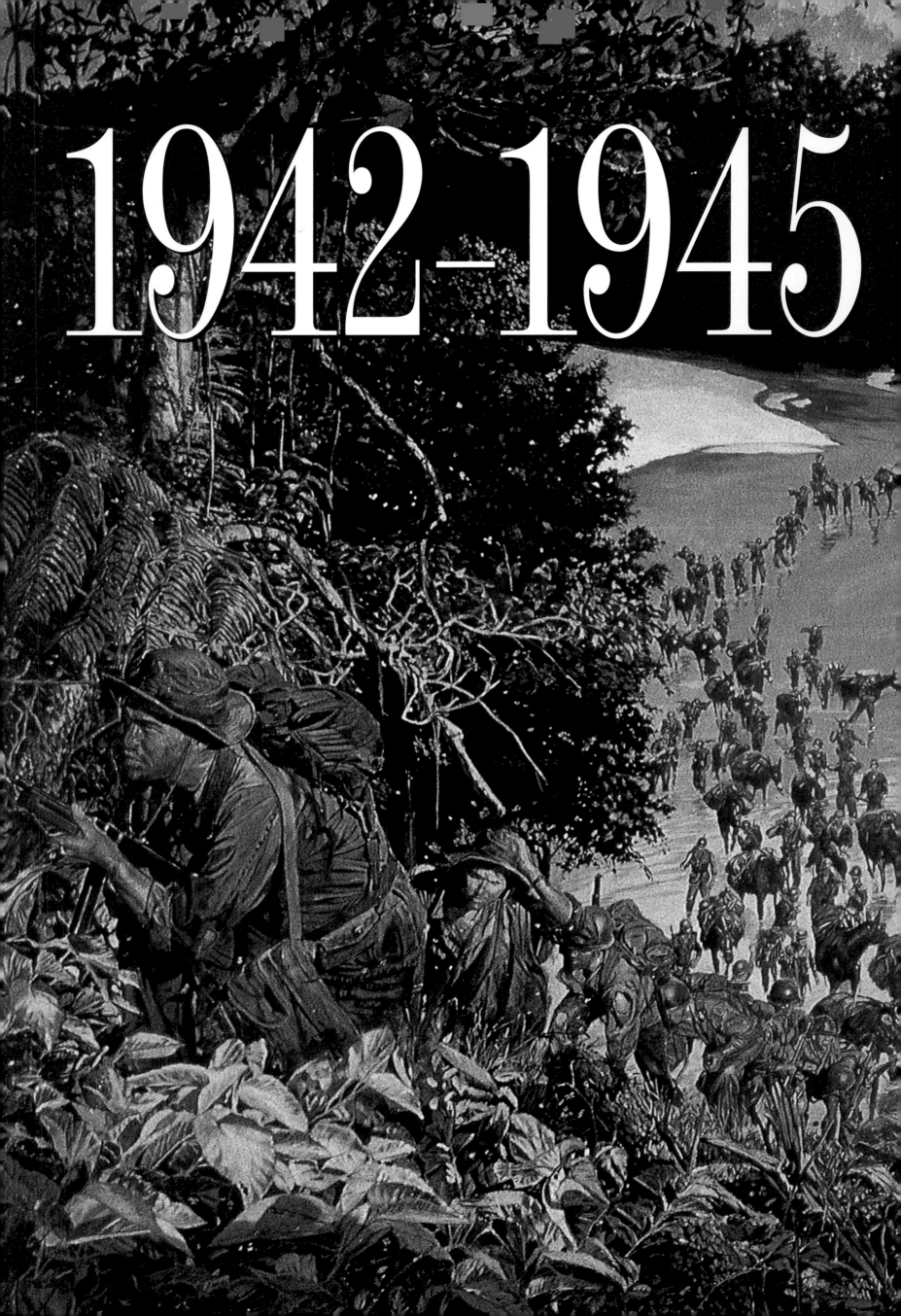

1942-1945

1942-1945
World War II
Watershed

Colonel John M. Collins, USA (Ret)

Members of a Marine Raider Battalion come ashore in a rubber raiding craft launched from a submarine in August 1942. This raid against the Makin Atoll in the Gilbert Islands was well behind Japanese lines. (National Archives)

When you come to a fork in the road, take it.
—YOGI BERRA, *THE BERRA BOOK*

America's Special Operations Forces diversified and developed exponentially during World War II, when imaginative leaders came to many forks in a widening road and dared to take all of them. Centers of gravity shifted overseas as soon as the United States assumed global responsibilities. Covert, clandestine, politically sensitive missions against strategically significant targets frequently demanded interdepartmental, multiservice, even multinational coordination. Sea, air, and amphibious SOF, which started to take shape, collaborated with each other as well as with complementary land forces in ways that made the whole greater than the sum of its parts.

Many impressive departures from the past were evolutionary rather than revolutionary. Incremental improvements were less dramatic than quantum leaps, but each made lasting contributions in important ways. Visionaries activated the U.S.-Canadian First Special Service Force to conduct surgical strike and sabotage missions in Nazi-occupied Norway and the Carpathian Mountains of Central Europe, but pressing requirements diverted that unique organization to perform light infantry feats in Italy instead. Merrill's Marauders, which operated behind Japanese lines in Burma, was the first U.S. regimental-sized organization to rely almost entirely on aerial resupply. Marine raiders led by Colonel "Red Mike" Edson and Lieutenant Colonel Evans Carlson conducted unprecedented

Lieutenant Samuel V. "Sambo" Wilson, an intelligence and reconnaissance platoon leader, led the way when Merrill's Marauders entered Burma's Japanese infested jungles in 1944. Lieutenant General Sam Wilson in May 1976 became the senior U.S. military intelligence officer as Director of Defense Intelligence Agency. (Lieutenant General Samuel V. Wilson)

51

Darby's Rangers came to grief during the Italian campaign. All three battalions disbanded in October 1944, after devastating misuse at Cisterna, where more than 750 sallied forth and six returned. ("Darby's Rangers," James Dietz)

hit-and-run amphibious assaults from open water in the Southwest Pacific. Alamo Scouts performed more than 100 deep penetration reconnaissance and raiding missions in New Guinea and the Philippines without losing a single man. Rangers that Benjamin Church and Robert Rogers pioneered never could have accomplished miracles like Lieutenant Colonel James Earl Rudder's stouthearted men, who scaled supposedly unscalable seaside cliffs under intense fire to neutralize German artillery that dominated Omaha and Utah Beaches during the Normandy invasion. The 6th Ranger Battalion, in conjunction with Alamo Scouts,

Above: Darby's Rangers, patterned after British Commandos, performed heroic deeds at Dieppe, France, in August 1942. Ranger Colonel Bill Darby was killed in action a week before World War II ended in Europe. (U.S. Army)

Right: England was teeming with American units in preparation for the invasion of Europe. A squad of Rangers, armed with Thompson submachine guns, take a break from serious training for a photo opportunity. (National Archives)

rescued more than 500 prisoners of war at Cabanatuan in the Philippines. Military PSYOP and civil affairs units began to play increasingly prominent roles

Three additional developments, which broke completely with the past, revolutionized SOF's repertoire: unconventional warfare; the first use of SOF aviation; and the first units specifically formed to identify obstacles in the surf, then destroy them, find alternative passageways

The military victory that was D-Day came at a heavy price. Here, crew members of the battleship USS Texas vie for positions from which to watch as Army Rangers come aboard for treatment of wounds sustained during the Normandy invasion. (U.S. Naval Institute)

Above: *Lieutenant Colonel James E. Rudder's 2d Ranger Battalion on 6 June 1944 seized a tiny foothold below a 100-foot cliff at Pointe du Hoc, France, then, despite demonic resistance, clawed their way up to neutralize an artillery battery that reportedly dominated Omaha and Utah Beaches. Barely 90 out of 225 made it to the top, where they discovered that no guns had ever been emplaced. (Texas A&M University)*

Left: *Rangers storm Omaha Beach on D-Day. ("Rangers Lead the Way," James Dietz)*

53

or, if those option prove infeasible, warn amphibious commanders that
alternative plans seem advisable. Those innovations, elaborated below,
confirm that World War II was indeed a Special Operations watershed.

Unconventional Warfare

Unconventional warfare (UW) involves efforts by underground movements and guerrillas to overthrow unpopular governments or oust
occupying powers. Related activities feature psychological operations,

espionage, subversion, sabotage, raids, ambushes, evasion, escape, and other clandestine, covert, or low-visibility operations. Small U.S. teams helped foment, sharpened the focus of, performed logistical functions for, and sometimes led politically sensitive insurrections in enemy-occupied Europe, southern Asia, and the Philippine archipelago during World War II. Unique requirements and unprecedented impediments demanded innovative ways to accomplish such hazardous missions for which there were no preexisting policies, no doctrine, and no pool of experienced personnel.

OSS Orchestration

The Joint Chiefs of Staff on 23 December 1942 formally gave UW responsibilities to the Office of Strategic Services (OSS). Major General William J. "Wild Bill" Donovan, its charismatic leader whose First Great War heroics merited a Medal of Honor and a Distinguished Service Cross, not only was a real go-getter, but enjoyed direct access to his friend Franklin Delano Roosevelt, the nation's President and Commander in Chief.

General Donovan ultimately approved three distinctive UW organizations with small cadres at their core. Basic missions were much the same and all prepared to expand capabilities logarithmically through close association with resistance groups in respective operational areas, but methods of operation varied considerably.

Detachment 101, slated for Burma, became the experimental model in March 1942 (it actually was the only detachment then in existence, but received an impressive designation to fool Japanese order of battle buffs). It originally contained twelve U.S. Army officers and nine NCOs under Carl Eifler, who was tailor-made for unconventional warfare. Colonel William R. (Ray) Peers, his no-nonsense successor, eventually commanded almost 700 U.S. troops and more than 10,000 Kachin tribesmen.

Three-man "Jedburgh" teams began to mushroom in Britain and Algeria during early springtime 1944. Their primary mission was to parachute into France, Belgium, and Holland beginning on D-Day, establish links between existing guerrilla groups and Supreme Headquarters Allied Expeditionary Forces (SHAEF), collect intelligence, then help Allied armed forces breach Hitler's Atlantic Wall. Jedburgh teams were named after a town near their training grounds in Scotland. Most writings note that each team included one U.S., one British, and one French or Dutch member, but only thirteen of 101 teams were configured that way. Seventeen were entirely or mainly French, thirty-two contained two Americans, and thirty-nine included two Brits.

Operational Groups (OGs) dropped into France shortly after D-Day to organize, equip, train, and command previously nonexistent guerrilla bands, then concentrate their power in accordance with strategically significant directives from SHAEF. Current Army Special Forces groups very nearly copy their OG predecessors, which assigned cutting-edge tasks to teams that contained two U.S. Army officers and thirteen enlisted men apiece.

"Wild Bill" Donovan had it all and gave every challenge his best shot. He was a lawyer, diplomat, public official, and proven combat leader who received every top U.S. award for valor and administrative ability. His slogan was, "Sure, let's give it a try!" When Donovan died, President Eisenhower said, "What a man! We have lost our last hero." (U.S. Army)

Colorful Carl Eifler, a great bull of a man, was a Los Angeles cop and U.S. Customs Service Border Patrol officer before he became OSS Detachment 101's first commander. General "Vinegar Joe" Stilwell, his boss, called Eifler "the Army's Number One thug." Thomas N. Moon penned a biography aptly titled The Deadliest Colonel. *(U.S. Army)*

Personnel Selection

Preliminary screening eliminated volunteers who obviously were unqualified for physical, mental, psychological, or moral reasons. Batteries of tests designed to uncover character flaws and weed out the least fit residue awaited "educated cutthroats" whose basic attributes emphasized leadership abilities, strength, agility, keen intellect, courage, and enthusiasm.

Arduous auditions during daylight hours and after dark strained each individual's stamina. Diabolical trials evaluated tact and tolerance under exasperating circumstances, given requirements to gain the confidence of skeptical guerrillas. Gung-ho, send-me-in-coach contestants who also displayed ingenuity and proclivities to improvise on the spur-of-the-moment got the highest grades. Intelligence collection requirements put a premium on analytical acumen (one contender who found a blonde wig and a hollow needle in a vacant room delighted inquisitors when he identified its most recent occupant as a "transvestite junkie"). Aspirants never could let their guards down because "charming" cadremen sought to break their cover during casual conversations and occasionally plied them with liquor on deceptively benign occasions.

Area-oriented, language-qualified, culturally aware candidates who qualified in all other respects made the final cut. Those who spoke French or Italian were common and the supply of Slavic linguists was adequate, partly because General Donovan trusted recent immigrants and other first-generation Americans. Oriental tongues in contrast were exceedingly scarce. Only two members of Detachment 101 had ever even visited the Far East, and none could converse in Jinghpaw, a Kachin dialect. Cooperative missionaries and indigenous translators fortunately filled otherwise unbridgeable gaps.

Tools of the Trade

Detachment 101, Jedburghs, and OGs required codes, ciphers, parachutes, homing beacons to guide aircraft toward drop zones, identification panels, signal lights, assorted demolitions, and other uncommon items as well as light infantry weapons and equipment. They additionally needed long-range radio transceivers that could connect isolated groups with far distant base camps and controllers. Available batteries were excessively heavy and plug-in power sources seldom were handy, so a clever inventor crammed two-way radio components, a hand-cranked generator, a telescopic mast, antenna wire, and repair parts into a 45-pound rucksack that any he-man could handle.

Weapon and motor vehicle instruction centered on enemy items commonly available to insurgents in target areas. Cross-training turned general practitioners into apprentice saboteurs, communicators, paramedics, and maintenance men. Specialists in those esoteric fields studied scouting, patrolling, raids, ambushes, evasion, and escape, so each team could function effectively if key members were killed or incapacitated.

British Major William E. Fairbairn, whose gutter fighting skills gave Tong hit men the shudders during thirty-three years of police work in Shanghai, taught close-quarter combat with and without the scalpel-sharp stiletto that he and E. A. Sykes co-designed for use by Commandos. U.S.

Ray Peers joined OSS Detachment 101 before it went to Burma, then replaced Carl Eifler as commander late in 1943. He later conducted covert operations in China, but always will be best known as the three-star general whose investigation of the 16 March 1968 My Lai massacre in Vietnam brought the principal culprits to justice. (U.S. Army Special Operations Command)

Close combat instructor William Ewart Fairbairn, born in 1885, looked benign at age 57, but was a master of mayhem who, beginning in 1942, taught OSS students how to kill quickly and quietly with bare hands, garrote, or knife. Knowledgeable associates agreed that nobody in that business was nearly as competent, much less better. (National Archives)

Lieutenant Rex Applegate, his apprentice, learned a hard lesson when "that dumb old bastard" told him to attack "for real" before dignitaries at what now is Camp David. He landed bottom side up in the audience.

Professional saboteurs demonstrated tricks of the trade. Buried telephone cables made of lead were simple to sever but easy for enemy repairmen to locate and splice, so instructors taught trainees to bore tiny holes that were hard to find, then short entire systems with a drop of acid or water. They also told trainees which explosives, fuses, detonators, primers, and delaying devices were best for any given job. Putty-like Composition C was particularly popular because a little went a long way, it was safe to handle, and molded easily. One golf ball-sized lump could bend a rail out of shape; one pound wrapped around a piston rod could put a locomotive out of commission.

Unorchestrated Orphans

Preparations for unconventional warfare in the Philippines were nearly nonexistent before Bataan fell on 9 April 1942. A few self-appointed U.S. leaders such as Lieutenant Colonel Russell Volckmann and Lieutenant Donald Blackburn organized or took charge of guerrilla groups in northern Luzon. Colonel Wendell Fertig did likewise on Mindanao. Similar U.S.-sponsored resistance sprouted on Samar and Cebu, but only the canniest freelancers survived because none enjoyed training and logistical benefits obtainable from a powerful godfather like Donovan's OSS

Most lived mainly from hand to mouth and improvisation was mandatory in many respects. Volckmann in July 1944, for example,

Lieutenant Colonel Russell Volckmann, who recruited, equipped, trained, and led five Filipino guerrilla regiments in northern Luzon, is seated on the right corner in September 1945 at a conference table facing Allied winners and losing Japanese General Yamashita. Volckmann later played a pivotal role in the creation of Army Special Forces. (National Archives)

Guerrilla chieftain Wendell Fertig, an Engineer Lieutenant Colonel in the U.S. Army Reserve, displeased Douglas MacArthur when he gave himself a brevet commission as brigadier general, but concurrently enhanced his prestige among Filipino subordinates. Fertig's henchmen held most of Mindanao before U.S. troops hit the beach in April 1945. (National Archives)

Sergeant Jose Calugas typified the tough soldiers of the Philippine Scouts. When the Japanese invaded the Philippines at Bataan, Calugas ran 1,000 yards under fire to another battery's position to put a gun back in action after its crew had been killed. (National Archives)

reestablished long-lost contact with General Douglas MacArthur's distant Southwest Pacific Area (SWPA) headquarters only because he cannibalized radio parts, "liberated" a Japanese generator, and linked the lot to a water wheel at the base of a 300-foot cascade. That makeshift station regrettably went off the air in November when a carabao washed over the waterfall and squashed the power plant during a typhoon. Lots of fresh meat was Volckmann's only consolation.

Counterproductive Rivalries

Turf battles persisted in every theater. DeGaulle's *Forces Francaises de l'Intereur* (FFI) and Communist-led *Francs-Tireurs et Partisans* (FTP) pursued incompatible political agendas. Tito's Partisans and Draza Mihailovic's Cetniks ruthlessly undercut each other in Yugoslavia. Hukbalahap guerrillas who sought to rule Luzon claimed they killed more Filipinos than Japanese. Moro warlords on Mindanao collided with rival Muslims as well as Christian contingents. Unconventional warfare forces from the United States accomplished far more with fewer resources than their most ardent supporters predicted, despite a standing start and the impediments just described. All requested, received, and distributed arms, equipment, and supplies that multiplied resistance capabilities immensely. All gave guerrilla leaders strategic, operational, and tactical advice. Each packet nevertheless produced unique results.

Burma

Detachment 101, the first in and first out, had to fight for acceptability. Lieutenant General "Vinegar Joe" Stilwell, the U.S. China-Burma-India theater commander, initially announced, "I didn't send for you and I don't want you," but when Japanese troops began to be intolerably troublesome, he told Colonel Eifler, "All I want to hear are booms from the Burma jungle."

Stilwell got his wish. A handful of Americans and hordes of cost-effective Kachins secured crucial parts of the Burma-Ledo Road between India and China, sabotaged enemy lines of communication that included a Japanese escape route into Thailand and, in those processes, killed or seriously wounded more than 15,000 hostiles, destroyed or captured more than 3,500 tons of supplies, rescued at least 550 Allied air crews, designated as much as 85 percent of all targets that U.S. Tenth Air Force attacked, furnished bomb damage assessments, and never lost a battle.

Lieutenant Alexander Nininger, Jr., a 1941 graduate of West Point, was killed 12 January 1942 in hand-to-hand combat while commanding a counterattacking unit of Philippine Scount infantry during the Japanese invasion of Bataan. He was awarded the first Medal of Honor in World War II. (National Archives)

Detachment 101 recruited and trained Kachin "hillbillies" from northern Burma, who were unbeatable in the bush. Mortar proficiency was part of their repertoire. Detachment 101's Kachin tribesmen never backed up to pay tables, because they collected most intelligence, provided most combat power, and suffered most casualties during operations to oust Japanese invaders. The OSS-101 Association, in partial recompense, has established a School of Agriculture, Forestry, and Vocations near Lasio for descendants of those gallant comrades. (U.S. Army)

OSS Jedburgh teams and Operational Groups had to gain the trust and respect of skittish freedom fighters before they could even begin to accomplish assigned missions in territory under Nazi German control, because survival was constantly at stake. The comradeship evident in this candid photograph indicates success in such regards. (U.S. Air Force)

Lieutenant Jack Singlaub, shown here in full battle regalia, on 11 August 1944 parachuted into heavily forested central France with Jedburgh Team James to battle Hitler's henchmen. His British smock concealed a snappy U.S. uniform that included a necktie. (Major General John K. Singlaub)

France

French guerrillas, led or advised and supported by "Wild Bill" Donovan's Jedburghs and Operational Groups, in June–July 1944 crippled locomotives and rolling stock (resistance forces destroyed fifty-two steam engines at Amberieu on D-Day alone); severed communication trunk lines that served German defenders behind Allied beachheads; blew bridges that survived earlier air attacks; harried enemy columns on the move; and otherwise delayed the redeployment of Field Marshal Rommel's strategic reserves. U.S. teams thereafter provided timely, accurate intelligence to General Patton's Third Army during its dash across France, guided guerrillas against bypassed pockets of Germans, and screened exposed flanks. Supreme Allied Commander General Dwight D. Eisenhower later noted that French resistance forces provided combat power equivalent to fifteen traditional divisions.

The Philippines

Guerrilla bands in the Philippines, isolated on widely separated islands and in constant contention with each other, never generated combat power equal to that of their counterparts in Burma and France. The overly ambitious Japanese High Command fortunately spread its armed forces too thinly to mount major counterinsurgency operations in most places, or they might have smothered organized opposition in its crib.

Filipino freedom fighters who followed U.S. leaders made important contributions despite those deficiencies, beginning with cogent intelligence reports. Colonel Fertig's irregulars seized crucial beaches before the first U.S. amphibious forces landed on Mindanao in April 1945, then acted as guides for the American landing forces, severed Japanese avenues of retreat, guarded U.S. lines of communication, and secured captured areas. Volckmann's formations, which duplicated most of those feats and performed a few that were uniquely their own, helped liberate northern Luzon, where General MacArthur counted them equal to a frontline division.

Notable Alumni

Cream of the crop Unconventional Warfare alumni were commonplace. Many Jedburghs and adventurous Operational Group veterans saw action in Norway, Greece, Yugoslavia, China, or Indochina before the curtain closed on World War II. Two junior officers became Directors of Central Intelligence: Jedburgh team chief Bill Colby (1973–1976), and case handler William J. Casey (1981–1987). Jedburgh Jack Singlaub, who bossed the super secret Studies and Observation Group (SOG) as a colonel in Vietnam (1966–1968), retired as a major general. Army Chief of Staff William C. Westmoreland picked three-star straight arrow Ray Peers to investigate the infamous My Lai massacre in 1969. U.S. Army Special Forces would have developed much later without boosts from Jedburgh Colonel Aaron Bank, along with Philippine freelancers Wendell Fertig, Russell Volckmann, and Donald Blackburn.

Classic Air Commandos

In the beginning, there was nothing, according to the Book of Genesis. God took six days to create heaven and earth, then rested on the seventh day. U.S. Army Air Force (AAF) visionaries in 1943 organized, equipped, manned, trained, and deployed aeronautical SOF in world record time, but could not rest when that work was done because aerial combat began on the seventh figurative day.

Japanese armed forces invaded Burma on 12 January 1942, easily defeated British and Chinese defenders, then occupied about four-fifths of that country before December. Flamboyant British Brigadier Orde C. Wingate, anxious to beat Japanese jungle fighters at their own game, launched Operation Longcloth in February 1943. One Chindit (British troops named after the mythological "Chindit," half lion and half griffin, that superstitious Burmese peasants believed guarded pagodas) brigade infiltrated on foot far behind enemy lines, played havoc for two months, then took a terrible drubbing, primarily because dedicated air support was woefully deficient in every respect.

Hap Arnold's Plan

Defeat didn't dampen Wingate's enthusiasm. Prime Minister Winston Churchill approved his audacious plan to airlift a full Chindit division deep into northern Burma during the 1943–1944 dry season (winter and spring). President Franklin D. Roosevelt and Army Chief of Staff General George C. Marshall then assured him that the AAF would furnish enough airlift, aerial firepower, and medical evacuation (medevac) capabilities to ensure success. AAF Commanding General Henry H. (Hap) Arnold, who was FDR's executive agent, assigned sky high priorities to Project Nine, which got off to a fast start, soon became the 1st Air Commando Group, and never slowed.

General Arnold pictured an autonomous, self-contained, composite organization that cut across traditional lines. He established basic objectives, then searched for a commander who could assemble the optimum mix of men and materiel expeditiously, given elemental guidance and a very long leash.

Arnold first interviewed Colonel Philip Cochran, who already was Milton Caniff's model for Flip Corkin in the comic strip *Terry and the Pirates*. Next came Lieutenant Colonel John Alison. Both were decorated fighter pilots with extensive combat experience. Both dreamed of additional glory. Both respectfully said, "Thank you, sir, for your vote of confidence, but include me out," or words to that effect, and the Great Man, loosely paraphrased, replied, "Sorry boys, but you're both in." He set standards and fended off troublesome bureaucrats, but directed them to work out details. "To hell with the paperwork. Go out and fight." No arguments there—they immediately scratched twelve typewriters off the original manifest.

All other personnel were handpicked volunteers, including glider jockey Jackie Coogan who, as a precocious child star, played The Kid in Charlie Chaplin's silent film *The Tramp*. The final head count was 523

Air Commandos from their onset in 1943 were blessed by General Hap Arnold, a politically savvy visionary and air power pioneer, whose open mind and position atop the Army Air Force totem pole gave them carte blanche to experiment with revolutionary organizations, tactics, techniques, and technologies. He, perhaps more than anybody else, deserves an honorary niche in the Air Commando Hall of Fame. (U.S. Air Force Art Collection)

General Hap Arnold, Army Air Force Chief of Staff, in 1943 hand-picked Colonel Philip Cochran (left), with Lieutenant Colonel John Alison as his right hand man, to organize the original air Commandos, then posted them to Burma, where they made military history. (U.S. Air Force)

Unconventional Air Commando Colonel Philip Cochran, with his rakish grin and 100-mission crush cap, was the model for comic strip character Flip Corkin (on right), who starred in Milton Caniff's Terry and the Pirates. The Congressional Record on 17 October 1943 and posters entitled "Pilot's Creed" preserved Flip's "noble sentiments." ("Terry and the Pirates" © Milton Caniff)

Above: *Admiral Lord Louis Mountbatten, who was deeply immersed in British Special Operations before he became Supreme Allied Commander Southeast Asia, protected the independence of U.S. Air Commandos against Tenth Air Force intrusions, perhaps partly because he recalled War Office efforts to disband embryonic British Commandos in 1940. (U.S. Air Force)*

Right: *A 1st Air Commando C-47 Gooney Bird early in 1944 practices towing two heavily-laden Waco gliders simultaneously before Wingate's Chindits boarded for a thrilling ride into Burma. (U.S. Air Force)*

officers and men, about one-fourth the number allotted traditional groups. Jacks-of-all-trades were more common than specialists. Fighter and bomber pilots, for example, were interchangeable. Enlisted light plane pilots maintained their own aircraft. Military bearing took a back seat because Colonel Cochran brooked relaxed relationships as long as his overworked gang got the job done.

Aircraft and Accessories

Eight types of aircraft that totaled 348 satisfied all conceivable needs. Cochran and Alison, abetted by Hap Arnold's "persuasive" powers and lots of luck, assembled the following inventory between mid-September and mid-October 1943:

- 13 C-47 Skytrains (Heavy Lifters)
- 12 UC-64 Norsemen (Utility Aircraft)
- 150 CG-4A Hadrians (Cargo Gliders)
- 25 TG-5 Frankforts (Training Gliders)
- 100 L-1 Vigilants; L-5 Sentinels (Light Planes)
- 6 YR-4 prototypes (Helicopters)
- 30 P-51A Mustangs (Fighters)
- 12 B-25H Mitchells (Bombers)

Everybody voted for C-47 transports, which could carry heavy loads and simultaneously tow two Waco gliders. UC-64 Norsemen, longtime workhorses in the Canadian arctic, got the nod for utility work. Little L-1 Vigilants designed to lift three stretchers made ideal aerial ambulances, but too few were available, so the medevac mix included newer but less capable L-5s, which could accommodate just one ambulatory casualty and needed almost twice as much takeoff space (900 as compared to 500 feet). Six highly classified Sikorsky YR-4 testbed helicopters with vertical takeoff and landing capabilities made their way from Wright Field, Ohio, to Burma only because Alison accidentally bumped into Harry Hopkins, an old acquaintance who was also one of FDR's confidantes. When Hap

Arnold asked Cochran how he accomplished that coup, the answer was, "Well, General, you just have to know the right people."

P-51 fighters and B-25 bombers split aerial firepower responsibilities: Mustangs provided top cover, strafing, and close-air support capabilities; Mitchells, armed with a nose-mounted 75mm cannon, eight forward-firing .50-caliber machine guns, and up to 3,000 pounds of bombs, packed a bunker-busting punch.

The 1st Air Commando Group acquired or created a raft of exotic accessories. Standard issue to every man included a Thompson submachine gun, a folding stock carbine, a .45-caliber pistol, and U.S. Army paratrooper uniforms with many pockets. Handymen fitted P-51s to fire experimental ground attack rockets, installed modified bomb racks on some light aircraft so they could drop supplies, and crafted rigs that enabled low-swooping C-47s to snatch gliders off the ground. Handheld cameras took aerial snapshots that Lieutenant Charles Russhon (Militon Caniff's *Charlie Vanilla*) developed outdoors at night because he had no portable darkroom.

On-The-Job Training

On-the-job training in theater prepared Cochran's air commandos for their baptism of fire. P-51s and B-25s began to fly combat missions in early February 1944. Wingate, by now a major general, accompanied one hot-shot bomber pilot who took full credit when he blasted the roof off a Japanese warehouse, then sheepishly admitted that he actually had aimed his 75mm cannon at a railway switch 200 yards short of that target. Gliders delivered folding boats, outboard motors, and petrol to help a footslogging Chindit brigade cross the Chindwin River, then returned to base after C-47s tooling along twenty feet above the surface snatched them off a sandbar. City slicker commandos devised wild schemes to coax balky mules into gliders until a simple farm boy said, "Why don't

Prototype YR-4 helicopters, the world's first whirlybirds in combat, performed search and rescue feats beyond the ability of any fixed-wing aircraft. The one depicted hovers above an Air Commando B-25 Mitchell bomber that belly landed in tall Burmese grass. (U.S. Air Force)

Lieutenant Colonel John R. Alison (center) was an ace fighter pilot with seven enemy aircraft to his credit before he became the 1st Air Commando Group's deputy commander. He and Colonel Cochran complemented each other perfectly. Together, they topped the first list of eight honorees who occupy the Air Commando Hall of Fame. (U.S. Air Force)

63

Cantankerous Chindit "Jeeps" load aboard an Air Commando transport en route to Broadway "air base" in Burma, March 1944. The 1st Air Commando Group's 319th Troop Carrier Squadron stenciled all of its aircraft with a question mark, which signified operations so secret that recruiters warned willing volunteers, "We can't tell you what the mission is, where you're going, or whether you'll ever come back." (U.S. Air Force)

we just try and see what happens?" Nothing untoward happened. Debrayed mules took to the air like Pegasus, accepted constraints that kept ears out of control cables, tolerated hobbles that kept them from kicking, relaxed in slings that kept them from slipping, and leaned left or right when gliders banked.

Every senior commander in the China-Burma-India theater tried to gobble up the embryonic air commando group, but patron saints intervened. General Arnold nominally assigned his brainchild to U.S. Tenth Air Force, but insisted that it remain operationally autonomous. He penned a "Dear Dicky" letter to that effect for consumption by British Admiral Lord Louis Mountbatten, the Supreme Allied Commander. Separate correspondence from Army Chief of Staff General George C. Marshall concurred. Those dispatches didn't dampen envy, but they prevented encroachment.

Operation Thursday

Wingate's aerial invasion of Burma, dubbed Operation Thursday, was a three-phase affair that first called for gliderborne advance parties to land unopposed after dark and build improvised airstrips in blind spots far behind enemy lines. C-47 "Gooney Birds" were to ferry in follow-on troops and supplies as soon as possible. The mission of that gung-ho Chindit-air commando task force thereafter was to give Japanese troops a bad case of fits.

Plans called for Chindits and air commandos to secure two landing zones (LZs) after dark on 5 March 1944, with forty gliders at LZ Broadway and forty more at LZ Piccadilly. Last-minute aerial photos at Piccadilly unfortunately revealed a field full of recently toppled teak logs, so sixty-one instead of forty loads headed for Broadway after Colonel Cochran leaped on a jeep hood and hollered at Piccadilly crews, "Hey, guys, you've got a better place to go!"

Barely half reached the objective area, partly because Chindits grossly overloaded most gliders with unmanifested ammunition, rations, and other consumables and partly because two gliders behind each tugging aircraft sometimes proved one too many. Overheated engines caused some "Gooney Birds" to abort, nylon tow ropes snapped during steep climbs, and whiplash from air streams severed others.

Broadway wasn't the parade ground that photos depicted because waist-high grass concealed deep buffalo wallows, tree stumps, dangerous debris, and crisscrossing runnels that Burmese woodsmen created wherever they dragged great logs. Alison, who safely set down one of the pathfinder gliders, outlined the LZ with smudge pots and lighted one flare to mark the release point. Overweight gliders, which swished down through the darkness at excessively high speed, soon littered the LZ with additional obstacles. One pilot walked away with scratches when his glider overshot with a baby bulldozer aboard, but two others that landed short killed every occupant, including the airfield construction crew and its chief.

Top, left: Eccentric British Major-General Orde Wingate, with copies of Plato and Aristotle in tow, confers with Air Commando Colonel Philip Cochran before Operation Thursday began in Burma. (U.S. Air Force)

Top, right: Phil Cochran briefs 1st Air Commando troops glider bound for Broadway in Burma, March 1944. John Alison, who led that assault, is holding a scroll, in the front row. Casual attire suited those professionals perfectly. (U.S. Air Force)

Center and above: Rome wasn't built in a day, but baby bulldozers that cleared wrecked aircraft, uprooted stumps, hauled huge logs, filled ditches, and leveled humps enabled engineers to build a lighted sod airstrip at debris-littered glider Landing Zone Broadway between dawn and dusk on 6 March 1944. Perhaps 100 C-47 transports landed and departed the very first night. (U.S. Air Force)

Congestion at Forty-Second Street and Broadway in New York City when the clock in Times Square strikes twelve on New Year's Eve has never matched the traffic jam on glider Landing Zone Broadway in Burma about midnight on 5 March 1944. (U.S. Air Force)

C-47 Gooney Birds in Air Commando employ served several purposes, of which medical evacuation was among the most important. Many seriously sick and wounded Chindit troops survived solely because they reached hospitals in time for lifesaving treatment. (U.S. Air Force)

Opposite: *Orde Wingate's Chindits in Burma relied almost entirely on aerial resupply, delivered mainly by parachute onto tiny drop zones that were hard to identify amid triple canopy jungles. It took talented Air Commando aviators to keep those tenuous lifelines open. (U.S. Air Force)*

Alison counted twenty-four dead, thirty-three badly injured, and only three salvageable gliders when dawn broke, but 539 men and three mules were fit for duty. Supplies totaled 15 tons. He turned to the only surviving engineer officer, an adolescent second lieutenant, and asked how soon he could clear the way for C-47s. The answer was, "If I have it done by this afternoon, will it be too late?" He wasn't kidding. Sixty-two Skytrains unloaded on a 4,600-foot earthen runway after sundown, plus ninety-two more the next night.

Impressive Payoffs

Operation Thursday terminated one week later, by which time air commandos had delivered 9,000 Chindits to busy Broadway and a nearby strip, along with more than 1,200 mules, 175 horses, and 250 sundry tons. Combat operations then commenced. The 1st Air Commando Group, small though it was, amassed an amazing combat record in just sixty-nine days between 12 March and 19 May 1944, when the summer monsoon began to swamp Burma. Neither Cochran nor Alison kept careful counts, but a few rough estimates and certified accomplishments belong in military history books.

No one will ever know how many tons of subsistence and medical supplies those guardian angels delivered by parachute and low-level free fall. Isolated recipients, who otherwise would have perished in Japanese-infested jungles, nevertheless gave grateful thanks every day. Multipurpose light planes flew reconnaissance sorties that gathered priceless intelligence. Those puddle jumpers also hopped into and out of implausibly small LZs,

The 1st Air Commando Group lost just one of its twelve candy-striped B-25H bombers during 422 combat sorties. Its thirty P-51A fighters, which employed the first air-to-surface missiles ever used in combat, lost only five during nearly 1,500 combat missions. Multipurpose pilots sometimes flew a P-51 in the morning and a B-25 after lunch. (U.S. Air Force)

from which they evacuated no fewer than 1,200 and perhaps as many as 1,500 casualties. Lieutenant Carter Harmon, who flew underpowered prototype helicopters in harm's way, conducted the world's first aerial search and rescue mission when he policed up a downed pilot and three walking wounded one at a time, while his tachometer screamed past the 300 rpm red line. Ensuing feats of comparable difficulty confirmed the value of rotary wing "egg beaters" in combat.

Fighter pilots and bomber crews made equally indelible marks. They not only demolished a slew of enemy locomotives, rolling stock, trucks, bridges, ammunition dumps, and buildings but, on 8 March gutted forty-eight Japanese aircraft on the ground— over 40 percent of all kills that Allied air forces racked up in Burma during that entire month. Air commando losses before the group disbanded contrastingly totaled five P-51s, one B-25, a few light planes, and one C-47 that came a cropper when it collided with a water buffalo on Broadway.

SOF in the Surf

Lung fish during the Devonian Period 400 million years ago incrementally turned fins into flippers, then into legs that eventually enabled amphibious descendants to spend lengthy periods ashore before they resubmerged. Predecessors of modern SEALs, who turned that process inside out, first put one toe in the water, then progressively developed procedures and equipment that enabled them to function almost as effectively in the surf as on terra firma.

It should have been clear at the onset of World War II that operations to defeat Axis Powers would demand a string of amphibious assaults in the Atlantic and Pacific Oceans plus the Mediterranean Sea. Beach reconnaissance and clearance units nevertheless started slowly and picked up speed at a snail's pace until traumatic experiences at Tarawa clarified urgent requirements in November 1943.

Above: *Scouts and Raiders icon Phil Bucklew, shown here in 1944, already wore two Navy Crosses, one for valor as a chief petty officer in North Africa during Operation Torch, the other as a lieutenant (jg) on Omaha Beach during D-Day landings in Normandy. (U.S. Navy)*

Right: *Army and Navy personnel, who completed rigorous training with Amphibious Scouts and Raiders (S&R) at Fort Pierce, Florida, display assorted uniforms and equipment in this 1943 photo. Note the signal lantern by their inflatable rubber boat. Graduates performed admirably in the Mediterranean and later in China. (U.S. Navy)*

Beach Recon Trailblazers

Army Captain Lloyd Peddicord and Navy Ensign John Bell in July 1942 started an Amphibious Scouts and Raiders (S&R) School that was basically in the beach reconnaissance business, first at Little Creek, Virginia, then at Fort Pierce, Florida. Original volunteers, including legendary Phil H. Bucklew, all were chief petty officers who previously belonged to "Tunney Fish," a group of physical education instructors whose boss was Commander Gene Tunney, former heavyweight boxing champion of the world. Brutal training programs weeded out all but the best Army and Navy candidates, who before graduation were well prepared to handle rubber boats and other small craft, surreptitiously inspect approaches, landing sites, and exits at night, collect and relay sensitive information to users, guide assault forces to objective beaches with hand-held signal lights, and perform other duties as directed.

The first group put principles into practice during Operation Torch on 8 November 1942, when Allied armed forces seized lodgments in Vichy French-occupied Morocco. Eight officers pinned on Navy Crosses and eight chiefs won commissions for sterling performances during that red-letter day. The Center for U.S. Navy Special Warfare in Coronado, California, is named after Phil Bucklew, who earned both. S&Rs thereafter led every assault landing in the Mediterranean theater.

The Scouts and Raiders School at Fort Pierce, Florida, took physical training seriously. All instructors were hard-nosed U.S. Army sergeants, several of whom embellished the curriculum with fiendish techniques they acquired from British Commandos in Scotland. (U.S. Navy)

Seven hearty Scouts and Raiders, who rigorously practiced handling rubber boats one moonless night in 1943, return to Fort Pierce, Florida, shortly after sunup. (U.S. Navy)

Obstacle Clearance Trailblazers

Lieutenant Mark Starkweather and sixteen companions completed a crash course in cable cutting, demolitions, and small boat handling between mid-September and late October 1942. Then, in the dead of night on 11 November, they took a Higgins boat trip up the Wadi Sebou near Casablanca, where they destroyed a huge boom and antishipping net that blocked waterborne access to Port Lyautey (now Kenitra) and the adjacent fighter airbase. All participants escaped, despite stormy weather and bombardment from a stone fort that commanded naval avenues of advance and withdrawal.

Terrible Tarawa

Embryonic beach clearance capabilities attracted painful attention on 20 November 1943, when the absence of reef-blasting abilities made U.S. Marines pay an exorbitant price in the West Central Pacific. Armored amphibious tractors (LVTs), sufficient only for the first three waves, made it across coral shelves at low tide, but follow-on forces aboard LCM and LCVP landing craft foundered in shallow waters far from shore. Tanks wallowed, while heavily laden troops waded 400–500 yards under withering fire before they reached the beach. Killed and wounded during that frightful trek constituted 20 percent of the 2d Marine Division.

Captain Jeffrey C. Metzel, a visionary who worked for the Chief of Naval Operations, anticipated requirements to recon and clear beaches. His boss, Admiral Ernest J. King, issued an implementing directive on 6 June 1943. Naval Combat Demolition Units (NCDUs), which got off the starting blocks first, satisfied needs in the European Theater through invasions in Normandy and southern France. Underwater Demolition Teams (UDTs) began to sprout in the Pacific before that year ended.

Ingenuity was a Scouts and Raiders characteristic. Novel inventions include the depicted boat, which originally was the pontoon of a defunct seaplane that previously belonged to Vichy France. That ungainly looking craft, with S&R stalwarts aboard, participated in the Seventh U.S. Army's mid-August 1944 amphibious assault on the French Riviera. (U.S. Navy)

Marine follow-on forces at Tarawa atoll waded a quarter mile through bloody water that was waist high or deeper, because landing craft, unlike amphibious tractors, unexpectedly foundered on the surrounding coral reef at low tide. That costly wakeup call expedited the development of U.S. beach reconnaissance and obstacle clearance capabilities. ("Tarawa, 20 November 1943," Tom Lovell, Marine Corps Art Collection)

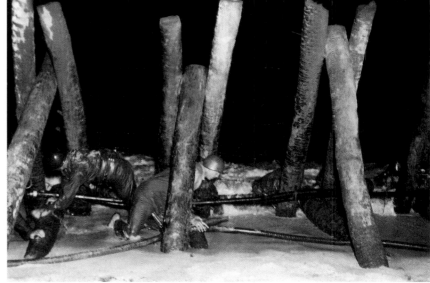

Naval Combat Demolition Units

Charismatic Lieutenant Commander Draper L. Kauffman, whose life story reads like pulp fiction, in June 1943 established a combat demolition school on North Hutchison Island near Fort Pierce, Florida, where the water was always warm and his pupils could experiment with explosives in private. He started from scratch and improvised every step of the way, given no doctrine and little guidance, but his mission clearly demanded special people, special equipment, and special procedures with which to investigate invasion beaches and clear approaches so landing craft could slice through the surf unimpeded by manmade or natural obstacles.

Gung-ho Seabees from Naval Construction Battalions, all volunteers, filled most student billets at first. Hard-nosed instructors, with guidance from a few British commandos, administered gut-wrenching physical training programs that Kauffman borrowed from neighboring Scouts and Raiders. He, in turn, kept candidates constantly busy, sometimes round the clock. One block of instruction called Hell Week was hard to distinguish from all other hectic activities. Faint-hearted aspirants fell by the wayside, while stronghearts who couldn't spell "Quit" learned to succeed under stressful conditions. Officers and men endured identical miseries, because mission accomplishment required mutual respect and teamwork.

Kauffman's curricula concentrated on ways to handle high explosives safely, determine which were best suited for particular jobs, wire them together to suit circumstances, and detonate the whole lot simultaneously. Raw materials that could be optimized for particular purposes ran the gamut from nitrostarch, ammonium nitrate, Composition C2, and TNT through fuses, blasting caps, crimps, galvanometers, and reels of primacord. Waterproofed M-2 igniters were in short supply, so NCDUs encased M-1 models in condoms, which NCDU logisticians bought by the gross. Brits, who complained that Yanks are "overpaid, over sexed, and over here," would have been outraged if they had known.

The Demolition Research Unit experimented with assorted drone delivery vehicles, but human handlers proved much more reliable. Bangalore torpedoes and explosive-filled hoses worked best on reefs and sand bars. Satchel charges were better suited for many man-made obstacles.

Top, left: Lieutenant Commander Draper Kauffman kneels right front before a group of Naval Combat Demolition Unit graduates whom he trained primarily for employment in the European Theater of Operations. His trail-blazing NCDU tactics and techniques, which paid off handsomely in combat, culminated at Omaha Beach in Normandy. (U.S. Navy)

Top, right: The graduating class completes combat demolition unit training by attaching explosive tubing to beach obstacles during night maneuvers at Amphibious Training Base, Fort Pierce, Florida, May 1944. (Naval Historical Center)

Naval Combat Demolition Units dealt daily with explosives during training at Fort Pierce, Florida, and after graduation. This exhibit shows TNT blocks (top left) and tetrytol blocks linked by primacord (top right). The center row, left to right, displays fuses, lighters, and electric blasting caps. A roll of safety fuse occupies the foreground. (Histoire & Collections, "Spearheading D-Day" by Jonathan Gawne and National Archives)

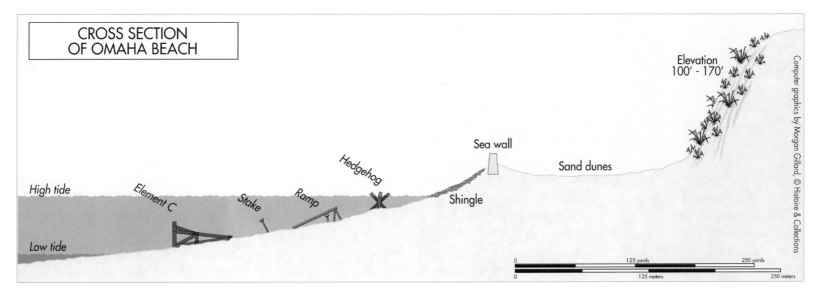

CROSS SECTION
OF OMAHA BEACH

Elevation
100' - 170'

Sea wall

Sand dunes

Hedgehog

Shingle

High tide

Element C

Stake

Ramp

Low tide

Computer graphics by Morgan Gillard © Histoire & Collections

0   125 yards   250 yards
0   125 meters   250 meters

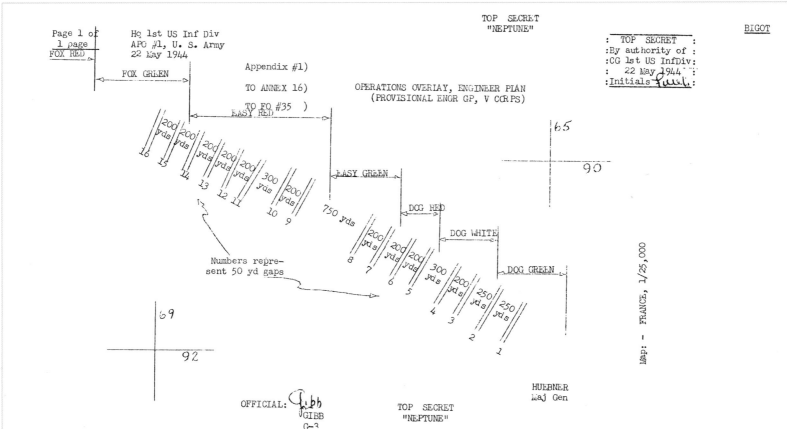

The cross-section of Omaha Beach at the top typifies underwater obstacles that Naval Combat Demolition Units and Army Engineers prepared to destroy. The overlay below plots all sixteen gaps they hoped to open by H-Hour +20 minutes. Two large crosses (bottom left, top right) indicate grid coordinates where the overlay fit atop the proper sheet of a 1:25,000 map. (Histoire & Collections, "Spearheading D-Day" by Jonathan Gawne and National Archives)

Opposite: U.S. Navy Underwater Demolition Team combat swimmer Chief Petty Officer John Regan, clad only in swim trunks, belt, and sheath knife, gets a hard-earned rest after setting explosive charges to clear beach obstacles in advance of the amphibious assault of Balikpapan, Borneo, in July 1945. (National Archives)

George Kistiakowsky, a civilian consultant who was about to become Project Manhattan's top implosion expert, packaged tetrol cubes in flexible tubes that users could wrap around steel beams. Lieutenant (jg) Carl Hagensen produced a more popular product when he stuffed 2-pound blocks of C2 (a plastic explosive) into sausage-shaped canvas sacks with a hook and eye at each end. An infinite number of so-called Hagensen Packs connected by primacord could be detonated concurrently.

Standing Operating Procedures prescribed one officer and five men per rubber boat, which left ample room for explosives. Physical training activities made trainees buck strong offshore currents almost daily, but swimming never was a big deal, because teams fully clad in fatigues, boots, steel pots, and life vests habitually paddled to target areas and back in the dead of night.

Underwater Demolition Teams

Rear Admiral Richmond K. Turner, who commanded the Fifth Amphibious Force at Tarawa in November 1943, expedited the development of Pacific-based Underwater Demolition Teams shortly thereafter. UDT and NCDU

Top, left: *Underwater Demolition Team swimmers, who went into combat clad in face masks, trunks, sneakers, and carried a K-Bar knife for protection, were commonly called "Naked Warriors" because they contrasted so starkly with fully uniformed NCDUs. Occasional applications of grease paint, not displayed here, were the principal embellishment. (U.S. Navy)*

Top, right: *UDT combat swimmers lined up at twenty-five-yard intervals off enemy beaches await high speed recovery during World War II. Well-tuned torsos, powerful kicks, and perfect timing were required. Recruiting advertisements might have read, "Professionals only. Amateurs need not apply." (U.S. Navy)*

Landing Craft Personnel, Ramped (LCPR), which normally mounted two .50-caliber machine guns apiece, primarily transported Underwater Demolition Teams from ship to shore and back again during World War II. The third platoon of UDT-4 is using the fearsome boat depicted for cast and recovery practice. (U.S. Navy)

mission statements and tools of the trade were much the same, but organizational structures and operational procedures differed considerably.

NCDUs primarily prepared to help U.S. amphibious assault forces seize a foothold in Normandy. UDT targets in contrast encompassed a slew of widely separated islands in the Central and Southwest Pacific. One set of stepping stones led to the Philippines, the other to Japan. Thirty-four UDTs, which contained thirteen officers, eighty-five men, and four platoons apiece, eventually covered that vast waterfront. Each team occupied a high-speed troop transport that embarked four specialized landing craft (LCPRs) for its exclusive use.

UDT procedures developed on Maui departed radically from those that Commander Kauffman prescribed at Fort Pierce: daylight operations replaced actions after dark; swim trunks replaced combat clothing; swimming became a major mission component; high-speed cast and recovery became commonplace; and face masks and flippers increased freedom of action.

"Frogmen" snooping at Kwajalein in January 1944 proved that daylight recons were more fruitful than those after dark, provided naval aircraft and shipboard gun batteries suppressed enemy fire. Ensign Lewis F. Luehrs and Chief Petty Officer Bill Acheson, who searched in their skivvies and sneakers after ragged coral outcrops threatened to deflate their rubber boat, registered such success that skinny dipping and sunlit operations became standard practices.

NCDU craft and crews that lingered like sitting ducks in hostile gun sights while swimmers inched into and out of the water risked one-way

trips to Davy Jones's locker. All UDT hands therefore welcomed innovative cast and recovery techniques that allowed muscular men to roll off at high speed and reboard at the end of elasticized loops while helmsmen whipped by at full throttle (timid observers called practitioners "half fish and half nuts").

Swimmers, who often wore blue-green grease paint as well as shorts, shoes, cork gloves, knee pads, flippers, and face masks, circled themselves with black stripes every six inches between neck and ankles to estimate water depths until creative thinkers devised a vastly superior string system. Team members unreeled long lines knotted at known intervals to measure horizontal distances, dropped a plumb at each marker to determine depth, plotted positions of enemy minefields as well as underwater obstacles, and grease-penciled findings on Plexiglas tablets. The UDT on-site commander then relayed results to amphibious planners at higher headquarters.

Performance in the Pacific

Underwater Demolition Teams during 1944–1945 spearheaded every major amphibious operation in the Central Pacific: Saipan, Tinian, Guam, Palau, Iwo Jima, and Okinawa. NCDUs, such as Lieutenant (jg) Francis R. (Killer) Kaine's stouthearted men in General MacArthur's Southwest Pacific bailiwick, hopped from the Admiralties up the coast of New Guinea, over to Mortai, thence to the Philippines, Tarakan, and Brunei Bay in Borneo.

Casualties were miraculously light, despite numerous close calls. Japanese bullets, for example, rained into the water at Saipan, lost momentum a foot or two beneath the surface, then fluttered past face masks like New Year's Eve confetti. Artillery and mortar bursts turned fish belly up, but wounded few combat swimmers. Laughter commonly relieved tensions. When Draper Kauffman and a nearly nude comrade came ashore at Saipan covered with psychedelic paint, one astounded

Top, left: String Line Reconnaissance, an unsophisticated yet surprisingly accurate form of hydrographic survey, enabled clandestine UDT swimmers to map gradients and pinpoint the location of underwater obstacles that obstructed final approaches to enemy beaches during World War II and later during the conflict in Korea. (U.S. Navy)

Top, right: A column of water shoots skyward to mark the site of an explosion set by an Underwater Demolition Team at Guam in August 1945. (U.S. Naval Institute)

UDT trainers during World War II soon discovered that finely honed physical conditioning was essential, because combat swimmers out of shape could easily dislocate a shoulder when snare men aboard a high speed recovery boat jerked them out of the water at the end of a loop. (U.S. Navy)

75

A boat filled with UDT members and theiur equipment is lowered from USS Humphreys *in preparation for the assault on Okinawa, 1945. (Naval Historical Center)*

UDT members daub aluminum paint on each other as camoflage against Japanese sharpshooters looking to pick them off as they removed obstacles from the paths of the pending assault on Okinawa. (Naval Historical Center)

Draper Kauffman checked out of the SOF community with two Navy Crosses to his credit at the end of World War II. He achieved Regular Navy status twelve years after commissioning and, as a rear admiral in 1965, became the 44th Superintendent of the Naval Academy, where he continued to mold young minds. (United States Navy)

Marine rifleman shouted, "Hey guys, this beach ain't ready for cabanas yet, but !@#$% tourists are already gathering!" The first assault wave that hit Guam's White Beach found a sign that said, "WELCOME, MARINES . . . USO TWO BLOCKS, COURTESY UDT 4."

Bloodbath at Omaha Beach

Six months before D-Day (6 June 1944) Phil Bucklew, Grant Andreasen, other stealthy Scouts and Raiders, and British counterparts began to take soundings off the stretch of French coast that became Omaha Beach. They scarfed up bucketfuls of sand ashore for trafficability experts to scrutinize and, for good measure, memorized landmarks along the skyline that might help them guide assault troops ashore.

Operation Neptune planners accordingly designated contiguous landing sites along a 7,800-yard stretch flanked by cliffs. Top Secret orders directed beach clearance parties to blow sixteen gaps (two apiece

on five sectors, six on extra-wide Easy Red Beach) by H+20 minutes at low tide, when obstacles in the surf would be exposed.

Twenty-one Naval Combat Demolition Units that totaled 105 officers and men clearly could not accomplish the aforementioned missions unaided. Barely two weeks before the big day they therefore joined two Army combat engineer battalions in an Army-controlled Special Engineer Task Force (SETF). Sixteen gap assault teams embraced a thirteen-man NCDU and twenty-seven Army combat engineers apiece, plus two tanks and a tank dozer. Eight gap support teams and two command teams, of which only five contained NCDUs, formed ready reinforcements. All crossed the English Channel aboard Landing Craft Tanks (LCTs), then, within sight of Omaha Beach, transferred to smaller LCMs, each of which towed a rubber boat full of explosives and related paraphernalia.

Chaos ensued from the onset. Half of the gap assault teams arrived at least ten minutes late, after rising tides began to swamp the deepest

The main mission of NCDUs at Omaha Beach was to demolish underwater barriers. The most common obstacles included tetrahedrons or hedgehogs that consisted of three heavy steel rails welded together in crisscross fashion, sharp stakes, and seaward slanting log ramps. Most impediments were mined. All could easily rip the bottom out of landing craft. ("Naval Demolition Men Blowing up Obstacles," Mitchell Jamieson, Navy Art Collection)

Small rubber boats loaded with extra explosives accompanied Naval Combat Demolition Units into shallow water at Omaha Beach shortly after H-Hour on D-Day, but enemy rifles, machine guns, and mortars immediately sank many and crews abandoned most of those still bobbing about, because they drew withering fire. ("Naval Demolition Units Reaching Beach," Mitchell Jamieson, Navy Art Collection)

This rare photo of Chris Lambertsen wearing a LARU was taken under water by a movie camera in 1948 while he demonstrated how to exit and reenter the submarine USS Quillback from Sleeping Beauty, *a one-man British motorized minisub that could deliver combat swimmers to enemy beaches far more stealthily than rubber rafts on the surface. (Dr. Christian J. Lambertsen)*

barriers, largely because the switch from LCTs to LCMs took longer than anticipated. Strong winds and coastal currents coupled with poor visibility deposited all but five teams far from designated sectors. Those hardest hit lost most of the buoys they needed to mark cleared gaps.

Ten of the sixteen U.S. tank dozers were dead on arrival, and Wehrmacht defenders immediately disabled three more. Sunken landing craft, smashed trucks, stalled tanks, and floating debris inhibited movement. Troops who sought shelter behind obstacles in the surf made it impossible for demolition teams to do their job. Enemy fire cut fuses on some Belgian Gates faster than demolition men could install them. Vehicles mangled primacord lines. One German mortar blast that triggered premature detonation killed many unfortunate waders. SETF consequently cleared only six of sixteen planned gaps by D-Day afternoon and partially swept three others. Only one, however, was clearly marked, which diminished its usefulness at high tide. Most of five infantry regiments made it ashore before dark, but armor and artillery fared less well. Barely 100 out of 2,400 programmed tons of supplies were on the beach. SETF casualties exceeded 40 percent, which included thirty-one killed and sixty seriously wounded NCDU participants.

Compensation came in the form of a secure lodgment that cracked the crust of Hitler's awesome Atlantic Wall on D-Day and paved the way for exploitations that defeated Nazi Germany eleven months later. Awards and decorations that gapping teams won included fifteen Distinguished Service Crosses for Army engineers, seven Navy Crosses for NCDUs, and one of three Presidential Unit Citations that U.S. naval forces received during Operation Neptune.

Defenders along Hitler's so-called Atlantic Wall often blocked constricted exits inland with Belgian Gates, which were welded steel antitank obstacles on rollers. It took special training and as many as sixteen Hagensen packs to demolish each one of those devilish contraptions, which weighed about three-tons apiece and measured perhaps ten feet high by eight feet wide. ("Placing A Charge on a 'Belgian Gate'," Mitchell Jamieson, Navy Art Collection)

Trailblazing Lambertsen

Precocious Christian J. Lambertsen pioneered the first practical aqualung in 1940, when he was a 23-year-old medical student. His closed-circuit Lambertsen Amphibious Respiratory Unit (LARU), which endlessly purified and recycled exhaled carbon dioxide to replenish oxygen supplies, enabled users to stay submerged for long periods without leaving telltale bubbles on the surface. The United States Navy inexplicably disdained that innovative device, whereas General Wild Bill Donovan's OSS snapped it up before Chris graduated, then enlisted the "boy wonder" immediately after he garnered his MD diploma. OSS Operational Swimmer Groups thereafter embraced Lambertsen's trailblazing infiltration and exfiltration techniques that welded LARU with small submersibles in novel ways.

The U.S. Naval Special Warfare community owes a debt of everlasting gratitude to Chris Lambertsen because nobody has made wider, deeper, or more lasting contributions to aquatic SOF. His fertile mind nearly sixty years ago began to mark paths that twenty-first-century SEALs and Special Boat crews currently follow. General Charles R. Holland, in his capacity as Commander in Chief of U.S. Special Operations Command, in 2000 consequently decorated Professor Lambertsen with the highest civilian award that USSOCOM can confer.

The U.S. Naval Special Warfare Community justifiably genuflects before Chris Lambertsen, the father of U.S. combat swimming. Second Lieutenant Lambertsen, M.D., posed for this portrait in February 1944, shortly after he pinned on Army Reserve Medical Corps insignia and became a full time member of the OSS Maritime Unit. (Dr. Christian J. Lambertsen)

Demobilization Blues

Pell-mell demobilization at the end of World War II decimated or disbanded U.S. Special Operations Forces. Army SOF took huge hits. All three air commando groups that eventually entered the inventory disappeared, along with most beach reconnaissance and clearance capabilities. U.S. flag officers, who scorned "elite" forces of any kind, said "good riddance," although pressing requirements would reemerge much sooner than they imagined. British oracle B. H. Liddell Hart's rueful remark that "the only thing harder than getting a new idea into the military mind is to get an old one out" summed up their myopic attitude perfectly.

Talented Chris Lambertsen in May 1945 posed third from the right in row one with students at the OSS Operational Swimmer Base in Ceylon, where he conducted courses in combat swimming and submersible delivery vehicles. He occasionally accompanied beach and river reconnaisance parties along Burma's Arakan coast to practice what he preached. (Dr. Christian J. Lambertsen)

1946-1972

1946-1972
First Rejection and Resurrection

Colonel John M. Collins, USA (Ret)

Fight on, my merry men all,

I'm a little wounded, but I am not slain;

I will lay me down for to bleed a while,

Then I'll rise and fight with you again.

—*"Johnnie Armstrong's Last Good-night"*
St. 18, Dryden's Miscellanies, 1702

Few U.S Special Operations Forces escaped chopping blocks after Japan capitulated in August 1945. Only six of thirty-one Underwater Demolition Teams (later telescoped into four), no Naval Combat Demolition Units, no Amphibious Scouts and Raiders, and no Air Commando Groups or psychological operation units remained after the bloodletting stopped. Eighteen airborne Ranger companies that superseded Ranger battalions in September 1950 disappeared less than one year later. Civil Affairs groups that helped U.S. occupation forces rehabilitate West Germany, Japan, and Austria evaporated when those duties were done in 1949, 1952, 1955 respectively.

Institutional Innovations (1946-Early 1960s)

SOF in every U.S. Service, like Johnnie Armstrong, bled a while, then reentered the fray despite official misuse, neglect, and active disapproval at very high levels. True believers with 20/20 foresight, who saw Special Operations as an essential national security instrument, took two steps

83

Above: *Brigadier General Robert McClure was the prime mover who turned dreams into reality in 1951–52, when he assembled an unbeatable group of far-seers and overcame stubborn opponents to win approval for U.S. Army Special Operations Forces whose forte was unconventional warfare. (U.S. Army)*

Above: *A captain commands each Army Special Forces A Detachment, like the one displayed here with radios, generators, medical kits, and demolitions. A warrant officer (1st lieutenant until 1987), two weapons NCOs, two engineers, two medics, two communicators, and two operations/intelligence NCOs complete the twelve-man package. (National Archives)*

forward and one back (sometimes one forward and two or three back) into the early 1960s, then tested roles, functions, and organizational structures in crucibles of combat throughout Southeast Asia.

Birth of the Green Berets

The National Security Council in May 1948 gave the newly minted Central Intelligence Agency full responsibility for "assistance to underground resistance movements, guerrillas, and refugee liberation groups . . . in threatened countries of the free world." A memorandum from the Joint Chiefs of Staff to Secretary of Defense James V. Forrestal the following August recommended that the "primary interest in guerrilla warfare should be that of CIA in peacetime and [the National Military Establishment] in wartime," but miniscule U.S. Army abilities to put that principle into practice during combat operations in Korea (1950–1953) made their proposition moot.

■ **SPECIAL PEOPLE:** Brigadier General Robert A. McClure, whose psychological warfare office in the Pentagon encompassed other so-called special operations, early in 1951 launched a campaign to win Army approval of unconventional warfare (UW) forces modeled after OSS predecessors. His staff featured Colonel Aaron Bank, a former Jedburgh, and Lieutenant Colonel Russell Volckmann, a guerrilla group commander in the Philippines during World War II. The two UW veterans developed concepts and force postures designed to cope cost-effectively with threats for which traditional troops were poorly prepared, while super salesman McClure pushed all the right politico-military buttons.

The collective wisdom of that farsighted trio called for a small, highly skilled cadre that could assemble, coach, and manipulate a guerrilla army of vastly greater size. Their dreams came true in May 1952 when the 10th Special Forces Group, oriented to Soviet-occupied Europe, began to receive the first of 1,800 authorized personnel at Fort Bragg, North Carolina. Most arrivals filled cutting-edge A Detachments (to use current terminology) that originally contained fifteen men, but by the mid-1950s stabilized at two company grade officers and ten experienced NCOs apiece. Each thereafter could split down the middle, yet vest both halves with light weapons, demolitions, communications, combat intelligence, and paramedical capabilities. Lean, mean B Detachments controlled two or more A Teams as required, while equally austere Cs handled two or more Bs. Group headquarters, which steered elements deployed in two or more countries, prepared overarching plans, issued orders, supervised implementation, furnished logistical support, and maintained contact with higher headquarters.

Personnel selection standards were sky high long before Barry Sadler's ballad crowed, "One hundred men we'll test today, but only three win the green beret." Superb quality consequently offset skimpy allocations. All Special Forces candidates were mature males, volunteers, already parachute-qualified or willing to attend jump school. Group tables of organization and equipment generally authorized sergeants first class (then E-6) or buck sergeants (E-5). Many were a grade or two lower, but

only the best made the cut. The Lodge Act (Public Law 597, 30 June 1950) furnished a handful of hardy East Europeans who were doubly welcome because they doubled as team interpreters in addition to their other duties. Preferred characteristics in any case coupled compassion when warranted with willingness to kill enemies without compunction. British Lieutenant General R. S. S. Baden-Powell, who composed the Boy Scout oath and law, would have applauded acceptance criteria that rewarded candidates who were physically strong, mentally awake, and morally straight. Faint hearts who faltered before or after enlistment fell by the wayside.

■ **SPECIAL PREPARATIONS:** A Psychological Warfare Center and School at Fort Bragg simultaneously integrated efforts to attack enemy minds as well as bodies in accord with a mission statement that directed the Center Commander not only to develop doctrine, procedures, tactics, and techniques for use by PSYWAR and Special Forces, but to test and evaluate related equipment. That document further told the school commandant to conduct individual and unit training.

The marriage of convenience between psychological and unconventional warfare caused heartburn in both camps, whose advocates claimed top priority. Emphasis slanted toward PSYWAR at the onset because that was Robert McClure's baby, but before long flip-flopped in favor of numerically superior Special Forces.

The school's Special Forces Department first concentrated on fundamentals, then on raids, ambushes, sabotage, subversion, evasion, escape, and other topics that pertain to guerrilla operations deep within

Above: *Jedburgh Major Aaron Bank, clad in a German uniform, posed with two U.S. comrades on each side early in 1945, shortly after he recruited about fifty "hit men" from POW stockades, then formed a tiny task force code-named Iron Cross in response to instructions from OSS chief "Wild Bill" Donovan. Most of his volunteers were disillusioned* Fallschirmjäger *(paratroops), SS, or both. Their original mission was to kill or kidnap Hitler. Iron Cross disbanded when the Third Reich began to disintegrate, but not before some members, including the five shown here, disguised themselves as a German signal platoon, glider landed with captured Volkswagens, then surreptitiously collected tactical intelligence for the 17th Airborne Division when it leaped across the Rhine in March 1945. Colonel Bank subsequently helped design Army Special Forces and, at age fifty, took command of the 10th Special Forces Group on 19 June 1952, when one warrant officer and seven enlisted men were present for duty. (Colonel Joseph W. LaGattuta, who trained with Task Force Iron Cross)*

Opposite, bottom: *Master Sergeant Stanley S. Reed, a skilled jungle fighter mountaineer, and unconventional warrior fluent in several languages, typified mature, area-oriented, thoroughly professional noncommissioned officers who populated Army Special Forces in the early 1960s. Abilities to employ finesse as well as force were priceless assets. (U.S. Army)*

85

President John Fitzgerald Kennedy, in his capacity as Commander in Chief, blessed Army Special Forces on 12 October 1961, when ramrod straight Brigadier General Bill Yarborough trooped their unique capabilities before him. A Green Beret graced the grave when a mournful nation buried JFK at Arlington Cemetery two years later. (Lieutenant General William P. Yarborough)

Post-World War II UDTs (and SEALs later on) relied on open-circuit breathing apparatus that left a trail of telltale bubbles on the surface. This combat swimmer, heavily laden with a demolition pack, wears a double-hose regulator, three oxygen tanks, and an early style wet suit that were standard issue in the mid-1950s. (U.S. Navy)

In advance of the invasion, Underwater Demolition Team personnel paddle ashore at Wonsan to destroy a North Korean minefield, on 26 October 1950. (Naval Historical Center)

hostile territory. Cross-training exposed all students to every A Team specialty, although none could attain the technical competence of communication specialists and medics. Aid men, for example, completed a thirty-eight-week course at the Army Medical Center before they took their final exam in an animal laboratory, where resident doctors graded abilities to amputate limbs, suture wounds, and otherwise attend casualties.

■ **PRESIDENTIAL IMPETUS:** Doubting Thomases at the top of the Army's totem pole, who saw armed combat through traditional glasses, treated Special Forces like a bastard stepchild through the 1950s, despite Communist insurgencies that threatened to engulf Laos, Cambodia, and Vietnam. John Fitzgerald Kennedy, who replaced President Eisenhower as Commander in Chief, conversely perceived requirements for "a whole new kind of strategy, a wholly different kind of force, and therefore, a new and wholly different kind of military training." He bought Special Forces lock, stock, and barrel on 12 October 1961, when Brigadier General (later three star) Bill Yarborough demonstrated politically astute, culturally attuned, militarily adaptable, otherwise unavailable capabilities that were precisely what JFK had in mind. Yarborough apologized because the green berets his troops wore were not authorized. "They are now," the President said.

Foreign internal defense (read counterinsurgency) in Southeast Asia supplanted unconventional warfare as the foremost Green Beret responsibility at that juncture. Fortune smiled for a few more months, until Lee Harvey Oswald assassinated President Kennedy in November 1963. Bureaucratic battles between Special Forces and the traditional Army resumed thereafter, but the conceptual seeds that McClure, Bank, and Volckmann planted produced capabilities that the Defense Department currently prizes.

Naval SOF Diversify

Underwater Demolition Team 1 cleared paths for U.S. amphibious assault troops at Inchon, Korea, in September 1950. With UDT-3, it reconnoitered landing sites farther north; assisted minesweepers along east and west littorals (primarily at Wonson and Chinnampo); conducted salvage operations; and cleared escape routes from Hamhung Harbor when Chinese "volunteers" drove U.N. forces into the Sea of Japan the

A member of UDT-13 prepares a demolition pack before entering the 50-degree water off San Clemente Island, California, during beach-clearing maneuvers, February 1955. (Naval Historical Center)

following December. Johnny-come-lately UDT-5 cut a few economically valuable North Korean fishing nets, and ad hoc naval "commandos" (sometimes with South Korean guerrillas) continued to mount occasional coastal raids, but customary UDT missions were scarce, so mentors sought ways to diversify.

Vice Admiral Robert P. Briscoe, who commanded Amphibious Forces, Atlantic Fleet, in 1951, conceived a composite unit that put UDTs, coastal raiders, electronic warfare specialists, and special boats in one package. That project evaporated before it got well started, but other innovations improved UDT capabilities exponentially, led to triphibious SEALs, and revolutionized naval SOF transportation.

■ **COMBAT SWIMMERS:** Combat swimmers who lack artificial air supplies can remain submerged four or five minutes at most, no matter how heartily they hyperventilate beforehand. Cold water quickly debilitates the best of those who plunge in without protective clothing. UDTs waited longer than they should have for artificial lungs and insulated suits,

Right: *President John F. Kennedy reviews the men of UDT-21 on board USS* Enterprise *on 14 April 1962. (Naval Historical Center)*

Above and below: *Frogman Francis "Red Dog" Fane, who saved UDTs from extinction after the Korean War, taught his men how to hold their breath four to five minutes under water, then introduced them to Jacques Cousteau's Aqua-lung or open-circuit SCUBA (self-contained underwater breathing apparatus), which enabled much longer submersion, but left a telltale trail of bubbles on the surface. (National Archives)*

partly because budgetary cupboards were almost bare between 1946 and 1960, and partly because the "Not Invented Here" syndrome afflicted senior decision-makers.

Commander Francis Douglas Fane, known as "Red Dog" until his hair turned white, began experimenting with Christian Lambertsen's ingenious LARUs and other artificial lungs in 1947 to determine how deeply combat swimmers could dive and how long they could submerge without harmful effects. He was strapped for cash, so by 1953 settled on open-circuit SCUBAs that featured bulky oxygen tanks and bubbled badly, but cost less than closed-circuit competitors and were easy to use. SEALs waited well into the 1980s before enlightened procurement officers with somewhat more generous budgets began to stock Draeger LAR V systems that were affordable as well as stealthy.

Hypothermia, characterized by subnormal body temperatures, afflicts combat swimmers who remain immersed too long even in tepid water. Impaired abilities to perform simple tasks such as tying knots occur first, followed by lethargy, stupor, retarded respiration, internal bleeding, heart failure, and death when rectal thermometers register 78 degrees Fahrenheit or less.

Frogmen in frigid seas during the Korean War originally wore soggy wool sweaters and long johns in fruitless efforts to stay warm. First-generation latex garments that followed were somewhat better, but leaks commonly destroyed insulation and reduced maneuverability when cold brine filled one or both legs. Military wet suits that trap a layer of warm water next to the skin subsequently incorporated commercial and recreational SCUBA technologies. Watertight dry suits over thermal underwear, coupled with special protection for hands, feet, and heads, later extended feasible areas of operation into the arctic.

President Kennedy on 25 May 1961 told a joint session of Congress that, given asymmetrical threats on a grand scale, he would "rapidly and substantially" amplify U.S. abilities to conduct paramilitary operations and engage in "sub-limited or unconventional war." Chief of Naval Operations Admiral Arleigh Burke, who already was on that wicket, authorized SEAL

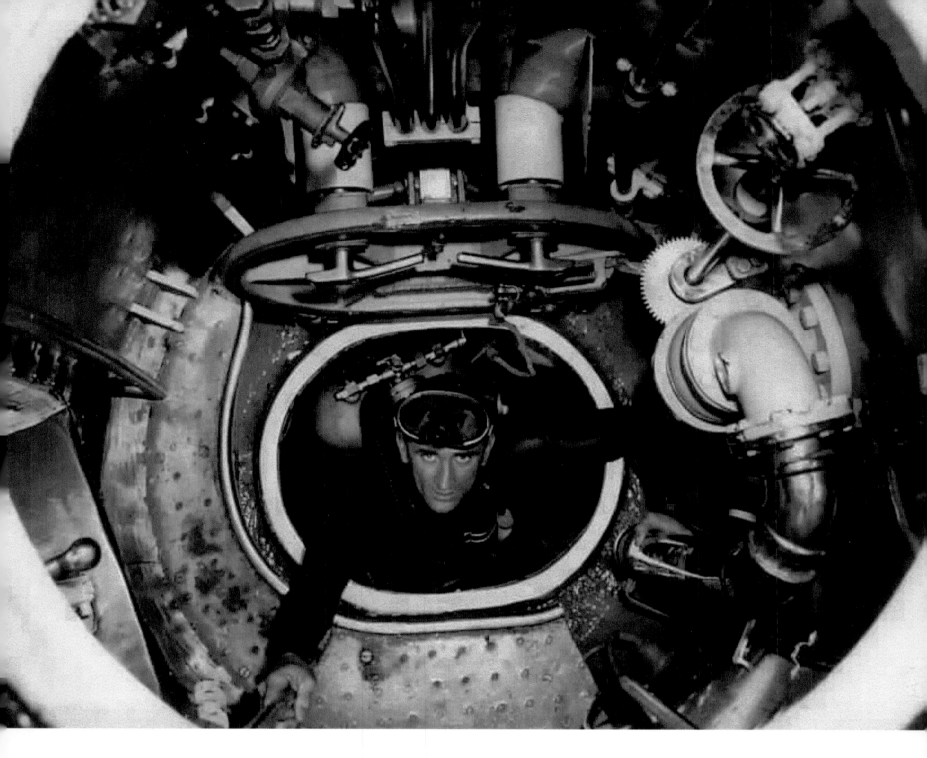

teams on 11 December 1961. Team One's top slot went to Lieutenant David Del Giudice on New Years Day 1962, followed by Team Two with Lieutenant John Callahan at the helm less than one week later.

Army Special Forces at Fort Bragg initially tutored both teams on the fine points of scouting, patrolling, raids, ambushes, and sabotage above the high-water line, plus martial arts and familiarization with selected foreign weapons. "Jumping frogs" who made five leaps from aircraft in flight above Fort Benning, Georgia, sprouted parachute wings. SEALs consequently were ready, willing, and able to scout the north coast of Cuba before and during the missile crisis a few months later and both teams were primed for action in Vietnam the following year.

■ DELIVERY VEHICLES: SEAL Teams One and Two rode submarines to and from the Cuban coast, but on-call transportation most often involved inflatable rubber rafts and geriatric landing craft of World War II vintage until 1963. Boat Support Unit One, which belonged to Captain Phil H. Bucklew's Naval Operations Support Group, thereafter operated and maintained Light and Medium SEAL Support Craft (LSSCs and MSSCs). Modernization accelerated later that year with high-speed, highly maneuverable Nasty Class Norwegian patrol boats that mounted various combinations of 40mm, 20mm, and .50-caliber guns, recoilless rifles,

SEALs and Underwater Demolition Teams formed symbiotic relationships with submarines before the Cuban missile crisis in 1962 and have maintained close links ever since. The UDT combat swimmer shown here on a launch and recovery mission in the 1960s is entering a submarine escape trunk. (U.S. Navy)

Opposite, bottom: Hypothermia occurs when human body temperature drops below normal (98.6 degrees Fahrenheit). Combat swimmers in seas between 60 and 40 degrees originally wore rubber wet suits like those shown, which trapped a thin layer of warm water next to their skin. Synthetics with better insulation properties currently are in use. Watertight dry suits over thermal underwear are essential in frigid waters. (UDT/SEAL Association)

UDT trainees practice high-speed swimmer cast and recovery from a rubber inflatable boat off Roosevelt Roads, Puerto Rico. (Naval Historical Center)

Aerial infiltration was a viable option for SEALs and UDT swimmers aboard CH-46 Sea Knight helicopters as early as 1964. Men dropped feet first through a "hell hole" in the helo's centerline, then maintained a firm body position until splashdown. Best results were obtainable when the chopper's forward speed in knots equaled its altitude in feet. (U.S. Navy)

mortars, rocket launchers, and flame throwers tailored to meet estimated threats and mission requirements.

Doug Fane, who dropped and retrieved UDT teammates from tiny hovering helicopters in 1947, opened the search for airborne infiltration and exfiltration techniques, which put an "A" in the acronym SEALs. Experimentation thereafter ceased for several years until larger choppers expanded possibilities. Insertion options by the early 1960s included free falling into water, preferably from about 10 feet at a forward speed of about 10 knots. Fixed-wing transports stood ready to deposit SEALs and equipment on the surface en masse.

Aerial extraction proved far more complex than pickups that flip swimmers into speeding boats like anglers net fish. The Fulton Recovery System, which employs fixed-wing aircraft to snatch individuals from terra firma and reels them aloft one at a time, is ill-suited for most SEAL team purposes. Loops at the end of flexible ladders lowered over water were losers because, as one participant explained, waves bounced them about erratically and anybody on the rungs blew off like an arrow from a bow when the next man grabbed the ring. Better devices still awaited development.

Shoe leather put the letter "L" in SEALS from the onset. Easily deliverable light vehicles, however, soon facilitated overland travel farther and faster than the best conditioned men ever could travel on foot. Teams One and Two, in short, were well qualified to perform triphibious missions within a matter of months after activation.

Rebirth of Air Commandos

Necessity, the Mother of Invention, came through in the clutch when she reinvented Air Commandos in all but name during the Korean War. The sense of urgency was so intense, however, that unlike first-generation Green Berets and SEALs, all Special Air Mission (SAM) crews learned their lessons in a School of Hard Knocks and through on-the-job training, first in Korea, then on a global basis.

■ **COMBAT IN KOREA:** Hard-charging Captain Harry C. (Heinie) Aderholt, as Commanding Officer of Detachment B, 21st Troop Carrier Squadron, was the right man at the right place at the right time when Kim Il Sung's troops swarmed across the 38th Parallel into South Korea in June 1950.

Above: *Captain Heinie Aderholt put Air Force SOF back in business during the Korean War. He truly belongs in the Air Commando Hall of Fame, along with World War II role models Philip Cochran and John Alison, whose methods of operation he admired and improved. (U.S. Air Force)*

Above: *Free spirit Heinie Aderholt, still hard at it as a SOF colonel in Vietnam, was an unexcelled innovator, improviser, and inspirational leader. Bureaucratic battles with powerful proponents of a "higher, faster, bigger bang for the buck" Air Force repeatedly deferred promotions, but he finally pinned on brigadier general stars in May 1974. (U.S. Air Force)*

Left: *Another version of aerial infiltration via helicopter was done by rapelling. Here, members of a SEAL team rapel from a hovering helicopter into the jungles of Vietnam in January 1967. (Naval Historical Center)*

Heinie Aderholt's hearties flew from forward airstrips littered with combat debris like the North Korean tank silhouetted in the foreground after U.S. Armed Forces broke out of the Pusan Perimeter during early autumn 1950. So doing reduced wear and tear on aircraft and crews, decreased turn-around times, and increased sortie rates remarkably. (U.S. Air Force)

His C-47 Gooney Birds touched down on 1 August at Taegu inside the tiny Pusan perimeter near the southernmost tip of the Korean peninsula and immediately began to resupply desperate U.S. and allied troops who were making last-ditch stands.

Heinie's mission changed abruptly in mid-September, after U.N. forces landed at Inchon, rolled up outflanked aggressors like a rug, and raced north. Operation Avery dropped indigenous civilian agents astride principal north-south corridors to determine whether enemy troops were withdrawing in disarray or were still combat ready. The first parachutists generally returned safely but, because they lacked portable radios, most of their findings were obsolete before they trickled back to debriefing centers.

Chinese "volunteers" during late November 1950 marshaled in Manchuria, then crossed the frozen Yalu River en masse. Where those massive formations were headed became a mystery by mid-December because they advanced less rapidly than U.N. defenders retired until great gaps separated friends from foes. General Walton Walker, the U.S. Eighth Army honcho who hoped to hold Seoul, gave intelligence types

seventy-two hours to clarify situations. Aderholt, in response, devised an ingenious scheme: he girdled his Gooney Birds with black and white stripes, painted wing bottoms to match, gave twelve two-man teams pastel smoke grenades, and scattered them across Korea's wasp waist. Agents who observed Chinese battalions or larger groups sent red signals when easily identifiable C-47s flew overhead. Yellow smoke indicated North Korean contingents of similar size, while green signified negligible enemy traffic of any kind. Flights on the deck in the dead of night under overcast skies in mountainous terrain gave aircrews goose bumps, but all survived and results were gratifying.

The most glamorous agents were patriotic Daughters of the Morning Calm, personally recruited by South Korean President Syngman Rhee's wife. "They were the artists, the starlets, the musicians, accomplished people, the very best," Aderholt recalled. They jumped at night, he continued, when "the weather was forty or fifty degrees below zero. They would go out in little cotton-padded shoes and a cotton-padded suit, and you would think that they didn't weigh enough to get them to the ground." Some

0-77766

Versatile C-46 Air Commando transports, which enjoyed greater lift capacity than C-47 Gooney Birds, infiltrated agents behind enemy lines, dropped flares, disseminated leaflets, and flew loudspeaker missions. The C-46 that a double agent grenadier destroyed in flight looked just like this one. (U.S. Air Force)

disguised as refugees parachuted into hostile territory as many as four times during December 1950 and the spring of 1951. One comely lass, who engaged in pillow talk while she lowered a loose-lipped Chinese colonel's libido, relieved him of facts that enabled General Matthew B. Ridgway to counter the impending offensive of an entire Chinese corps.

Detachment 2, 21st Troop Carrier Squadron continued to drop spies as far north as Manchuria until that mission terminated in 1952 because Communists began to catch agents as soon as they hit the ground. Bleary-eyed airmen even so continued round-the-clock schedules that entailed

Above: *SOF aerial delivery specialists who crewed C-119 Flying Boxcars helped sustain isolated French outposts in Indochina during the early 1950s until Communist General Vo Nguyen Giap's guerrilla bands overwhelmed last-ditch defenders at Dien Bien Phu. (U.S. Air Force)*

Right: *PSYWAR leaflets, initially dropped from 2,000 feet, then from 500 feet to increase accuracy, featured pictures more than words, because North Korean troops and Chinese Communist "volunteers" were largely illiterate. Loudspeaker broadcasts from low-flying aircraft proved more effective, according to reasonably reliable intelligence reports. (U.S. Air Force)*

94

"white hat" missions during daylight and "black hat" duty after dark. The same crew that chauffeured President Rhee, the U.S. ambassador, General Ridgway, or other potentates before breakfast might deliver freight until sundown, grab forty winks in their aircraft, then resume their hectic pace at night. Gooney Birds became the world's first, last, and only C-47 bombers after Aderholt replaced external cargo bundles with 75-gallon napalm canisters. He impersonated a malicious Santa Claus one Christmas morning when he dumped the first load on an enemy headquarters.

The 581st Air Resupply and Communication Wing (ARCW), which commenced operations from the Philippines and Seoul City Airport (K-16) in July 1952, was a composite organization that incorporated defanged B-29 Superfortresses, SA-16 amphibians, three air transport types, and two distinctively different whirly birds. ARCW's main mission was to prepare, reproduce, and disseminate theater-level psychological warfare (PSYWAR) materials, but its diversified aircraft inventory opened up a much wider range of options that included special reconnaissance; agent drops; insertion, extraction, and logistic support for guerrilla bands; and battlefield illumination, plus search and rescue. Loss rates were low despite high risks, but exceptions to that rule were spectacular. One C-46, for example, blew to bits in flight when a double agent waved goodbye, tossed a live grenade into its cargo compartment, then waltzed out the door on gossamer wings. MiGs on the night of 15 January 1953 shot down *Stardust 20*, a PSYWAR B-29 making its final leaflet run not far from Manchuria. Survivors suffered mental and physical anguish in Chinese prisons until tormenters turned them loose thirty months and twenty days later (4 August 1955), the last U.S. POWs to return from captivity.

■ **POST-KOREA AIR OPERATIONS:** Collaboration between the United States Air Force and Central Intelligence Agency in the battle against communism commenced in Korea, then began to take on global dimensions before that conflict wound down. Politically sensitive, low-profile intervention in French Indochina, isolated Tibet, and Fidel Castro's Cuba typify the diversity of air SOF involvement.

ARCW's C-119 Flying Boxcars ferried weapons, equipment, and supplies to French and Foreign Legion troops during final stages of a protracted struggle to prevent Communist control of Indochina. ARCW also trained CIA's Civil Air Transport (CAT) crews, all to no avail, because France capitulated after its disastrous defeat at Dien Bien Phu in May 1954.

Detachment 2 of Major Heinie Aderholt's 1054th Observation, Evaluation, and Training Group on Okinawa from 1957 to 1960 helped CAT give aid and comfort to Tibetan guerrillas on the Roof of the World, where "lowlands" averaged 13,000 feet and heavily laden flights across the Himalayas could best be described as "hairy." Airdrops sustained the Dalai Lama during his escape to India in March 1959, but Chinese Communists gutted outgunned rebels the following year.

Omnipresent Aderholt early in 1961 helped prep anticommunist Cuban exiles on the fine points of B-26 bombers before the Bay of Pigs fiasco and obtained permission from President Anastasio Somosa to base those aircraft in Nicaragua. President Kennedy's politically

Two jet black SA-16 amphibians, posted to Spook City on extended temporary duty outside Seoul in 1952, infiltrated and exfiltrated agents behind Chinese Communist lines after dark. They landed ashore wherever sandy beaches and enemy situations allowed, but otherwise set down in placid water at low tide. (U.S. Air Force)

Page 96–97: The 187th Regimental Combat Team, with two Ranger companies attached during Operation Ripper, dropped on 23 March 1951 at Munsan-ni 20 miles northwest of Seoul to keep fleeing enemy forces from reestablishing strong defensive positions beyond the unfordable Imjim River. The leap was too late to accomplish that mission, but the 2d Ranger Company (Airborne) on that date made history's only parachute assault by an all black unit. (U.S. Army Center of Military History)

Page 97, top: Cuban exiles crewed fifteen B-26 medium bombers that CIA acquired from a USAF aircraft "graveyard" outside Tucson, Arizona. Their primary mission was to neutralize Castro's tiny but sharp toothed air force before the Bay of Pigs invasion began on 15 April 1961. They failed, because last minute restrictions from the White House made that impossible. (U.S. Air Force)

Page 97, center: C-46 Air Commandos, lined up like ducks in a row at a U.S.-built air base on a remote coffee plantation in Guatemala, prepared to deliver exiled Cuban paratroopers before amphibious landings began at the Bay of Pigs. C-54 transports, such as the one parked far right, were pre-invasion cargo haulers. (U.S. Air Force)

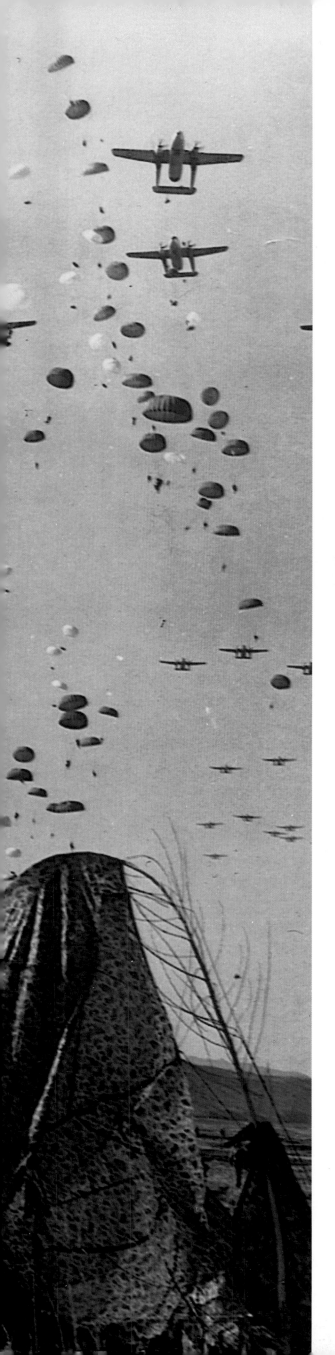

motivated decisions that severely limited employment unfortunately allowed Castro's cannon-firing T-33 trainers to blast bombers from the sky and left him firmly in place because, as he succinctly put it, the invaders "had no air support."

Proving Grounds (1961-1972)

Mountains, plains, jungles, swamps, grasslands, sea coasts, inland waterways, cities, towns, villages, and hamlets, coupled with determined, elusive foes on that geographic chessboard, made Laos, Vietnam, parts of Cambodia, and eastern Thailand perfect proving grounds for U.S. Special Operations Forces to practice every mission that now is legally mandated: special reconnaissance, unconventional warfare, foreign internal defense (counterinsurgency), direct action, counter-terrorism, psychological operations, civil affairs, search and rescue, humanitarian assistance, and unspecified clandestine activities. Army, Navy, and Air Force SOF individually performed some amazing feats, but most operations involved interservice collaboration.

Prelude in Laos

The Geneva Accords of 20 July 1954 legally neutralized Laos and granted independence, but persistent power struggles dashed U.S. hopes for a nonaligned nation between Communist North Vietnam and pro-Western Thailand. Chief of State Prince Souvana Phouma collided head-on with

97

Above: *An advisor of the 1st Special Forces Group instructs Vietnamese soldiers in aiming and firing the Springfield M1903 rifle in Ban Me Thout, Vietnam, March 1962. (National Archives)*

U.S. Mobile Training Teams in Laos between 1959 and 1962 initially were designated Ambidextrous, then Hotfoot, and finally White Star. All organized, equipped, and trained indigenous tribesmen to counter Communist Pathet Lao insurgents. Mortar proficiency was part of their repertoire. (Eugene Gavigan)

his half-brother Souphanouvang, the titular head of Pathet Lao insurgents who, with logistical aid from Hanoi, Moscow, and Beijing, seized northern provinces and established a strong underground in the panhandle.

The United States Government, which bankrolled Laotian Armed Forces (FAL) after 1 January 1955, established a Program Evaluation Office (PEO) in Vientiane and staffed it with pseudo civilians because the Geneva Accords forbade foreign troops in Laos, other than a small French training mission. Its counterinsurgency operations initially

U-10 short takeoff/landing (STOL) Helio Couriers, *which carried five passengers or a 1,700-pound payload, could operate from football field-size strips, fly as slowly as 25-30 mph, linger much longer than helicopters, and required a lot less maintenance. SOF in Laos used them for liaison, light cargo, forward air control, recon, and leaflet drops. (U.S. Air Force)*

O-1 Bird Dogs, like this one deep in Cambodia, flew low and slow at treetop level with an experienced SOG recon team chief or intelligence specialist in the back seat. Sharp eyes often discovered, and hand-held cameras recorded, carefully-concealed enemy activities and installations that U-2 spy planes and space satellites could not detect. (John Plaster)

Bull Simons (fourth from the left) answered calls to take charge wherever international crises developed. Laotian duty as a lieutenant colonel opened in July 1959, after he selected, organized, and trained 77th Special Forces Group personnel for Operation Ambidextrous (later "Hotfoot"). He headed "White Star" Mobile Training Teams in Laos beginning in 1961. (U.S. Army)

emphasized economic assistance on a grand scale, but inept procedures coupled with lackadaisical attitudes and widespread corruption among recipients promoted Communist propaganda without compensatory improvements in FAL capabilities.

Twelve Army Special Forces field training teams from Fort Bragg, all disguised as civilian contractors, arrived in late July 1959 along with Thai interpreters. They collocated their base with PEO then, in deference to French sensitivities, furnished low-key technical as opposed to tactical advice at four widely separated locations. The coup, countercoup, and intensified civil war that rocked Laos between August 1960 and the following May eliminated that source of friction because all French forces withdrew. Short-sighted policies that rotated U.S. SOF out of Laos every six months disrupted continuity, and patrician FAL officers who resisted retraining further impeded progress.

The U.S. Military Assistance Advisory Group (MAAG) that joined PEO in April 1961 after President Kennedy personally identified Laos as a jeopardized "domino" incrementally organized forty-eight White Star Mobile Training Teams that totaled more than 430 men under the command of crusty Lieutenant Colonel Arthur D. "Bull" Simons. Some teams featured combat advisors, while others furnished training camp cadremen. All U.S. military personnel arrived in civvies, but switched to military uniforms soon after the United States government acknowledged their presence.

The FAL never amounted to much no matter how hard White Star tutors tried, but primitive Hmong and Kha tribesmen, who eagerly soaked up instruction, showed great promise as guerrillas. Omnipresent Heinie

Aderholt's Detachment 2, 1045th Observation, Evaluation, and Training Group from Okinawa air dropped weapons and supplies to beef up their capabilities. How well White Star and its indigenous allies might have performed in tandem with Heinie's "sanitized" B-26 bombers at Takhli, Thailand, remains subject to speculation because President Kennedy canceled any U.S. use of combat aircraft in Laos after the Bay of Pigs fiasco, and multinational negotiations culminated in a second declaration of neutrality on 23 July 1962. The last White Star contingent departed on 6 October, North Vietnamese encroachers remained, and CIA thereafter assumed full responsibility for clandestine activities.

U.S. Special Operations Forces did very little to prevent eventual Communist victory in Laos, but compensatory rewards nevertheless were forthcoming. SOF established crucially important interdepartmental, interagency, international linkages; incrementally honed political, economic, cultural, and linguistic skills that enabled them to work well with allies whose customs at first were quite unfamiliar; emphasized finesse instead of brute force to the greatest extent feasible; substituted persuasion for compulsion whenever required; and concurrently tested weapons, equipment, unorthodox tactics, and techniques under realistic conditions in tropical environments. All "do's and don'ts" that Army and Air Force SOF learned in Laos were immediately transferable to protracted conflict in Vietnam, which already was picking up speed, but politico-military decision-makers in Washington, D.C., and Saigon unfortunately were slow to understand.

Army Special Forces in Vietnam

Land, sea, and air SOF in Vietnam received a bewildering array of missions from the day vanguards arrived in 1957 until rear guards departed fifteen years later. Frontier security, riverine warfare, cross-border operations, and novel airpower applications admirably illustrate diversity.

The Ho Chi Minh Trail, which linked North Vietnam's Red River Delta with the Republic of Vietnam (RVN) via Laos and Cambodia, was nothing more than a skein of rustic traces through a saw-toothed wilderness when it opened in the late 1950s. U.S. and RVN officials paid scant attention as long as porters, bicycles, and assorted beasts of burden carried all consignments marked for Viet Cong (VC) guerrillas, but trickles became torrents as soon as widened routes began to accommodate truckloads of North Vietnamese regulars, together with tons of ammunition and other supplies. Frontier security at that point became a salient mission for Army Special Forces.

Military Assistance Command Vietnam (MACV) on 26 November 1963 directed the then provisional Special Forces Group to detect, interdict, and harass enemy invaders, plug infiltration routes, and gradually expand areas of control along South Vietnam's lengthy frontier with Laos and Cambodia. That document contained two corollary responsibilities: recruit and train indigenous personnel for those purposes; and conduct PSYOP and Civil Affairs campaigns to bolster public support in border regions far removed from governmental centers. Plans called for RVN to assume full responsibility for each outpost when feasible, which would free U.S. Special Forces to open new sites.

Opposite: Hmong tribesmen in Laos, equipped only with hand tools, built undulating airstrips along razor sharp ridges a mile above sea level for use by intrepid SOF airmen. One, aptly named "Agony," was 600 feet long, replete with zigzag curves and, in one place, barely twenty feet wide. Operations there were exhilarating, even for experts in broad daylight. (U.S. Air Force)

North Vietnamese foot traffic on the Ho Chi Minh Trail started in the late 1950s, followed by pack bicycles that could carry larger loads than pint-sized Annamese elephants, which push and pull better than they bear heavy burdens. Sinewy porters beside seatless bicycles such as those shown commonly pushed 500-pound bundles hundreds of miles up and down steep inclines. (National Archives)

Bangiang River banks near Tchepone in the Laotian panhandle looked like a lunar landscape after U.S. bombers finally destroyed the triple-span bridge. Truck traffic thereafter ceased on that part of the Ho Chi Minh Trail, but barges ferried troops, weapons, equipment, and supplies to the far shore, where waiting motor convoys transshipped them to South Vietnam. (U.S. Army)

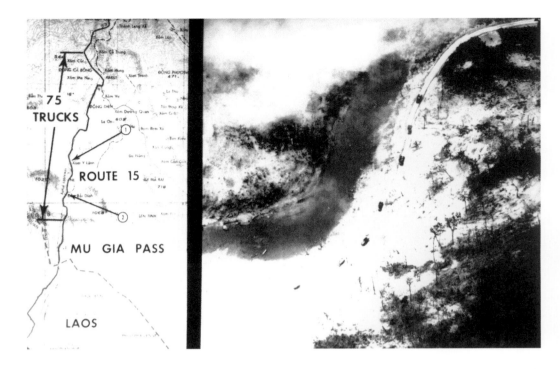

Right: This aerial photo of Communist truck traffic on the Ho Chi Minh Trail is rare, because convoys moved mainly at night over well-camouflaged routes. AC-130 Spectre gunships, other SOF aircraft, SOG, and B-52 bombers slowed but never stopped the incessant flow. (U.S. Air Force)

Above: Rickety bridges that French engineers installed in Laos, were too frail to accept even light vehicular traffic in the 1960s along what became the Ho Chi Minh Trail, but primitive bypasses and fords enabled North Vietnamese porters, pack bicycles, ox carts, and trucks to proceed across shallow streams almost unimpeded. (U.S. Army)

Below: An Army Special Forces "LRRPs" (Long Range Reconaissance Patrol) squad leader reviews a mission with his team before leaving its home base. (U.S. Army)

Duty at isolated camps that soon festooned the frontier was exceedingly dangerous. All were magnets astride preferred enemy avenues of approach far beyond range of the nearest divisional artillery. Serviceable roads and navigable waterways connected only a few compounds with civilization; some depended entirely on aerial delivery for supplies and reinforcements. Uneven quality characterized indigenous mercenaries, who constituted a large majority at every garrison. Fighters, for example, predominated at some installations, while weaklings and turncoats out-

numbered warriors elsewhere. Superstitious Montagnards performed well close to home, but became antsy when uprooted to fill blank files in unfamiliar territory where local communities were unable or unwilling to furnish sufficient recruits.

Heavily fortified fighting camps improved defensive capabilities considerably by 1967. Each featured inner and outer perimeters that enclosed a "keep," mutually supporting strong points, and overlapping fields of fire

Five of the twenty Medals of Honor awarded Army SOF during the Vietnam War were for heroic actions in defense of fortified camps. The first went to Captain Roger H. C. Donlon at Nam Dong, where Viet Cong attacked his A Detachment before dawn on 6 July 1964. "Suffering from multiple wounds," he "moved from position to position around the beleaguered perimeter, hurling grenades at the enemy and inspiring his men to superhuman effort." ("Field Communications in Foxhole," Mort Künstler)

Isolated frontier security outposts along South Vietnam's border with Laos and Cambodia were perennial hotspots where spine-tingling enemy attacks periodically interrupted deceptively peaceful interludes. (U.S. Army)

103

Above: *In 1964 Captain Roger H. Donlon of the 7th Special Forces Group was in command of a Special Forces base camp on the Laos border, consisting of Special Forces Detachment 726, a 311-man South Vietnamese "strike force" and their families, and sixty Chinese Nung guards. On 6 July 1964, despite being wounded four times, Donlon tenaciously fought and rallied his men to defend against a Viet Cong attack. He was awarded the first Medal of Honor in Vietnam. (National Archives)*

Top, right: *Captain Harry Cramer, posed rear center with his twelve-man A Detachment plus two field grade officers, was the first Special Forces fatality in Southeast Asia (21 October 1957). A Viet Cong mortar actually did him in, but the Vietnam Wall in Washington, D.C., omitted his name until 1983, because he officially died during an accidental explosion. (U.S. Army)*

Right: *South Vietnamese (ARVN) Special Forces troops swarm out of their transport to bolster American Special Forces at their mountain base atop Mt. Nui Ba Den, prior to a sweep in Tay Ninh Province. (U.S. Army Military History Institute)*

Opposite, bottom: *Posthumous Medal of Honor recipient Eugene Ashley, a medic, hastily assembled an assault force of Laotian volunteers to relieve the desperately engaged garrison at Lang Vei, then led five charges against heavily-armed hostiles in captured bunkers. His group poked a hole through which survivors escaped after an enemy artillery round killed him. (U.S. Army)*

across cleared spaces in every direction. Construction was completely underground wherever water tables allowed, except in the marshy Plain of Reeds and the lower Mekong Delta, where floating structures rose and fell with floods. Mounded earth, steel Conex containers, 55-gallon drums, and heavy logs made readily available, cost-effective materials.

Those citadels, positioned about thirty miles apart on the average, were too few to accomplish all assigned missions, but they established a permanent presence where MACV's divisions seldom if ever intruded. Viet Cong forces that dared to attack suffered far more than gallant defenders. Aggressive patrolling, coupled with compassionate concern for nearby inhabitants, undercut Communist influence. Airmobile reaction (Mike Force) companies, manned by Montagnards, Chinese Nungs,

Above: *Second lieutenant Charles Q. Williams of 5th Special Forces, serving as executive officer of a Special Forces camp at Dong Xoai, led the defense of the camp during a fourteen-hour attack on 9–10 June 1965. For his actions, including the destruction of a Viet Cong machine gun and crew with a bazooka, he earned the second Medal of Honor awarded in Vietnam. (National Archives)*

Left: *Paramilitary Civilian Irregular Defense Groups (CIDG), composed mainly of Montagnard tribesmen, manned most Special Forces fighting camps in Vietnam. Families were a fixture at many sites. Captain Vern Gillespie found time to frolic with Rhade children during a peaceful interlude at Buon Brieng (Darloc Province) in 1964. (U.S. Army Special Operations Command)*

Cambodians, and Vietnamese volunteers in various combinations, exploited small unit contacts, extracted compromised teams, conducted reconnaissance in force operations, and stood ready to reinforce besieged outposts on short notice.

Frontier security capabilities declined precipitously as soon as North Vietnamese Army (NVA) regulars rather than Viet Cong guerrillas posed primary challenges. The last of three Special Forces compounds in the A Shau Valley fell on 16 March 1966, never to be replaced. Lang Vei went next, with great loss of life when NVA tanks attacked in South Vietnam for the first time during the chaotic night of 7–8 February 1968. Casualties among twenty-four Green Berets on site included seven dead, three captured, and thirteen wounded, several of them seriously, in return for one

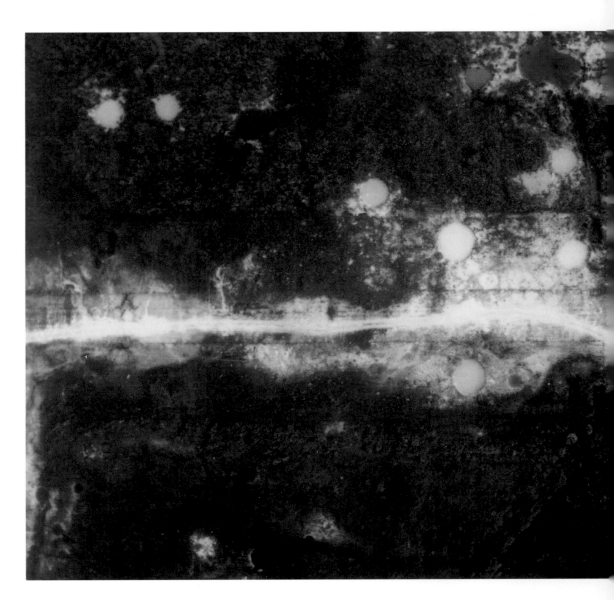

Above and top, right: *Major Bernard Fisher in March 1966 miraculously landed his A-1E Skyraider on bomb cratered A Shau airstrip, rescued a buddy who crash landed shortly before on the enemy's side of the runway (see circled wreckage), then took off safely through ferocious crossfire between Green Berets and North Vietnamese Regulars. Recompense for that incredible feat was a Medal of Honor. (U.S. Army)*

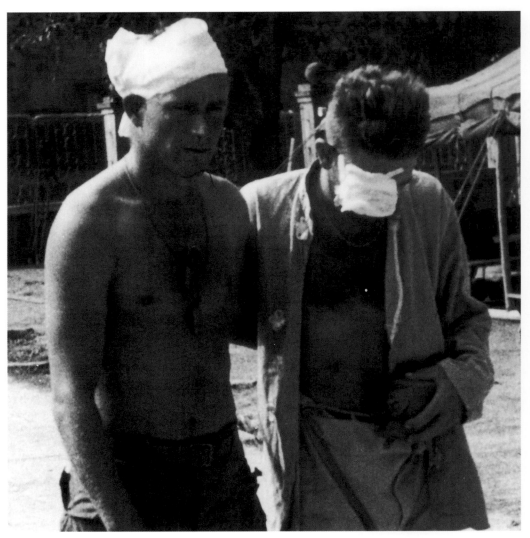

Above: *God surely was co-pilot on 12 May 1968 when Medal of Honor recipient Joe Jackson swooped his C-123 into enemy-held Kham Duc during rotten weather to rescue the last three U.S. survivors. A damaged aircraft reduced usable runway length to 2,200 feet, but he lifted off safely with all aboard, because apparent miracles protected him repeatedly. (U.S. Air Force)*

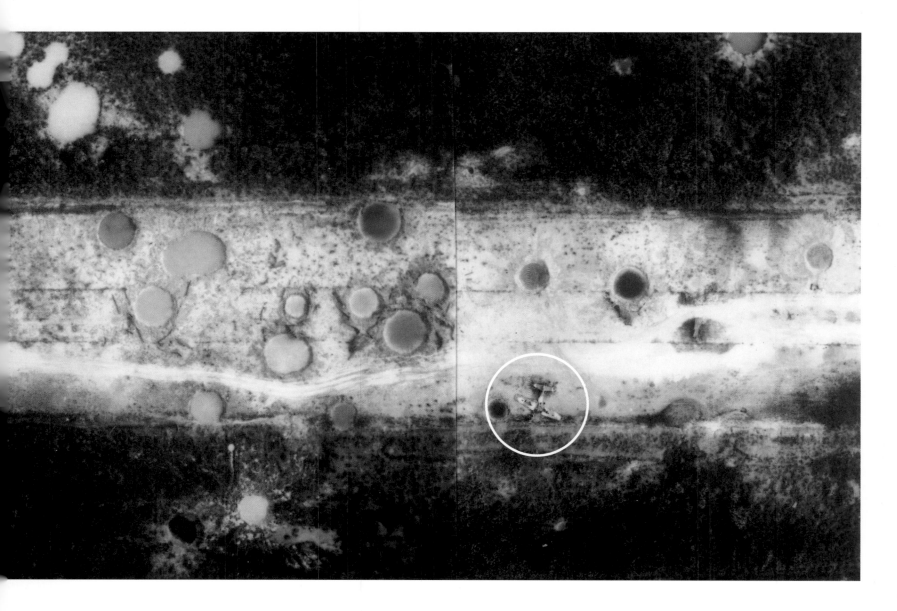

posthumous Medal of Honor (Sergeant First Class Eugene Ashley, Jr.), a Distinguished Service Cross, and nineteen Silver Stars. Assailants the following May obliterated Kham Duc, the last border camp in northwestern RVN. Lieutenant Colonel Joe Jackson and Major Bernard Fisher, both Air Commandos, received Medals of Honor for heroic rescues under mission impossible conditions at Kham Duc and A Shau respectively.

Left: *Kham Duc, located forty miles from the nearest friendlies, was the launch site for SOG's first incursion into Laos and the last U.S. frontier security post to fall in South Vietnam's I Corps Tactical Zone. Quantitatively superior North Vietnamese Regulars on 10 May 1968 swarmed down from dominant terrain, then overran the camp and airstrip. (U.S. Air Force)*

Opposite, bottom: *Lieutenant Colonel Dan Schungel, who commanded Company C, 5th Special Forces Group, and Lieutenant Miles Wilkins, Executive Officer of Team A-101, barely survived the bloody battle at Lang Vei in February 1968. Schungel wore a Distinguished Service Cross thereafter, while Wilkins received one of nineteen Silver Stars. (U.S. Army)*

107

SEALs wade through waste-deep muck in the Ca Mau Penisula. (U.S. Naval Institute)

MACV, in consonance with President Nixon's Vietnamization policies, began to pass frontier security responsibilities from U.S. Special Forces to host country counterparts in August 1969. Transfers that provoked disciplinary breakdowns and mass Montagnard desertions proceeded precipitously until 31 December 1970, when conversion was complete. Borders became more porous than ever thereafter.

Bluejackets and Brown Water

U.S. armed forces and their allies fought to control overflowing rice bowls and win the allegiance of millions in the marshy Mekong Delta, which covers 16,000 square miles between the Gulf of Thailand and the South China Sea. Few roads in that sodden environment were much better than footpaths and only one was paved. Inland waterways consequently handled most military traffic, even though tight turns, sand bars, swamp grass, fish traps, low bridges, and enemy-installed obstacles restricted maneuverability in many places. Conditions were worse in the Rung Sat Special Zone, a tidewater morass where hundreds of tiny islands, inundated trees with spidery roots, brambles, and ravenous insects abound, but that economically worthless plot in the northeastern corner was crucially important because it straddled the main shipping lane between Saigon and the sea.

Naval special warfare in that geographic quagmire progressed through three overlapping stages between 1966 and 1970, each more audacious than its predecessor. Game Warden operations initially harassed Viet Cong guerrillas; a joint Army-Navy Mobile Riverine Force

A SEAL team is inserted into the Mekong Delta in 1967. ("SEALs on Ambush," Marbury H. Brown, Naval Art Collection)

(MRF) subsequently conducted battalion-sized search and destroy sweeps; SEALORDS (Southeast Asia Lake, Ocean, River, and Delta Strategy) finally seized and held enemy territory.

Ambassador Henry Cabot Lodge's crystal ball was cracked when he concluded, "I would not be surprised to see the Mekong Delta totally cleared of Communist forces by the end of 1965," because NVA very nearly owned "Waterworld" and were gaining ground before that year ended. Enter Task Force 116, code named Game Warden, established 18 December 1965. Its shoot and scoot missions directed participants to enforce curfew, eviscerate Viet Cong "tax collectors," search junks and sampans in streams, deny guerrillas free use of waterways, and safe-guard the channel to Saigon.

The U.S. Navy owned no craft suitable for such purposes, so it purchased high-speed, shallow-draft River Patrol Boats (PBRs) powered by Jacuzzi-designed water jets that delighted civilian playboys. Aluminum soon replaced fiberglass hulls and lightweight ceramic armor shielded each pilot house and firing position, but protection depended mainly on speed and firepower that featured machine guns and grenade launchers. Three experimental air-cushioned hovercraft, dubbed "Dragon Boats" because bows displayed glaring eyes and ferocious fangs, rushed across the Plain of Reeds at 70 knots, but failed to pass practicality tests because they cost about $1,000,000 per copy versus $90,000 for PBRs and performed less well elsewhere.

Swashbuckling boat crews, not yet considered SOF, looked a lot like McHale's raunchy Navy of television fame but were "special operators" in

A SEAL team hastily disembarks from Boston Whalers before moving inland in the Rung Sat Special Zone in April 1968. Note the M60 machine gunes mounted on the bow of each boat to provide suppressing fire against Vietcong resistance when coming ashore. (Naval Historical Center)

Shallow draft Light SEAL Support Craft (LSSCs), powered by gasoline engines and water jets, were the first U.S. Navy boats explicitly designed for brown water warfare. Two-man crews with a SEAL squad on board maneuvered them throughout the Mekong Delta and Rung Sat Special Zone. (U.S. Navy)

Above: *SEAL raids against Viet Cong villages in the Mekong Delta and Rung Sat Special Zone south of Saigon were exceedingly risky under best case conditions, because accurate, real time intelligence reports were rare; indigenous friends, foes, and neutrals all looked alike; and dense vegetation facilitated ambushes. Who would surprise whom thus was seldom certain. (Naval Historical Center)*

Right: *Army Special Forces move into elephant grass after disembarking from a Navy boat as part of a joint Army-Navy Mobile Riverine Force (MRF) operation. (National Archives)*

every sense because they rode into battle aboard those offbeat boats and pioneered brown water tactics. Boat captains and their three-man crews all were bluejackets cross-trained as pilots, navigators, communicators, mechanics, and gunners. Underwater Demolition Teams (UDTs) and SEALs who loved coastal combat didn't take kindly to riverine warfare at first, but quickly bonded with highly professional PBR squads that delivered and retrieved them on countless occasions.

Crews and passengers were reasonably safe in the midst of wide rivers, but risks skyrocketed as soon as they entered narrow canals and meandering streams, where contact mines, choked channels, and likely ambush sites lay around every bend. River minesweepers (MSRs), aerial scouts, chemical defoliants, "Big Zippo" craft that spewed napalm, and "Douche boats" that blasted bunkers with 3,000 psi streams of water helped greatly. Many SEALs and PBR sailors owed their lives to straight-shooting Seawolf gunships that belonged to Light Attack Helicopter Squadron 3 (HAL-3), but close-quarter battle remained a fact of life. Witness, for example, Boatswain's Mate First Class James Williams, a boat captain and patrol officer in charge of two PBRs. He discovered elements of two North Vietnamese regiments aboard sampans and junks on 31 October 1966, made three passes through dense formations despite furious enemy fire, destroyed sixty-five enemy vessels, killed or wounded more

SEAL training for RVN soldiers in 1970. (National Archives)

Left: *SEALs and boat units in the Mekong Delta sometimes redeployed rapidly over long distances to corner Viet Cong adversaries. This Riverine Patrol Boat suspended beneath a CH-64 heavy lift helicopter floats through the air with the greatest of ease, like the daring young man on a flying trapeze. (U.S. Navy)*

Opposite, bottom left: *Every peasant family in the Mekong delta possessed a sampan instead of an ox cart or automobile, because almost all traffic moved by water. U.S. riverine forces routinely searched such vessels, then seized or sunk those that served insurgents. SEALs shown here dispatched one bunch of bad guys, then paddled back to their PBR in a commandeered boat. (Naval Historical Center).*

Opposite, bottom right: *A team of Rangers move out from their Navy support craft into the floodplain of the Mekong Delta. Many amphibious operations were conducted by Army-Navy Mobile Riverine Forces (MRF). (U.S. Army Military History Institute)*

("Seals on Ambush," Marbury H. Brown,
Navy Art Collection)

than 1,000 troops, captured another slew, and destroyed countless supplies during a three-hour battle. His reward was a Medal of Honor which, with a Navy Cross, two Silver Stars, three Bronze Stars, and three Purple Hearts, made him the U.S. Navy's most decorated enlisted man.

Game Warden results through 1966 were modest at best despite Williams's incredible feat because too few naval SOF monitored far too many miles. A joint Army-Navy Mobile Riverine Force (MFR) in February 1967 therefore commenced search and destroy operations on a much grander scale. Traditional forces provided most combat power, but special

An innovative approach to warfare in the watery Mekong Delta was the Mobile Riverine Force. Army troops and weaponry embarked on shallow draft Navy vessles. Here, an assault force scrambles ashore along the My Tho River in September 1967. (National Archives)

boat crews continued probes, UDTs continued to conduct hydrographic surveys and clear underwater obstacles, while SEALs collected priceless intelligence and attacked Viet Cong infrastructures, including key leaders.

Senior U.S. and allied officials gave the MRF credit for "saving the delta" during the 1968 Communist Tet offensive. Its capabilities declined precipitously the following year when the Army's 9th Infantry Division began to disband in response to President Nixon's Vietnamization policies. Resources and areas of responsibility progressively shrank until the MFR disappeared completely in August 1969.

Naval patrols in the Mekong Delta were comparatively safe on broad rivers, as pictured here. Situations, in contrast, were exceedingly dicey when they slithered down narrow streams with dense vegetation along both banks.("USN PBR on Patrol, Long Tau River, Rung Sat Special Zone," Charles Waterhouse, Navy Art Collection)

Above: *A SEAL team covers its approach on board a SEAL Team Assault Boat (STAB) in October 1968. (National Archives)*

Left: *A PBR boat crew stands armed and ready in support of its SEAL team that has gone ashore in the Mekong Delta, October 1968. (National Archives)*

Above: *SEALs and UDTs in Vietnam couldn't function without dedicated boat support, but boat crews didn't qualify as SOF. This account nevertheless recognizes PBR 105 boat captain James Williams, who richly deserved the Medal of Honor he received for his courageous actions in the Mekong Delta. DDG-95, an Arleigh Burke Class destroyer, bears his name. (U.S. Navy)*

Right: *Medal of Honor recipient James Williams on 31 October 1966 captained a Patrol Boat, Riverine (PBR), like the one shown here when he and a subordinate aboard an identical PBR sank a bevy of Viet Cong junks and sampans that embarked elements of two North Vietnamese regiments. The minigun on the bow laid down devastating firepower. (U.S. Navy)*

A SEAL Team One squad in the Mekong Delta prepares to swarm ashore and push inland from an armored Heavy SEAL Support Craft (HSSC). The baby cannon on this much modified Landing Craft Utility (LCU) helped keep Viet Cong guerrillas pinned down and on the defensive until U.S. raiders made contact. (U.S. Navy)

Vice Admiral Elmo "Bud" Zumwalt, Jr., anointed as Commander Naval Forces Vietnam on 1 October 1968, advocated an offensive rather than defensive strategy that could wrest initiative from communist adversaries. His brainchild, called SEALORDS, aimed to curb the flow of contraband from southeastern Cambodia to customers throughout the Mekong Delta. Naval forces included Swift Boats that previously patrolled the South China Sea coast, assault squadrons that formerly belonged to the Mobile Riverine Force, and Game Warden boat crews that covered more territory than ever before. Vietnamese Marines provided land power. SEALs and UDTs, who found a friend in Vice Admiral Zumwalt, performed minor miracles beyond his bold expectations.

Events moved so fast that by 2 January 1969 the last of four plugs was firmly in place along rivers and canals that generally paralleled Cambodia's border from the Gulf of Thailand to the so-called Parrot's Beak west of Saigon. Seepage continued, but arterial waterways in the Mekong Delta remained off limits to Viet Cong guerrillas and North Vietnamese regulars until Saigon fell in April 1975, three years after the United States Navy passed all riverine responsibilities to its South Vietnamese counterparts.

Cross-Border Operations

President Kennedy, displeased with the CIA's performance, had passed covert action responsibilities to the Defense Department during the summer of 1962, but transition postdated his untimely death. A Studies and Observation Group (SOG)—euphemistically dubbed to conceal its true purpose—reported directly to the Joint Chiefs of Staff from Saigon and, in January 1964, began to plan and conduct cross-border operations that eventually reached into Laos and Cambodia as well as North Vietnam. Its land, sea, and air components specialized in stealthy reconnaissance and surveillance missions; inserted secret agents to create qualms at the highest levels in Hanoi; performed psychological

Darkness compounded dangers in the Mekong Delta, where differentiating friends from foes was difficult even in daylight. Camouflage-painted SEALs, commonly called "the men with green faces," nevertheless specialized in ambushes after dark, aided by binoculars (which amplify light), first-generation starlight scopes, innovative tactics, and intensive training. ("Mekong Delta, SEAL Team Drop-off, Night Ambush," John Steel, Navy Art Collection)

Jack Singlaub amassed immense covert and clandestine experience in France, southern China, Indochina, Manchuria, and Korea before he became SOG's second chief in 1966. Retired Major General Singlaub's e-mail address appropriately is SOGBOSS. (U.S. Army)

115

warfare stunts that included "dirty tricks"; mounted hit-and-run maritime raids along the North Vietnamese coast; and interdicted enemy traffic on the Ho Chi Minh Trail.

Support forthcoming for SOG from on high was stone cold at worst and lukewarm at best, because traditionalists in the Pentagon and Military Assistance Command Vietnam viewed covert action as a sideshow. The Department of State and the antsy U.S. ambassador in Laos laid on political restrictions that all but declared the Ho Chi Minh Trail "off limits" for the first two years.

Above: *John Plaster, who later authored two authoritative books about SOG, displays some of the small arms and grenades that line-crossers commonly carried into Laos and Cambodia. Flash suppressors, sawed off weapons, and claymore mines were common.* (*John Plaster*)

116

Opposite, top: *SEALS and their supporting STAB crewmen make a high-speed run near the Cambodian border, 20 June 1970. (Naval Historical Center)*

Above: *SOG Hatchet Forces relied on heavily armed indigenous troops like Bru tribesman Cum Ba, shown here in a helicopter doorway ready to embark on a cross-border raid. Fierce loyalty and competence in the clutch were common characteristics. (John Plaster)*

Left: *Indigenous platoon- and company-sized SOG Hatchet Forces, properly dispersed for security purposes on an offshoot of the Ho Chi Minh Trail as seen here, constituted cross-border raiders and quick reaction reserves, but performed many other useful functions during forays into Laos and Cambodia. (John Plaster)*

It seems fair to say, however, that results might have been a mixed bag, even if superior headquarters had given SOG a freer rein and bigger budgets. Enemy counterintelligence specialists quickly scarfed up all but a few of 500 or so luckless South Vietnamese agents and turned a good many into double-crossers. PSYWAR experts enjoyed tactical fun and games, but strategically significant benefits were scarce. Maritime operations never were more than pinpricks. SOG's recon teams in sharp contrast developed priceless intelligence available from no other source. They also killed countless enemy soldiers (read thousands) and obliterated mountains of supplies in collaboration with dedicated air support and company-sized Hatchet Forces that consisted mainly of indigenous volunteers. A bevy of U.S. and

Opposite, bottom: *SOG's dirty tricks occasionally included trips "over the fence" clad in enemy uniforms. So doing risked forfeiture of protections that Geneva Conventions promise legitimate POWs, but Recon Team West Virginia, depicted here in North Vietnamese Army attire with Chinese weapons, seldom worried because no prisoners of war from SOG ever returned anyway. (John Plaster)*

Right: Two Air Force pararescue jumpers prepare for a jungle penetration from their hovering HH-53C helicopter, 14 April 1972. (National Archives)

Above: SOG's recon troopers in desperate straits sometimes escaped on "strings," which were nothing more than weighed ropes that hovering helicopters dropped to the ground through gaps in heavy foliage. Flights that followed extractions through teeny openings barely big enough to admit one man at a time would have frightened even escape artist Harry Houdini. (John Plaster)

allied airmen one step ahead of bloodthirsty pursuers deep in hostile territory still thank God that SOG's gutsy search and rescue crews returned them safely from white hot landing zones.

SOG's Rewards and Prices Paid

Approximately 2,600,000 men and women served in Vietnam between January 1965 and March 1973, of whom 243 received a Medal of Honor (.00009 percent). Nine Green Berets, one SEAL, and one Air Force Green Hornet Huey helicopter pilot, a hugely greater proportion of about 6,800 U.S. SOG personnel, were similarly decorated during the same period, four of them posthumously. Comrades recommended Sergeant First Class Bob Howard for that award three times in thirteen months before officials on high approved. The tiny recon company at Kontum, which rotated fewer than 300 men in and out during its years in combat, accumulated

Far left: *SOG Sergeant First Class Bob Howard, shown here after his battlefield promotion, was a warrior's warrior. The Medal of Honor he finally received after three recommendations merely capped a string of incredible feats that inspired friends and instilled fear in foes. (U.S. Army)*

Left: *Freckle-faced Staff Sergeant David Davidson, better known as "Babysan," lacked bulging biceps, a stubbly beard, and a hairy chest, but he was a superlative cross-border recon team chief. His luck ran out on 5 October 1970, when North Vietnamese troops terminated him on an isolated ridge in Laos during his third year with SOG. (John Plaster)*

A Special Forces advisor brings in a helicopter to extract a "Mike" Force (Mobile Strike Force) of Montagnard troops after a sixteen-day sweep near Bet Het in November 1969. These indigenous forces were very effective in conducting reconnaissance and combat operations. (National Archives)

MACV deliberately chose the euphemistic title "Studies and Observation Group" to keep its offensively-oriented cloak and dagger outfit under cover, but SOG's diabolical death's head patch would have been a dead giveaway (pun intended) if any member ever publicly displayed that ferocious emblem or similar insignia that subordinate elements prized. (John Plaster)

more Medals of Honor than any unit of comparable size in U.S. history, given equivalent ground rules. (James Andrews's twenty raiders received the first six ever issued after they hijacked a Confederate train in 1863, but on looser terms.)

SOG paid a high price in lifeblood for its assaults on the Ho Chi Minh Trail. More than 160 unsung heroes were killed in action or died of wounds. Purple Hearts numbered several hundred; oak leaf clusters were common—SFC Howard, for example, was severely wounded on eight separate occasions. None of the eighty missing in action resurfaced when North Vietnam released 591 U.S. prisoners of war early in 1973. The toll was far higher among SOG's fiercely loyal Nung, Montagnard, Cambodian, and South Vietnamese teammates, who comprised a majority on most cross-border missions, but nobody kept count. Was it worth it? Every warrior who participated would do it again, given the opportunity.

Special Air Operations

Super-secret, high-priority Jungle Jim programs, which opened in a remote corner of Eglin AFB, Florida, on 14 April 1961, introduced the jet-propelled, biggest bang for a buck Air Force to low-tech Air Commandos who possessed counterinsurgency capabilities that neither Strategic nor Tactical Air Command (SAC and TAC) could duplicate. Adventuresome volunteers, in tandem with Army Special Forces from the onset,

Above: *Low, slow A-1E Skyraiders which, unlike fuel-gulping jet fighters, could cover good guys on the ground for an hour or more per sortie, commonly answered SOG's distress calls. Huge ordnance loads, coupled with abilities to deliver knockout blows from treetop level, made them perfect platforms for the closest possible air support in the tightest possible places. (U.S. Air Force)*

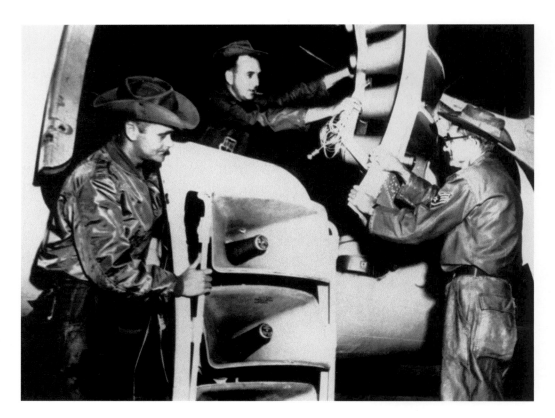

Right: *Air Force Special Operations Forces in Vietnam employed several PSYOP platforms to broadcast messages, deliver leaflets, or both. Air Commandos in jaunty hats manned the C-47 Gooney Bird shown here, which featured loudspeakers. (U.S. Air Force)*

initially flew sixteen geriatric C-47 Gooney Bird transports, eight B-26 medium bombers retrieved from a bone yard, and eight T-28 trainers that masqueraded as ground attack aircraft, all modified to suit special purposes under peculiar conditions. Operations to and from austere airstrips in the dead of night prepared them for assorted missions that elucidations below merely typify.

SOG's "private air force" flew surreptitious reconnaissance sorties, delivered agents and dropped supplies deep inside North Vietnam, supported deception programs, and provided close air support replete with forward air controllers for isolated parties in mortal peril. No missions, however, were more thrilling for all concerned than those that inserted clandestine teams over the fence from South Vietnam into communist-infested Laos and Cambodia, then extracted them when goings got excessively hot.

Courageous South Vietnamese crews flew antiquated, unmarked, lightly armed H-34 Kingbee helicopters that could stay aloft after hellacious enemy automatic weapons drilled holes from stem to stern. Retrievals commonly took place during daylight hours because air-ground coordination was iffy after dark, but Nguyen Van Huang, better known as Mustachio, flew into a firestorm all by himself one pitch black night in 1966 with no navigational instruments save his own sharp eyes, found a SOG recon team in desperate straits, whisked every member from harm's way, then returned unscathed despite eighty-eight holes in his aircraft.

The U.S. 20th Special Operations Squadron, nicknamed Green Hornets, first flew CH-3 Jolly Green Giants, then switched to UH-1F Hueys, half of which carried rockets, two multibarreled miniguns and, in some cases, grenade launchers. Pilots routinely popped into and out of pinhole-sized clearings surrounded by towering trees, but one of the most hair-raising rescues took place on 26 November 1968, when SOG Recon Team Chisel, with its back to a Cambodian river, faced NVA Regulars on the other three sides. First Lieutenant Jim Fleming was short on fuel after long hours in the air, but answered their SOS anyway. He inched onto the river bank while his tail rotor churned white caps, but the group ashore couldn't break contact, so he backed off with all guns blazing, lingered until Claymore mines bought time for him to flare in again against fearful

Opposite, top: Rugged A-1E Skyraiders, which originally served the U.S. Navy, carried more munitions than four-engined B-17 Flying Fortress heavy bombers did during World War II. No other Vietnam era attack aircraft in the USAF inventory crammed lethal payloads, accuracy, durability, and loiter times into one package nearly as well. (U.S. Air Force)

Bottom, left: Fearless South Vietnamese crews in obsolescent, lightly-armed, unmarked H-34 Kingbee helicopters flew countless cross border missions for SOG. Rough cut men and machines by all accounts were completely competent and incredibly tough. Recompense included a princely 3,000 piaster ($25) bonus for each insertion and extraction. (U.S. Air Force)

Bottom, right: HH-3 Jolly Green Giants, like this one hovering over a hole in the jungle, specialized in short notice rescue and recovery operations on hot landing zones at all hours of day or night. Intrepid crews saved SOG recon teams many times under awesome circumstances. (U.S. Air Force)

121

First Lieutenant James Fleming, a hotshot helicopter pilot who sported a "bushstache," was still in his work clothes when a friend snapped this picture immediately after Jim saved SOG Recon Team Chisel from certain death in Cambodia and safely delivered all hands to Duc Co. (John Plaster)

odds, then lifted off with all six SOG team members on board. Bullets broke his windshield and his bird was bone dry when it reached Duc Co after dark. All hands, however, were safe. Part of his recompense was a Medal of Honor. Grateful survivors furnished the rest.

Fixed-wing transport aircraft retooled as gunships were godsends to Army Special Forces frontier security outposts and other beleaguered forces. First-generation AC-47s, which cruised at a leisurely 120 knots, theoretically were vulnerable while they orbited at 3,000 feet with one wingtip tilted toward a given spot on the ground. Equipment excluded night vision devices and line-of-sight visibility between cockpit and target was poor, so pilots had to wait for signals below before they tripped triggers on three six-barrel miniguns. Darkness nevertheless concealed their locations aloft and those old, slow aircraft could loiter for hours until called. Strong men shuddered when Puff the Magic Dragon roared, stuck out its scarlet tongue, and belched fifty to a hundred 7.62mm bullets per second in short bursts. Awesome displays could continue as long as forty-five flares and the 24,000-round basic load lasted.

AC-130 Spectre gunships, which flew much higher and faster, boosted combat capabilities by orders of magnitude beginning late in 1967. AC-119 Flying Boxcars that bolstered the inventory a bit in 1969 sported two

Above: *AC-130 Spectre gunships, shown here belching death on insurgents below, were an immense improvement over capabilities obtainable from AC-47 Puff the Magic Dragons. Range, altitude, firepower, target acquisition capabilities, and survivability all were vastly superior. No other nation in 2002 possesses a comparable weapons system. (National Archives)*

Left: *Army Special Forces noncoms inspect a mini-gun aboard an Air Force AC-130 Spectre Gunship. (National Archives)*

20mm cannons and four miniguns, but their performance otherwise was little better than Puff's, and in some respects was worse. The fiercest Spectre mounted two 7.62mm machine guns, two 20mm cannons, and two 40mm cannons, or one 40mm and a low-recoil 105mm howitzer affectionately dubbed Big Bertha. Better yet, they came equipped with light-intensifying devices that turned night into day, laser range finders,

Opposite, top: *Puff the Magic Dragon's three miniguns gave great comfort to friends in dire need and put the fear of God into bad guys on the ground. C-47 Gooney Birds became obsolescent well before the Vietnam War, but AC-47 firepower was state-of-the-art through the mid-1960s. (U.S. Air Force)*

Top: *The firepower aboard SOF gunships was awesome. Aircraft loaded with linkless belts of armor-piercing 20mm Vulcan cannon ammunition shown here could spit out 100 rounds per minute. Targets received shellackings, even if other onboard weapons never fired a single shot. (U.S. Air Force)*

Above: *AC-130A Spectre gunships armed with four 7.62mm miniguns, plus 20mm and 40mm cannons, killed hundreds of trucks along the Ho Chi Minh Trail. Some mounted a 105mm howitzer, beginning in 1972. Sensors included Forward Looking Infrared Radar (FLIR) and Black Crow, which could detect spark plug emissions from idling enemy vehicles. (U.S. Air Force)*

and supersensitive sensors, especially forward-looking infrared radar (FLIR) that detected vehicular and body heat. Resultant offensive options not only made it possible for Spectres to kill tanks and trucks hidden under camouflage nets and triple canopy trees along the Ho Chi Minh Trail, but enabled them to engage assailants around isolated camps without waiting for defenders to holler, "They're already through the front gate!"

Audacious Disappointment

> *Old Mother Hubbard went to the cupboard*
> *To get her poor dog a bone.*
> *But when she got there, the cupboard was bare,*
> *And so the poor dog got none.*

That's precisely what happened to a grand group of Special Operators who set out to rescue at least seventy U.S. POWs inside Son Tay Prison near Hanoi on 20–21 November 1970. That illustrious team, with Air Force Brigadier General Leroy Manor in overall charge, featured Colonel "Bull" Simons, Lieutenant Colonel Elliot "Bud" Sydnor, and incomparable Captain Dick Meadows. Together, they prepared meticulous plans and conducted more than 170 rehearsals before President Nixon personally approved the mission that "Headhunter" Blackburn

originally conceived as a desk-bound commando in the Pentagon. They did everything right, but everything went wrong at the last minute because, unbeknownst to the would-be rescuers, custodians had transferred all prisoners to another camp not far away. U.S. sharpshooters greased more than forty North Vietnamese during a firefight that lasted less than thirty minutes before the broken-hearted assault force withdrew with one bullet wound and one broken bone.

The failed raid nevertheless produced meaningful pluses along with monumental disappointment: pumped up POWs, who got word through prison grapevines, knew they weren't forgotten. North Vietnamese leaders

This low-level oblique aerial photograph shows infamous Son Tay Prison the way it looked to a pilotless drone before Dick Meadows' fourteen-man assault force aboard an HH-53 Jolly Green Giant helicopter deliberately crash landed in the main compound. (U.S. Air Force)

Far left: Blackburn's Headhunters, *by Philip Harkins, lionized guerrilla chieftain Don Blackburn a decade before he became SOG's first top dog in 1965. Brigadier General Blackburn, from his perch in the Pentagon, conceived the Son Tay Raid five years later. That gambit failed, but nevertheless gave U.S. POWs in North Vietnam a new lease on life. (U.S. Army)*

Left: *Colonel "Bull" Simons, who characteristically dotted every "I" and crossed every "T," briefed raiders one last time to make sure they had it right immediately before all departed on that ill-starred mission to rescue U.S. POWs in Son Tay Prison near Hanoi. (Benjamin F. Schemmer)*

Above: *SOF raiders took full advantage of "Barbara," a miniature model of Son Tay Prison that the CIA prepared in minute detail for use during meticulous planning and preparation processes. Banana 1, the HH-3 helicopter that carried Dick Meadows' assault force, landed in a space about the size of a volleyball court within the 140x185 foot compound. (U.S. Army Special Operations Command)*

Right: *An MC-130E Combat Talon code named Cherry 1 led heliborne assault forces (shown here in practice formation) 337.7 miles over northern Thailand, southern Laos, and western North Vietnam in the dead of night to Son Tay. Cherry 2 served as a low-level escort for five A-1Es that furnished fire support. Major John Gargus, the navigator aboard Cherry 2, authored the AFSOF chapter in this book. (U.S. Air Force)*

quickly discarded scattered camps and concentrated all U.S. prisoners thirty to fifty per room in downtown Hanoi's crowded Hoa Lo Prison, where security was airtight but solitary confinement was infeasible. Occupants for the first time consequently could converse, care for each other, hold church services, and occupy endless hours with educational classes that included math, foreign languages, even culinary arts. Those improvements immeasurably boosted morale and, in some cases, preserved sanity until freedom finally arrived two years later.

Members of the Son Tay raiding force are shown aboard a helicopter inbound for the North Vietnamese POW compound not far from Hanoi. They had rehearsed the operation for months beforehand. (John F. Kennedy Special Warfare Museum)

Courage in the Clutch

Twenty-eight Army Special Forces, SEALs, and Air Commandos received Medals of Honor for conspicuous courage above and beyond the call of duty in Vietnam at the risk of life while engaged in action against an enemy of the United States. The illustrative trio of enlisted recipients cited below not only performed incredible feats, but lived to wear the award.

Staff Sergeant Roy Benavidez, assigned to Detachment B-56, 5th Special Forces Group (Airborne), on 2 May 1968 volunteered to rescue a desperately embattled twelve-man A Team in jungles near Loc Ninh after Viet Cong defenders dispersed three previous extraction attempts. That landing zone clearly was too hot, so he vectored his chopper to an alternative clearing about 75 yards away, hopped out while it hovered, was wounded three times before he reached the exhausted survivors, took charge nonetheless, then directed suppressive fires so he could carry or drag casualties to the waiting helicopter.

Roy Benavidez earned his Medal of Honor the hard way at Loch Ninh on 2 May 1968. A doctor mistakenly declared him dead from thirty-seven puncture wounds and serious lacerations, a broken jaw, exposed intestines, a collapsed lung, and eyes caked shut with blood. President Reagan told reporters, "You wouldn't believe [this] if it were a script" when he read the citation. (U.S. Army)

127

The Son Tay raid, which lasted twenty-seven minutes, ended when HH-53 Apple Two, dimly illuminated by an enemy surface-to-air missile that detonated overhead, scooted for safety before daybreak on 21 November 1970, with Lieutenant Colonel Bud Sydnor and thirty-three other raiders on board. (U.S. Air Force)

Colonel Arthur D. "Bull" Simons in civies discusses the failed Son Tay raid. He illustrates a point by using a map of the target area. (U.S. Army Center of Military History)

The situation turned really sour when Benavidez hobbled back to recover the dead team leader and classified documents. Enemy sharpshooters hit him in the back and belly, killed his pilot, and the "bird" crashed. He pulled stunned survivors from the wreckage, organized a defensive perimeter, and directed air strikes that enabled another helo to land. The gutsy sergeant thereafter engaged in hand-to-hand combat and sustained three more serious wounds before he transferred all casualties to serviceable transportation. Then, and only then, he crawled aboard himself, bloodied but unbowed.

Barrel-chested Engineman Second Class Mike Thornton, a physical marvel of immense strength and stamina, served his fourth tour in Vietnam with the U.S. Naval Advisory Group. His mission, together with Lieutenant Tom Norris and three indigenous SEALs, was to reconnoiter an enemy naval base just south of the Demilitarized Zone and perhaps snatch a prisoner on Halloween night, 31 October 1972, but the incompetent skipper of a Vietnamese Navy junk put them ashore in a hornet's nest several miles farther north.

The badly outnumbered band stumbled across a battalion-sized bivouac shortly after it started inland, then hightailed it back to the beach, where all hands hid until two enemy sentinels sounded alarms. One sentry fled, but Thornton butt-stroked the other with his rifle, quizzed him concerning their true location, and relayed results to

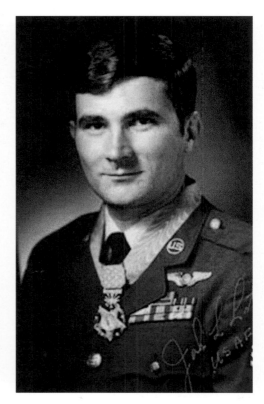

Norris, who called for naval gunfire from the cruiser USS *Newport News* before a terrible head wound knocked him unconscious and disfigured his face. Thornton, bloodied by grenade fragments, shouldered his officer's limp body, ran 400 meters through soft sand, rushed through the surf, added a badly injured Vietnamese SEAL to his load, towed both comrades into deep water, administered first aid, and swam for more than two hours fully clad until rescuers arrived. Who else could have done that? Maybe nobody.

Airman First Class John L. Levitow, who was loadmaster aboard the AC-47 gunship *Spooky 71*, demonstrated unbelievable bravery during actions to safeguard besieged Long Binh Army Base near Saigon on the night of 24 February 1969. One of his many tasks was to set ejection and ignition controls on parachute-delivered, two-million-candlepower flares that illuminated targets for ground troops and attack aircraft as well as *Spooky*'s minigunners. It was risky business because magnesium, which burns at 4,000 degrees Fahrenheit, was timed to ignite twenty seconds after other crewmen pitched each tube out the door.

Levitow had just passed a fully-primed flare to a partner when a Viet Cong mortar round hit the right wing, riddled the aircraft with holes, wounded all five men in the cargo compartment, put *Spooky* in a steep spiral, and plopped the sputtering tube into live ammunition. Badly lacerated, bleeding heavily, partially paralyzed, and flopping around inside the tilted fuselage, he tried to grab the careening flare with bare hands while it spewed toxic fumes, failed, then fell on it, hugged it to his body, crawled to the open door, hurled it out instants before it blazed, then collapsed unconscious. His reward for that selfless action, which saved the entire crew from incineration, was the only Medal of Honor that any Air Force enlisted man received during more than a decade of U.S. military involvement in Vietnam. Airman 1st Class William Pitzenbarger belatedly joined Levitow at the pinnacle in December 2001.

Top, left: SEAL Petty Officer Mike Thornton's Medal of Honor belongs in the Guinness book of records, because he rescued friend Tommie Norris, who subsequently received an identical decoration for rescues the previous April. No similar chain of events ever occurred before or since. (U.S. Navy)

Top, center: SEAL Lieutenant Tom Norris lost half of his face and would have lost his life without sidekick Mike Thornton's intervention. Thornton was present when Norris later received a Medal of Honor for earlier actions, during which he led overland and waterborne patrols that, within four days, rescued two downed pilots deep in enemy territory. (U.S. Navy)

Top, right: AC-47 loadmaster John Levitow's threshold of pain far surpassed that of most mortals when, despite concussion and more than forty wounds from an enemy mortar round, he threw himself bodily on a burning magnesium flare, dragged himself to the open cargo door, and hurled out that lethal device before it fully ignited. (U.S. Air Force)

1973-1991

1973-1991
Second Rejection and Resurrection

Colonel John M. Collins, USA (Ret)

DIETZ

Above: *General James Lindsay, the first Commander in Chief of U.S. Special Operations Command, symbolically strengthened USSOCOM's ties with the past in 1987 when he modified the unofficial spearhead emblem that General Wild Bill Donovan's Office of Strategic Services (OSS) designed during World War II. (U.S. Special Operations Command)*

Pages 130–131: *Members of the 7th Special Forces group disembark an Air Force SOF transport in Honduras, 1988. (Gary L. Kieffer)*

Left: *A portrait of a contemporary Special Forces soldier. ("Silent Warrior," James Dietz)*

The Phoenix, a mythical bird, once symbolized immortality. Only one such ever existed at any given time and, after a long life, each burned itself to death in a nest of aromatic wood, whereupon a successor miraculously emerged from the ashes.
—ADAPTED FROM AESOP'S FABLES

Special Operations nearly died when the Vietnam War wound down, but unlike the mythical Phoenix, it didn't do so voluntarily. Thrifty committees on Capitol Hill, abetted by military moguls who mimicked post–World War II predecessors, were collectively responsible for hatchet jobs in the early 1970s. SOF remnants, figuratively

Opposite: *More than 700 Rangers in C-141 Starlifters hit the silk above Torrijos-Tocumen International Airport east of Panama City shortly after 0100 hours on 20 December 1989. They quickly overwhelmed opposition with assistance from one AC-130 Spectre gunship and an AH-6 Little Bird light attack helicopter, both of which began to prep the drop zone while the lead man in each transport aircraft stood in the door. ("Jump into Night, Torrijos Airport," Al Sprague, Army Art Collection)*

Iranian mobs milled around the U.S. Embassy in Teheran after radical Iranian "students" beholden to the Ayatollah Khomeini seized sixty-seven hostages on 4 November 1979, released fourteen, and held fifty-three of them captive inside the walled compound. Dick Meadows' advance party cased the joint for rescuers who, due to unforeseen circumstances, failed to arrive the following April. (AP/Wide World)

covered with ashes, languished in Limbo for the next fifteen years until two military fiascos prompted congressional legislation that gave Special Operations Forces statutory responsibilities and authority. Bureaucratic battles continued, but steady improvement gradually overcame diehard opposition within the Department of Defense.

The Vietnam War created a wave of public revulsion across the United States well before U.S. involvement ceased. Congress, in response, sharply slashed the budgets of every military service during fiscal year 1970 and doled out dollars sparingly for several more years. Special Operations Forces suffered most severely, because potentates in the Pentagon viewed counterinsurgency and unconventional warfare as improbable missions for at least the next several decades and SOF played minor roles in plans to defend NATO Europe against Soviet aggression.

SOF-manning levels in every service plummeted far below authorized strengths after funding finally leveled out below one-tenth of one percent of the Department of Defense's budget. Nine active Army Special Forces group equivalents shrank to three loaded with low-ranking, under-trained neophytes. Impecunious SEAL teams and UDTs struggled to maintain previously stratospheric standards. The Department of the Navy at one point considered transferring them to the U.S. Naval Reserve or scrapping the lot, along with the only special operations submarine. Air Force SOF literally were flying on one wing and a prayer when amputations stopped.

Foreseeable Failures

Humiliations were predictable, given grievous shortcomings throughout the U.S. Special Operations community and politico-military employers who understood little and cared less about SOF capabilities and limitations. Fruitless efforts to rescue American hostages in Teheran came first, followed by bolixes in the Caribbean.

Major Generals Edward C. "Shy" Meyer and "Barbwire Bob" Kingston conceived and, after extensive lobbying, sold superiors on Special Forces Operational Detachment Delta (SFOD-D), an all-Army organization dedicated to counterterrorism. Activation at Fort Bragg occurred on 17 November 1977 with Colonel Charlie Beckwith as the first commander. Shy Meyer, then the Army's Deputy Chief of Staff for Operations, later became Chief of Staff. Bob Kingston, who commanded the John F. Kennedy Center for Military Assistance at Fort Bragg, North Carolina, later wore four stars as Commander in Chief, U.S. Central Command. Robert Kupperman, a counterterrorism specialist with the Arms Control and Disarmament Agency, contributed during Delta's concept formulation stage. Beckwith leaned on two close friends: retired Lieutenant General Sam Wilson, a Merrill's Marauder veteran, and civilian consultant Earl Lockwood.

Disaster at Desert One

The first practical test came on 24 April 1980, when Delta headed toward Teheran as part of a makeshift joint task force to rescue fifty-three hostages still incarcerated inside the U.S. Embassy compound since the previous

Two small, unused buildings that belonged to the JFK Special Warfare School at Fort Bragg were Delta's original digs in 1977. Brigadier General James Lindsay, then XVIII Airborne Corps Chief of Staff, soon thereafter donated the Post Stockade, which consisted of several solid structures on nine isolated acres inside a double chain link fence. (National Archives)

134

November. Interservice training before departure was superficial. Air Force C-130s arrived first at Desert One, an intermediate staging base in the Iranian outback, where they waited in darkness to refuel eight Navy Sea Stallion helicopters with Marine Corps pilots in each cockpit. Two choppers malfunctioned en route, a third on site, so Charlie Beckwith aborted the mission because no fewer than six were essential. Eight men died after a hovering helicopter collided with a C-130 while frustrated rescuers prepared to withdraw. Beckwith and the senior helicopter officer present agreed to abandon all five remaining Sea Stallions, which flames and exploding ammunition threatened to engulf. Forces from the world's greatest superpower, which faced no opposition of any kind, in short shellacked themselves because they were shy one measly chopper.

Top, left: *Then Major General Edward C. "Shy" Meyer was point man for Delta Force in the mid-1970s when many senior officials in the Pentagon strongly resisted activation proposals. U.S. Army counterterrorism capabilities might have been stillborn, or Delta's gestation period at best might have been prolonged, without his potent persuasive powers. (General Edward C. Meyer)*

Top, center: *"Barbwire Bob" Kingston, shown here as an Army Special Forces colonel at Fort Bragg, conceived and discussed concepts for a counterterrorist outfit much like Delta Force in the early 1970s, long before senior officials seriously began to debate missions and required capabilities. (General Robert C. Kingston)*

Top, right: *Green Beret Colonel "Charging Charlie" Beckwith, a warrior who won his spurs the hard way in Vietnam, later honed his skills as A Squadron commander, British 22d Special Air Service (SAS) Regiment. He took charge of Delta Force on 19 November 1977. (Benjamin Schemmer)*

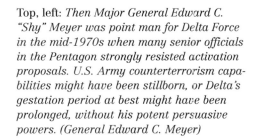

Eight Navy RH-53D Sea Stallion helicopters loaded aboard the aircraft carrier Nimitz *in the Arabian Sea, launched about dusk on 24 April 1980, then headed for the Desert One refueling site in central Iran, 600 nautical miles away. None returned. (U.S. Air Force)*

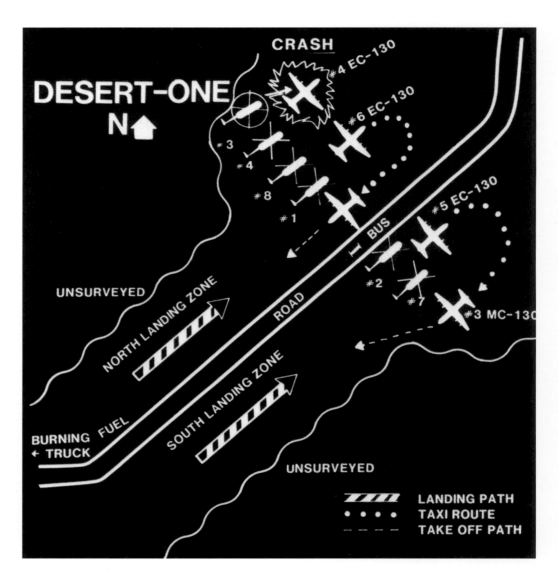

Aircraft on the ground at Desert One in Iran were tightly packed, as this schematic diagram indicates. The top center disaster site where a hovering Sea Stallion helicopter collided with an EC-130 is clearly visible. (U.S. Air Force)

Retired Army Special Forces Major Dick Meadows, every Green Beret's idol, infiltrated Teheran with Sergeant First Class John "Scotty" McEwan and several other Special Forces veterans, flawlessly scouted the U.S. Embassy compound, and reconnoitered urban routes thereto during Desert One. They unfortunately waited in vain to guide Delta Force rescuers who never arrived. This 1969 photo shows SOG Captain Meadows in Laos. (Colonel Robert Killebrew)

Glitches in Grenada

Pro-Cuban Marxists seized control of Grenada in March 1979, suspended the constitution, and tightened ties with the Soviet Union. An international airport, munitions storage facilities, barracks, training camps, and other components of a base from which to foment and support revolutions in the Caribbean Basin soon took shape. The Reagan Administration, which took an exceedingly dim view of such proceedings, invaded in October 1983 at the behest of several Caribbean countries after rambunctious radicals overthrew the Grenadian Government, which wasn't leftist enough for their liking.

The helicopter heap depicted by no means adequately illustrates the debacle at Desert One. Five brave airmen and three Marines died, flames destroyed an EC-130, none of the six Sea Stallion choppers on site survived, and Iranian radicals held fifty-three U.S hostages for nine more months. (U.S. Air Force)

136

Superb Army Rangers, SEALs, and Delta forces that formed the tip of the spear faced badly outclassed foes (whose opposition, however, was led by a seasoned Cuban colonel whom Fidel Castro rushed to the island just before the invasion began). An implausibly short fuse and faulty intelligence nevertheless put two of Murphy's Laws into play from the onset: "Nothing is as easy as it looks; anything that can go wrong will go wrong" at the worst possible moment.

Excessive urgency at the highest levels allowed four days to mount Operation "Urgent Fury" between Friday, 21 October and H-Hour for participants at 0500 the following Tuesday. Planners reserved no time whatsoever to review alternative concepts of operation, rehearse, and adjust. Unhappy consequences ensued.

Air Force combat controllers on the night of 23 October expected sixteen SEALs in Boston Whaler assault boats to transport them from the destroyer USS *Clifton Sprague* to Point Salines airport, where they were to reconnoiter surroundings, forward results up the chain of command, emplace beacons, and guide in Army Rangers aboard C-130 transports during wee hours the next night. Four overburdened SEAL parachutists, six hours behind schedule, unfortunately drowned when they dropped into roiling seas after dark instead of at dusk. Survivors tried again the next night, but unanticipated foul weather and high sea states, plus equipment failures, led to mission failure.

Task Force 160 (the Night Stalkers) at Fort Campbell, Kentucky, alerted shortly before supper on Sunday afternoon, arrived in objective areas ninety minutes late on Tuesday morning because feverish helicopter crews had to disassemble their birds; load and reload aboard C-5 Galaxy transports until all concerned were satisfied; pick up passengers at Pope Air Force Base, North Carolina; head for Barbados, which boasted the nearest Caribbean airfield that could handle C-5s; reassemble their Black Hawks; and finally fly 170 miles to Grenada under their own power.

Current intelligence concerning the lay of the land as well as enemy strengths, equipment, locations, dispositions, and inclinations to fight, was woefully deficient in many respects, although activities on Grenada that were inimical to U.S. security interests had been plainly visible for three years. Recent aerial photos replete with grid squares supplemented antiquated tourist maps of the island in some cases, but lacked contour lines and heavy vegetation often concealed key features.

Most Rangers expected to airland at Point Salines, but had to leap extemporaneously because neither aerial nor on-site reconnaissance revealed that bulldozers, barrels, and other paraphernalia littered the only runway. Delta's mission, which was to free political prisoners at Richmond Hill Prison, came a cropper when unanticipated enemy firepower downed the lead helicopter and put three others out of commission with one dead and several seriously wounded. Three more Black Hawks crashed and three Rangers died because nobody knew beforehand that suitable landing zones were absent along cliffs on three sides of the People's Revolutionary Army (PRA) training ground at Camp Calivigny.

Prudent planners never send a boy to do a man's job, but orders nevertheless directed a few lightly armed SEALs to seize and hold the

Ernesto "Che" Guevara, a guerrilla warfare guru and Fidel Castro's sidekick, was a source of inspiration to pro-Communist factions on Grenada in 1983. Souvenirs that U.S. Special Operations Forces accumulated after fighting ceased included four portraits on this romanticized postcard that a Cuban soldier pasted inside his footlocker. (Commando Operations, Time-Life Books)

Faulty topographic intelligence and failure to anticipate massed firepower from nearby Fort Frederick produced a fiasco at Richmond Hill Prison, where sixty Delta Force troopers aboard six Black Hawk helicopters sought to rescue political prisoners. That mission came a cropper after a hail of bullets downed one vulnerable bird and badly damaged all others. (National Archives)

Above: *Rangers expected to land at Point Salines Airport in southwest Grenada but, because heavy obstacles blocked the runway, parachuted in instead, dropping from only 500 feet to minimize exposure to enemy fire. (U.S. Air Force)*

main radio station on Grenada and a few more to rescue Britain's Governor General and his staff, whom goons held under house arrest. Both succeeded as long as resistance remained light, but PRA troops soon ran the first outgunned group into the sea and U.S. Marines had to divert an entire company from its primary mission to rescue the second contingent.

Hasty planning wasted precious lives and expensive property during "Urgent Fury." U.S. Atlantic Command, unfamiliar with standard SOF procedures, scheduled assaults during daylight instead of after dark. Promulgators learned what experienced Special Operators knew all along. The proper answer to the question, "Do you want it right, or do you want it right now?" invariably should be, "We want it right," unless postponement invites greater trouble than prompt action.

The Advent of USSOCOM

Thumb-in-the-eye, knee-in-the-groin bureaucratic battles over the future of U.S. Special Operations Forces began in the Pentagon before the debacle at Desert One and continued unabated despite embarrassing glitches in Grenada. True believers whose persistent efforts finally legitimized SOF and paved the way for eventual acceptance should reside forever in USSOCOM's Hall of Fame.

Noel Koch, the Principal Deputy Assistant Secretary of Defense for National Security Affairs, along with Colonel George McGovern (his military assistant) and civilian Lynn Rylander, lit intellectual candles to enlighten senior Pentagon officials starting in 1981, but high-ranking officials with closed minds blew out those flames before they could spread. Koch and his frustrated cohorts eventually concluded that "sometime, but not now" clearly meant "never, never, never" when the topic concerned proposed SOF reforms.

Key players on Capitol Hill, fed up with foot dragging, made similar deductions more or less simultaneously. Congressman Dan Daniel on the House Armed Services Committee, coached by his lieutenant Ted Lunger and savvy Lieutenant General Sam Wilson, led the charge. Sam Nunn, then Chairman of the Senate Armed Services Committee, and colleague Bill Cohen picked up the cudgel in 1985. Army generals Shy Meyer, Sam Wilson, and Bob Kingston provided crucial participants with respected advice and council throughout protracted debates. Pro-SOF Benjamin Schemmer, who owned and edited the influential *Armed Forces Journal*, publicly sharpened issues when he pounded a gong that was impossible for adversaries to ignore. Schemmer currently supports Special Operations as Editor in Chief of this tome.

Congress, like Hercules who cleansed stinking Aegean stables as one of his seemingly impossible labors, on 14 November 1986 promulgated Public Law (P.L.) 99-661, which created an Assistant Secretary of Defense for Special Operations and Low-Intensity Conflict (ASD SO/LIC) with policy and resource oversight responsibilities. Congress further decreed a United States Special Operations Command and told its Commander in Chief (CINCSOC) to develop SOF doctrine, strategies, and tactics;

Above: Sam Nunn (D-GA) and colleague Bill Cohen (R-ME), who respectively were Chairman and a bridge-building member of the Senate Armed Services Committee, championed Special Operations in the mid-1980s. Congressman Dan Daniel (D-VA) did likewise in the House of Representatives. Gifted assistants helped them craft legislation that gave SOF a statutory power base. (U.S. Special Operations Command)

Opposite, top: Most Rangers hit the ground at Point Salines, Grenada, in broad daylight, well behind schedule. They secured the airfield, occupied the nearby Cuban construction camp, then made a beeline for Saint George's Medical School a few miles to the east to safeguard U.S. students who had witnessed the parachute assault with pride and apprehension. (Commando Operations, Time-Life Books)

Retired Lieutenant General Sam Wilson, in his capacity as SOF elder statesman in the mid-1980s, was the respected adviser of senators, congressmen and key members of their staffs who crafted legislation that created an integrated U.S. Special Operations community. (Lieutenant General Samuel V. Wilson)

139

validate requirements; establish priorities; ensure combat readiness; prepare budget requests for SOF-peculiar weapons, equipment, supplies, and services; train assigned forces; monitor the preparedness of Special Operations Forces worldwide; and otherwise promote professionalism.

P.L.100-180 lowered a second boom on 4 December 1987 because congressional conferees "felt forced by bureaucratic resistance within the Department of Defense to take very detailed action on mandating the urgently needed reorganization and reform of special operations and low-intensity conflict capabilities, policies and programs." The ASD SO/LIC became the principal civilian advisor to the Secretary of Defense (SECDEF) on such matters, with direct access to that Great Man or his deputy. Persistent programming and budgeting problems led to P.L. 100-456, which, on 29 September 1988, gave CINCSOC control over all funds for forces under his command, so senior Army, Navy, and Air Force officials could no longer divert dollars from SOF to conventional forces.

Blind Homer, who lived in perpetual darkness, knew full well that "there is many a slip twixt the cup and the lip." Slips aplenty in fact followed passage of those three federal laws. Congress, for example, intended that CINCSOC command all Active and Reserve Component SOF in the United States, but one sea service complied reluctantly, the other scarcely at all.

Navy leaders fought to retain control of SEALs (which absorbed Underwater Demolition Teams in 1983), Special Boat Units, and Swimmer Delivery Vehicle Teams on grounds that they provide crucially important capabilities not otherwise available to fleet commanders. Many SEAL officers were reluctant to switch because, unlike Army and Air Force SOF, they occupied a specialist category that had promised reasonable promotion prospects since 1970. Recent funding increases moreover lent credibility to a Naval Special Warfare Master Plan that painted rosy pictures of their future. Pockets of resistance consequently persisted after compulsory transfers took place on 1 March 1988. The U.S. Marine Corps, which successfully insisted that none of its units fit official definitions of SOF, limited involvement to a few individuals on CINCSOC's staff. Marine Corps Commandant General James Jones in July 2002 announced intentions to contribute combatants, but their size, configuration, roles, and missions remained uncertain when this book went to press.

No cape-clad magician could intone "Presto! Chango!" and pull perfected SOF out of his plug hat in a puff of purple smoke because elite military capabilities, unlike legislative intentions, take time to mature, especially when resistance is strong. Newly created USSOCOM and SOF round the world nevertheless soon began to benefit from better personnel management, arms, equipment, and training within organizational structures that promoted interdepartmental, interagency, interservice, and international team play. The SOF community, which served as a test bed for innovative products and procedures, incrementally acquired characteristics that die-hard domestic critics grudgingly admired and foreign adversaries feared.

Operation "Earnest Will" (1987-1988)

Egomaniacal Iraqi President Saddam Hussein, nominally a Sunni Muslim, in 1980 attacked neighboring Shiite Iran. The resultant war of attrition, which lasted eight years and challenged freedom of transit throughout the Persian Gulf, indirectly involved petroleum-dependent countries everywhere.

Iraqi assaults on oil facilities at Abadan, Dezful, and Ahwaz, along with tankers en route, cut Iranian shipments in half by 1986, whereupon Iran retaliated in kind, mainly with contact mines and Silkworm antiship missiles. Actions escalated sharply the following year when Iran, enraged because Saudi Arabia and Kuwait were bankrolling "Iraqi brothers," began to interdict tankers that served those two countries. President Ronald Reagan on 10 March 1987 agreed to reflag eleven Kuwaiti tankers under the Stars and Stripes after the Emir asked for assistance, then widened the scope to ensure safe passage of all petroleum-laden ships to and from friendly Persian Gulf ports.

The first Operation Earnest Will convoy came to a halt on 21 July 1987 when a tethered mine tore a huge hole in the oil tanker *Bridgeport*.

Top, left to right:
General Robert C. Kingston, whose diversified SOF experience totaled ten years including unconventional warfare in Korea and Southeast Asia, was a strong contender to become the first CINCSOC. Many admirers considered him best qualified, but he had retired in December 1985 and recall to active duty never materialized. (General Robert C. Kingston)

General James J. Lindsay, the first CINCSOC (June 1987–May 1990), wore a Distinguished Service Cross and a Silver Star with four Oak Leaf Clusters. He commanded a Special Forces A Detachment as a captain. Infantry assignments thereafter culminated with command of the 82d Airborne Division and XVIII Airborne Corps. (USSOCOM)

General Carl W. Stiner logged about six years with SOF before he became the second CINCSOC (June 1990–May 1993), first as a captain with the 3d Special Forces Group, then as a major general in charge of the Joint Special Operations Command. He ran U.S. combat operations in Panama during Operation Just Cause as a three-star general. (USSOCOM)

Middle, left to right:
General Wayne A. Downing had six Special Ops assignments after he was promoted to lieutenant colonel. Earlier combat experience in Vietnam, coupled with senior SOF responsibilities during Operations Just Cause and Desert Storm, prepared him well for assignment as the third CINCSOC (May 1993–February 1996). (USSOCOM)

Captain Henry H. Shelton served with the 5th Special Forces Group in Vietnam. He commanded the 82d Airborne Division and XVIII Airborne Corps as a two- and three-star general before he became the fourth CINCSOC in 1996. "Hugh" left that slot the following year when President Clinton made him Chairman of the Joint Chiefs of Staff. (USSOCOM)

General Peter J. Schoomaker, the fifth CINCSOC (November 1997–October 2000), accrued extensive SOF experience starting with Delta Force in the late 1970s. He returned to Delta in several capacities including Commander, served as a SOF staff officer in the Pentagon, then commanded the JSOC and U.S. Army Special Operations Command (USSOCOM)

Bottom, left:
General Charles R. Holland, an AC-130 pilot, broke the mold on 21 October 2000 when he became the first Air Force CINCSOC. Rungs on his SOF ladder first featured seventy-nine combat missions with the 1st Special Operations Wing at Udorn, Thailand. He later was JSOC's Deputy Commanding General, then occupied top slots at SOCPAC and AFSOC. (USSOCOM)

Army Task Force 160's MH-60 Black Hawk helicopters saw yeoman service during Operation Earnest Will, primarily for resupply and medical evacuation purposes (sometimes for search and rescue). This one hovers above the Hercules, an oil rig servicing barge refitted as a waterborne base that greatly increased SOF flexibility. (U.S. Army Special Operations Command)

Agile U.S. Army Little Bird helicopters working in tandem from U.S. Navy ships sank or disabled several Iranian gunboats and mine layers during Operation Earnest Will in 1987–1988. Miniguns and rockets, coupled with forward-looking infrared radar (FLIR) that enabled occupants to see through darkness and fog, gave them a distinctive edge. (U.S. Army Special Operations Command)

Active protection thus became mandatory. Special Operations Forces got golden opportunities to strut their stuff because Navy and Marine Corps inventories contained nothing nearly as suitable as SEAL shallow-draft boats and the Army's MH/AH-6 Little Bird helicopters, which performed best after dark when Iranian minelayers did their dirty work.

Three surgical operations in quick succession without a single U.S. casualty made these saboteurs back off. Sea and air SOF working in tandem discovered, disabled, boarded, searched, and sank the minelayer *Iran Aja* on 21–22 September 1987. Three weeks later, three Little Birds shot it out with and sank three Iranian gunboats that lurked in the dark to ambush unwary petroleum tankers near Middle Shoals Buoy. Four destroyers, in retaliation for Silkworm attacks on two tankers, bombarded an Iranian gas-oil separator (GOSP) on 19 October. SEALs thereafter secured a damaged oil-drilling platform in shallow water, left a demolition team to complete destruction, then seized valuable intelligence materials from another site nearby.

Routine SOF scouting and patrolling continued without further combat until December 1988, when Earnest Will forces rode herd on one last tanker convoy. SEALs and Little Birds performed admirably on every occasion, but Persian Gulf storms buffeted available boats so badly that USSOCOM easily validated requirements for replacements with better sea-keeping capabilities.

Operation "Just Cause" (1989-1990)

General Manuel Noriega, who specialized in electoral fraud, murder, illicit drug dealings, corruption, and civil rights violations, seized control of Panama in 1983. He tightened ties with leftist Cuba, Nicaragua, and Libya, savagely suppressed rioters in 1987, subsequently crushed a coup, and in response to sanctions, declared war on the United States in December 1989. President George Herbert Walker Bush responded with Operation Just Cause, which sought to defang armed forces loyal to Noriega, arrest him, and restore order in that strategically important country.

General Maxwell Thurman, the Commander in Chief of U.S. Southern Command, kicked off Operation Just Cause just after midnight on 20 December 1989 with Army Lieutenant General Carl Stiner as his right-hand man. General Stiner went on to serve as USSOCOM's second Commander in Chief from June 1990 until May 1993.

SOF's main missions were to help neutralize Panamanian Defense Forces (PDF) and capture Noriega. Tributary instructions told them to block Noriega's land, sea, and aerial escape routes; keep potential reinforcements out of Panama City; seize three major airports; secure Atlantic and Pacific terminals of the Panama Canal; rescue a CIA agent incarcerated in Modelo Prison; and disable major telecommunication transmitters.

Army Rangers aboard a U.S. Navy Combat Harbor Patrol Division inshore patrol craft from Naval Station Rodman, Panama, prepare to disembark on a search for simulated "aggressor" troops. They are participating in a joint Army-Navy riverine/jungle warfare exercise along the Chagres River in Panama in 1983. Practiced joint operations and working knowledge of the Panamanian landscape were to prove helpful six years later during operation Just Cause. (Naval Historical Center)

Page 144–145: Army Rangers parachuted in to seize key objectives in support of Operation Just Cause in Panama 1989. ("Energetically... Rangers in Panama," James Dietz)

Page 145: MH-60G Pave Hawk helicopters (Black Hawks with in-flight refueling probes) delivered eight to ten Rangers apiece at H-Hour to block access routes between Panama City and potential reinforcements, then provided fire support with twin 7.62mm miniguns. (U.S. Air Force)

Army Major General Wayne Downing's Joint Special Operations Task Force (JSOTF) deservedly drew accolades for well-choreographed actions that involved SEALs, Special Boat units, Army Rangers, Special Forces, Delta, PSYOP, Civil Affairs, and Air Force Special Tactics teams on a grand scale. USSOCOM's Army and Air Force component commands furnished a wide array of fixed- and rotary-wing aircraft for reconnaissance, surveillance, aerial fire support, and transportation. Contingency preparations entitled "Blue Spoon," which began almost two years ahead, gave prospective combatants ample opportunity to iron out wrinkles. Links between SOF and non-SOF participants were infinitely closer than loose lashups during Operation Urgent Fury in Grenada.

JSOTF accordingly accomplished all assigned missions with alacrity. U.S. Special Operations Forces took less than twenty-four hours to stifle most organized resistance. JSOTF's forces quickly controlled Omar Torrijos International Airport, adjacent Tocumen military airfield, and the PDF airbase at Rio Hato. Disciplined shooters had clear shots at 167 terrified cadets who popped up unexpectedly inside Rio Hato's NCO Academy, but took them captive instead. SOF safely evacuated panicky passengers, some of whom PDF held hostage, after a Brazilian airliner arrived without warning just before Just Cause began. No reinforcements reached PDF Headquarters inside the *Comandancia*, which housed Noriega's paramilitary Dignity Battalion and other fanatics. PSYOP-style telephone calls nicknamed "Ma Bell" induced almost 2,000 enemy troops in fourteen rural garrisons to surrender without firing a shot. Delta Force troops, dressed like Darth Vader, spirited Kurt Frederick Muse out of Modelo Prison in 360 seconds. SOF squelched television transmitters high above Panama City by 1500 hours on D-Day and silenced Radio Nacional's

Top: *Macho de Monte (Mountain Men) of Manuel Noriega's elite 7th Rifle Company looked and acted as tough as the death's head on crossed bayonets they displayed outside their headquarters at Rio Hato, Panama, but Colonel Buck Kernan's Rangers mopped them up in less than two hours along with 6th Company counterparts during Operation Just Cause. (U.S. Army)*

AM/FM stations a few hours later. JSOTF chased wily Noriega all over the Isthmus before he sought sanctuary in the Papal Nuncio's residence. Civil Affairs and PSYOP units helped stabilize Panama before and after Noriega surrendered at 2044 hours on 3 January 1990.

Special Operations Forces, which accounted for slightly more than 15 percent of the Just Cause troop list (4,400 of 27,000), suffered half of all killed in action and nearly 30 percent of all wounded (11 of 23 KIA; 93

of 324 WIA). Those counts almost included Ranger Colonel (now four-star general) Buck Kernan, who extinguished every electric light at Rio Hato when he hit a power line that set his parachute on fire. A shootout that wags later christened Operation Lavatorio de Caballeros took place in a men's room at Panama City's International Airport. Two toughs standing on toilet seats inside stalls survived when Rangers rolled in a grenade, then shot soldiers who came through the door. One thug met his Maker immediately thereafter; a watchful Ranger wasted the other, who toppled from a second-story window.

Sixty-two SEALs at Punta Paitilla Airport on Panama Bay took the worst pounding. Repeated rehearsals indicated that they could easily overcome night-shift maintenance crews plus a few civilian "Rent-a-Cops," disable Noriega's Learjet, and block the runway to prevent his escape. Well-laid plans unfortunately went astray when barricaded gunmen with automatic weapons ambushed one platoon, killed four SEALs in the open, and wounded eight more. Whether airfield seizure was a suitable SEAL mission has been subject to debate ever since, but the main culprit most likely was what Prussian strategist Carl von Clausewitz called "the fog of war."

War With Iraq (1990-1991)

Three armor-heavy Republican Guard divisions beholden to Iraqi despot Saddam Hussein rumbled into Kuwait shortly after midnight on 2 August 1990. Rapid buildups put eight more divisions in place as far south as the Saudi Arabian border less than a week later, at which time Saddam formally annexed that oil rich kingdom as Iraq's nineteenth province. U.N. Security Council Resolutions immediately renounced his power play; President Bush drew an imaginary line in the sand; and a multinational coalition installed Desert Shield against further aggression, then launched Operation Desert Storm to liberate Kuwait.

Desert Storm put icing on the Special Operations cake that planners and practitioners baked during Just Cause. Political inhibitions and military reluctance limited roles that top-level decision-makers allowed SOF to play, but great diversification nevertheless is evident in this smorgasbord. The vanguard of SEALs that arrived on 12 August 1990 comprised the first segment of a tripwire along the border between Saudi Arabia and Kuwait. Army Special Forces gave clandestine intelligence collection tips to, and guided the efforts of, Kuwaiti freedom fighters who furnished more useful information than any other source in that occupied country.

The shooting war began on 17 January 1991, when terrain-hugging Pave Low helicopters replete with night vision devices led Apache gunships that demolished two Iraqi early warning radars and opened air corridors into the heart of Iraq. SOF CH-47 Chinooks planted beacons to mark cleared flight paths for land attack aircraft that followed. Green Berets, in concert with Saudi and Egyptian engineers, breached several Iraqi minefields and bridged an above-ground pipeline that impeded access from Saudi Arabia into Kuwait. MC-130 Combat Talon crews

William F. Kernan, shown here as a Ranger colonel, later became Commander in Chief of Joint Forces Command and the first non-Navy Supreme Allied Commander Atlantic. The Secretary of Defense on that occasion said, "We can expect to see Buck Kernan residing where Rangers feel most at home— at the battle's cutting edge. . ." (General William F. Kernan)

Opposite, bottom left: *Delta Force soldiers and men from the 7th Infantry Division went to work at the* Commandancia, *headquarters of the Panamanian Defense Force in Panama City. They accomplished assigned missions there in short order, with few serious casualties on either side. (U.S. Air Force)*

Opposite, bottom right: *Cannons aboard AC-130 Spectre gunships and AH-6 Little Birds armed with rockets and miniguns worked over the* Commandancia's *heavily-walled citadel from top to bottom, but dents in that sanctuary were mainly superficial after sound and fury subsided. (U.S. Air Force)*

Thank God for combat search and rescue crews! That thought must have been in Navy Lieutenant Devon Jones' mind when he raced toward an MH-53J Pave Low helicopter sixty miles northwest of Baghdad on 21 January 1991. Two A-10 Warthogs smoked an Iraqi truck that tried to grab him first. (U.S. Air Force)

MC-130 Combat Talons delivered eleven BLU-82 bombs during Operation Desert Storm, first to obliterate Iraqi minefields, then for psychological purposes. Overpressures from each 15,000-pound warhead approached 1,000 pounds per square inch near ground zero. Lethal effects covered the equivalent of three football fields in all directions. (U.S. Air Force)

obliterated five other minefields with humongous BLU-82 "Daisy Cutter" bombs. Heliborne combat swimmers destroyed twenty-nine antiship mines in the Persian Gulf. SEALs who probed Kuwaiti beaches to make Saddam Hussein anticipate amphibious assaults diverted two Iraqi divisions that otherwise could have opposed overland offensives during Desert Storm. SEALs captured the first POWs on 24 January when they seized an offshore oil platform loaded with belligerent Iraqis and liberated Qarah Island.

Special Forces, with variable degrees of success, conducted strategic reconnaissance missions deep inside Iraq to monitor the movement of enemy ground forces that might attack VII or XVIII Airborne Corps. The Iraqis never had one effective Scud surface-to-surface missile launch against Israel after Delta Force and Special Tactics teams were inserted deep into western Iraq by SOF aviation beginning on 7 February. Their work kept Israel out of the war. SOF helicopters inserted Special Forces teams at two sites along VII Corps avenues of advance, where they tested soil and took photographs to ascertain trafficability conditions.

AC-130 Spectre gunships furnished awesome aerial fire support. All fourteen crew members aboard "Spirit 03," who selflessly continued to assist Marines at Khafji after dark gave way to daylight on 31 January 1991, went to a watery grave in the gulf when Iraqi surface-to-air gunners scored a direct hit. Iraqi troops grabbed most other downed aircrews before SOF's search and rescue teams arrived, but three recoveries were spectacularly successful.

Valorous deeds routinely receive standing ovations from admiring audiences, whereas virtuosos behind the scenes remain largely unsung.

Accolades below accordingly recognize bravura performances by SOF liaison teams, psychological operations (PSYOP) specialists, and civic action units.

The 5th Special Forces Group, commanded by Colonel Jim Kraus, sent 109 linguistically competent Coalition Support Teams (CSTs) to assist Saudi General Sultan bin Abdul Aziz, whose Joint Arab Islamic Force consisted of troops from twenty-three nations with disparate languages, customs, religions, arms, equipment, doctrines, and capabilities. Commander in Chief H. Norman Schwarzkopf, who regularly received combat readiness reports that underscored allied capabilities and limitations, hailed Green Berets as the glue that held his incongruent coalition together

Teams installed radio links from division down to company level, then conducted individual and unit training that featured tactics, fire coordination, close air support, minefield breaching, maintenance, and medical evacuation. Special Forces officers and NCOs filled about half the Tactical Operation Center slots in all six Kuwaiti brigades. After combat began, each CST controlled U.S. air strikes, which not only simplified targeting but reduced the likelihood of casualties from "friendly" fire by coalition partners. Green Berets guided the Syrian Corps through U.S. 1st Cavalry Division lines after dark and took two objectives when Iraqi resistance stopped Pan-Arab troops.

Well-conceived psychological operations cement ties with friends, convert fence straddlers, and meddle with enemy minds to the wielder's advantage. Colonel Tony Normand and Lieutenant Colonel Dan Devlin, with a wealth of practical experience between them, concocted PSYOP plans and programs that reaped strategic, operational, and tactical benefits during Desert Shield and Desert Storm, despite stringent politico-military restrictions.

Saddam Hussein, for example, encouraged members of the Muslim world to overthrow "corrupt" rulers, promised to redistribute wealth among "have" and "have not" nations, and pledged to protect Islam against U.S.-led infidels. U.S. PSYOPers in response helped develop, and universally respected Islamic sources disseminated, messages designed

Above: *Egomaniacal Iraqi President Saddam Hussein, who escaped harm during Operation Desert Storm, has remained a menace ever since. U.S. Special Operations Forces undoubtedly will play prominent roles in any attempt to topple his ever more malicious regime, as President George W. Bush promised during the summer of 2002. (AP/Worldwide)*

to discredit those claims. Implementing themes typically emphasized Saddam's willingness to sacrifice Iraqi Armed Forces; his disregard for the suffering of Iraqi civilians; his amassment of personal fortunes at their expense; his waste of national resources; his repression of minorities; his cynical manipulation of sacred Islamic tenets; and his brutal attacks on Muslim brothers. It's impossible to prove cause-effect relationships, but this much is certain: Syria's President Hafiz al-Assad, who scarcely admired the United States, donated 17,000 troops and 300 T-72 tanks to the cause, Libya's Mu'ammar al-Qadhafi remained quiescent, and a dozen other Muslim countries far and wide joined the coalition.

Precise effects of PSYOP on Iraqi troops were equally hard to pin down, but a few facts are indicative. Voice of the Gulf AM/FM broadcasts and mobile loudspeakers, which bombarded Iraqi audiences around-the-clock, mingled music with demoralizing situation reports that clearly were correct. Nearly thirty million leaflets that littered the landscape told potential defectors how to surrender, furnished maps that pinpointed collection stations, and promised no harm to those who complied. Terrified troops often abandoned weapons and decamped when leaflets warned that B-52 bombers would soon assail their positions. Nearly three-fourths of more than 85,000 POWs said PSYOP influenced decisions to surrender. These results would have saved many lives and significantly shortened the war even if those figures were grossly inflated.

USSOCOM's Civil Affairs units performed imperative post-combat missions in collaboration with Islamic counterparts when they directed the delivery of emergency food, water, and medical supplies to Kuwait on

liberation day, then helped the Kuwaiti government restore health, transportation, and electrical facilities, repair utilities, reestablish police forces, and extinguish some of the 650 flaming oil wells that Iraqi arsonists torched. Statistical lists included the distribution of water, 12,500 tons of food, 1,250 tons of medicine, 750 vehicles, and 245 electrical generators.

Lieutenant Colonel Raphael Perl, a full-time analyst with the Congressional Research Service and weekend Civil Affairs warrior in the U.S. Army Reserve, received orders to reinstate sanitation facilities. No manual contained convenient checklists but, on his own initiative, he planned essential operations with Kuwaiti representatives in Washington, D.C., assembled a mountain of materials in the United States, supervised preparations for shipment, accepted cargos on the far shore, formed an unprecedented convoy that contained 50 trash trucks and 300 sanitation specialists, instructed polyglot drivers who spoke no English, then led that caravan across the desert to Kuwait City, where occupants controlled ailments that result from unsanitary conditions and kept the rat population down.

Comfort for Kurds

Yogi Berra was right when he quipped, "It ain't over till it's over," because it surely wasn't over when Desert Storm stopped on 28 February 1991. Barely one month elapsed before Iraqi troops crushed rebellious Kurds and created refugee problems of epic proportion in snow-covered mountains that straddle the Turkish frontier. Hundreds of civilian men, women, and children who lacked adequate food, water, clothing, and shelter died daily from amoebic dysentery, acute dehydration, cholera, and other diseases until mid-April, when shocked observers finally intervened.

Brigadier General Richard Potter, who deployed an Army Special Forces Task Force across a 3,600-square-mile area of responsibility, summed up its accomplishments as follows: "No other brigade-size element could have . . . taken responsibility for 600,000 Kurds; organized a relief effort; stabilized the situation; dealt with the international political

151

and cultural ambiguities; and produced success with no compromise or embarrassment to the United States. . . . Colonel Bill Tangney [the 10th Group Commander] masterfully transitioned his units from combat operations to humanitarian endeavors and turned seemingly hopeless situations into success stories." Well said. Tiny teams worked miracles in squalid camps such as Cukurea, where SOF medics saved all but three of 250 desperately ill children that civilian doctors considered incurable.

Historical Lessons Learned

The scribbled names of American soldiers are big and black on the walls of the fortress at Verdun. One of them says:

> **AUSTIN WHITE, CHICAGO, ILLINOIS, 1918**
> **AUSTIN WHITE, CHICAGO, ILLINOIS, 1945**
> **THIS IS THE LAST TIME**
> **I WANT TO WRITE MY NAME HERE.**

A third rejection with no promise of resurrection isn't SOF's first choice either, but all concerned should bear in mind that U.S. armed forces have suffered sharp cutbacks after every major war since the

152

American Revolution. Nothing in tarot cards says it can't happen again, so Special Operators who hope to feel knives last and least instead of first and foremost must make themselves indispensable across the conflict spectrum or repeatedly risk unpleasant historical experiences.

Prospects for permanent acceptance would improve immensely if SOF deeds as well as words permanently convince Secretaries of Defense, the Joint Chiefs of Staff, and commanders in chief of combatant commands that humans are more important than hardware when it comes to Special Operations; that quality is more important than quantity; that Special Operations Forces can neither be mass produced nor be created rapidly after emergencies occur; that SOF and traditional armed forces are complementary; that misuse invites unconscionable casualties; and that refusal to use SOF under advantageous circumstances may boomerang unfavorably. Special Operators in turn must constantly demonstrate great worth because bureaucratic opponents behind every bush still disapprove. SOF policymakers from top to bottom moreover should remember that there are no substitutes for sky-high recruiting and reenlistment standards accompanied by rigorous training, without which U.S. Special Operations Forces never could truly call themselves "special."

Army SOF furnished food, clothing, shelter, medical support, and other life-sustaining assistance to countless noncombatant Kurds in miserable refugee camps along the mountainous frontier between Iraq and Turkey in the frigid spring of 1991. Mortality (especially among children) would have been incomparably higher without their help. (U.S. Army Special Operations Command)

Opposite: *Bald eagles and Old Glory have long symbolized the United States around the globe. The Commander in Chief of U.S. Special Operations Command picked this montage to grace the cover of USSOCOM's 2002 calendar, because it beautifully symbolizes the irrefutable strength and fierce resolve of past, present, and future SOF in every service. (U.S. Special Operations Command)*

153

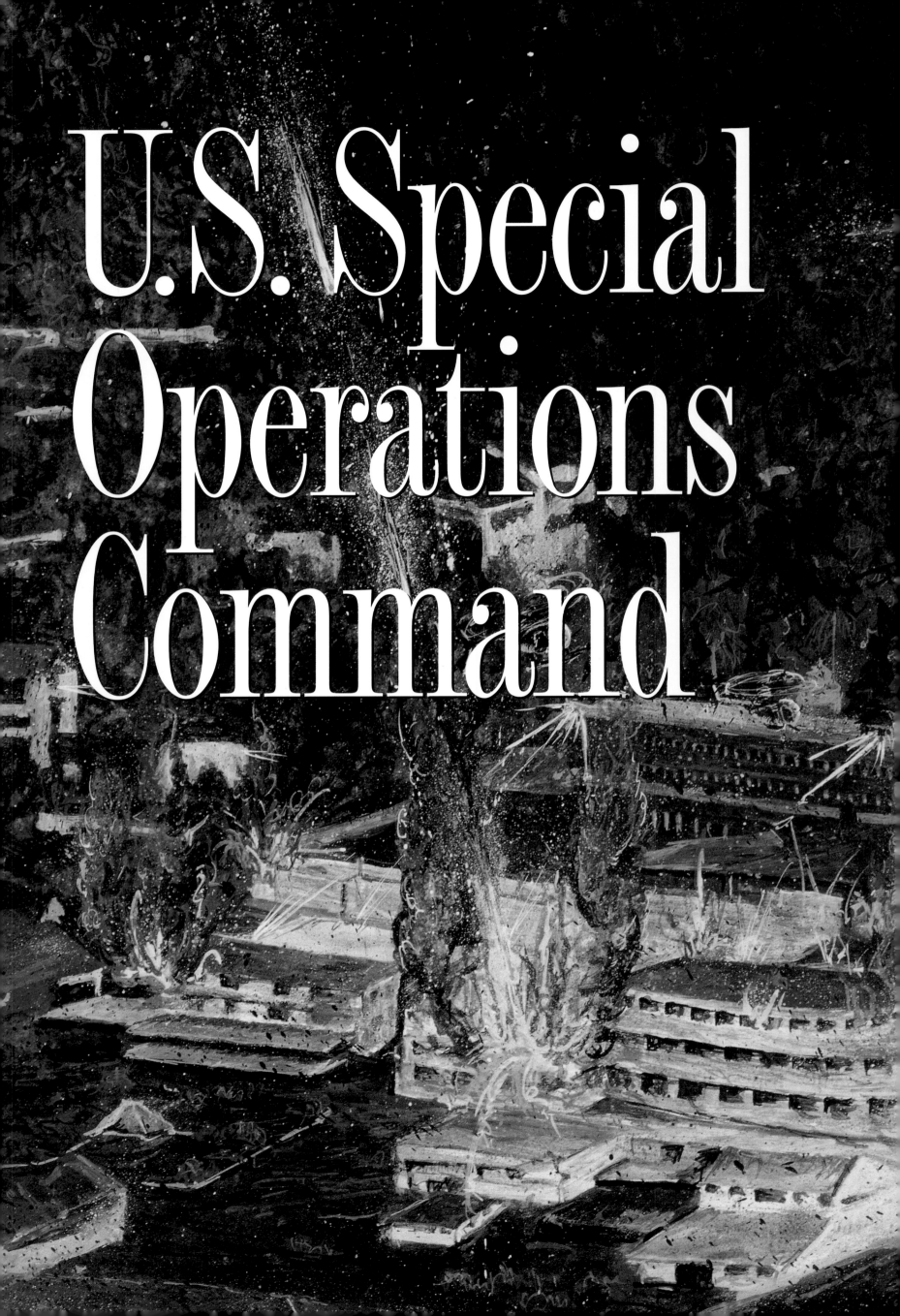

U.S. Special
Operations
Command

U.S. Special Operations Command

Benjamin F. Schemmer

enowned for their language skills and cultural sensitivity almost as much as for their legendary military tradecraft, America's Special Operations Forces have become the "instrument of choice" and now are widely acknowledged as a "diplomacy multiplier" whose impact on international security far outweighs their meager numbers. Fewer than 200 four-to-twelve men teams from the Army's 5th Special Forces Group (Airborne), for instance, each accompanied by a few men from the Air Force's 720th Special Tactics Group, liberated Afghanistan from Al-Qaeda terrorists and Taliban oppression—and they accomplished that within ninety days of their first insertion into the country on 19 October 2001. It was a remarkable accomplishment unique in the annals of warfare—and all the more notable because no war plan existed for such a campaign when New York's World Trade Center and the Pentagon were struck by terrorists on 11 September 2001.

Barely 48,000 strong (including Reserve and National Guard units), the men and women of U.S. Special Operations Command endure what are probably the highest operational tempos among all of America's armed forces. They are as busy in peace as they are in war.

Regionally oriented, SOF units or teams operated in more than four of every five of the globe's 198 nations during fiscal year 2001. In an average week, 4,938 special operations personnel were deployed away from their home stations to a total of 146 countries. They have become America's "global scouts."

These "quiet professionals," as they are best known, are all special volunteers in an all-volunteer force, specially trained people with a remarkable inventory of skills, all a cut above the best of the 1,388,100 Americans who wear a military uniform. Roughly four out of five of all

Offical seal of the United States Special Operations Command when the modified the spearhead emblem of the Office of Strategic Services (OSS) was adopted in 1987. (U.S. Special Operations Command)

Pages 154–155: Delta Force operators landed from an MH-6 Little Bird helicopter on the roof of Modelo Prison across from PDF headquarters in the Commandancia; raced down to the cell of imprisoned CIA agent Kurt Muse; yelled, "We're here to get you out"; and rescued him within six minutes as H-hour unfolded in Operation Just Cause. ("We're Here to Get You Out!" © by Bill Jackson, courtesy of the Unit Fund)

Left: U.S. Air Force Senior Airman Scott Heflin, a radio maintenance specialist with the 352nd Operational Support Squadron, Royal Air Force Mildenhall, United Kingdom, listens to radio traffic in the Joint Special Operations Task Force Element, Hoedspurit, which is a command and control center for the 352nd Special Operations Group deployed to Air Force Base Hoedspriut, South Africa. The 352nd Special Operation Group is deployed to South Africa in support of Operation Atlas Response. (U.S. Air Force)

Opposite: U.S. Navy SEALs from SEAL team 8 shoot M-4 carbine rifles on a firing range in Kuwait as part of the Southwest Asia buildup. (U.S. Special Operations Command)

157

Above: *An Army Special Forces team fast ropes from the back of an Army CH-47 Chinook helicopter to secure a building rooftop during an infiltration exercise at Fort Bragg, North Carolina. (U.S. Special Operations Command)*

Army Colonel Edward M. Kane, U.S. Army Special Operations Command G-3 Section, listens to Lieutenant James T. Scott, pointing with his upraised hand, as Brigadier General Stanley F. Cherrie listens during a briefing about the Operation Joint Endeavor Mission Eagle Division Tatical Operations Center, located on Tuzla Air Base, Bosnia-Herzegovina. Operation Joint Endeavor is a peacekeeping effort by a multinational Implementation Force (IFOR), comprised of NATO and non-NATO military forces, deployed to Bosnia in support of the Dayton Peace Accords. (U.S. Army)

soldiers, sailors, and airmen who volunteer for these high-risk units never make the first cut (even though most of them have already passed muster in their primary military skills, whether as a rifleman, pilot, or combat controller).

Their elite units range from Army Rangers, Special Forces, Civil Affairs and Psychological Operations personnel, and a Special Operations Aviation Regiment to Air Force Special Operations and Special Tactics squadrons to Navy SEAL (Sea-Air-Land) teams, Special Boat Squadrons and SEAL Delivery Vehicle teams.

They all serve under the umbrella of the United States Special Operations Command, activated in 1987 and headquartered at MacDill Air Force Base in Tampa, Florida. They train under and report adminis-

tratively report through four component commands. These are the Army
Special Operations Command at Fort Bragg, North Carolina, which
accounts for almost 60 percent of all U.S. Special Operations Forces; the
Air Force Special Operations Command at Hurlburt Field, Florida, about
one-quarter of all SOF personnel; the Navy Special Warfare Command at
Coronado, California, not quite 15 percent of SOF; and the Joint Special

*On the open ramp of a low flying C-130
Hercules assigned to Yokota AB, Japan, a
Special Tactics Team member coordinates a
drop during exercise Cobra Gold in
Surathani, Thailand. (U.S. Air Force)*

Operations Command at Fort Bragg, North Carolina, whose personnel come from all three service component commands. The command insignia are shown here.

The men and women in SOCOM's component commands, broken down by service and between active duty personnel and those in the reserve components, are shown in the accompanying table.

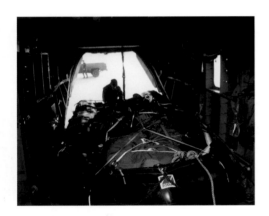

An Army Special Forces Zodiac raft is loaded into an MH-53J Pave Low III helicopter of the 20th Special Operations Squadron during a joint Army-Air Force exercise conducted by the U.S. Special Operations Command. (U.S. Army)

SOCOM PERSONNEL STRENGTH *(as of January 2003)*

COMMAND	TOTALS	PERSONNEL%
Active Duty Military	29,100	64
Reserve Components	14,500	30
Subtotal, Military	43,600	94
Civilian	3,000	6
SOCOM Total	46,600	100

SOCOM PERSONNEL STRENGTH BY SERVICE
(as of January 2003)

SERVICE	ACTIVE	RESERVE	TOTAL	%
Army	15,300	11,500	26,800	57
Air Force	8,700	1,800	10,500	23
Navy	5,100	1,200	6,300	14
Marine Corps	50	0	< 50	<1
Total Military	29,100	14,500	43,600	100

Even a cursory look at the command's unclassified organizational charts reveals the rich diversity of units and mix of skills found throughout its units. The ubiquitous nature of U.S. Special Operations Forces and the high operational tempo of their units is evident in the table on page 162 of their worldwide deployments in a typical year.

The men and women of Special Operations rank among America's busiest warriors. While few in number, they are in increasing demand by the nation's regional or war-fighting commanders, and the pace and scope of their operations has grown faster than any other element of the U.S. armed forces.

That high operational tempo has continued unabated. Late in December of 1999, it caused the Pentagon's Joint Staff to send a message

Opposite, bottom: A CH-3E Sea King helicopter from the 1550th Combat Crew Training Wing floats on the surface of Elephant Butte Lake, New Mexico, as members of a Navy SEAL team approach in an inflatable boat during the joint Air Force/Navy special operations exercise Chili Flag. (U.S. Air Force)

```
                              United States
                      Special Operations Command
                        MacDill Air Force Base, FL

        ┌──────────────────┬──────────────────────┬──────────────────────┐
   U.S. Army              Joint                  Naval                 Air Force
Special Operations   Special Operations   Special Warfare Command   Special Operations
    Command              Command              Coronado, CA             Command
  Ft. Bragg, NC        Ft. Bragg, NC                                Hurlburt Field, FL
```

U.S. Army
Special Forces Command
Ft. Bragg, NC

John F. Kennedy Special Warfare Ctr. & School
Ft. Bragg, NC

1st Special Forces Group
Ft. Lewis, WE

1st Special Warfare Training Group
Ft. Bragg, NC

3rd Special Forces Group
Ft. Bragg, NC

75th Ranger Regiment
Ft. Benning, GA

5th Special Forces Group
Ft. Campbell, KY

160th Special Operations Aviation Regiment
Ft. Campbell, KY

7th Special Forces Group
Ft. Bragg, NC

Civil Affairs (CA)/ Psychological Operations (PSYOP) Command
Ft. Bragg, NC

10th Special Forces Group
Ft. Carson, CO

4th PSYOP Group
Ft. Bragg, NC

350th CA Cmd (Prov.) #
Pensacola, FL

19th Special Forces Group*
Draper, UT

96th CA Battalion
Ft. Bragg, NC

351st CA Command #
Mountain View, CA

20th Special Forces Group*
Birmingham, AL

2nd PSYOP Group #
Cleveland, OH

352nd CA Command #
Riverdale, MD

7th PSYOP Group #
Muffitt Field, CA

353rd CA Command #
Bronx, NY

Special Operations Support Command
Ft. Bragg, NC

112 Signal Battalion
Ft. Bragg, NC

528th Special Operations Spt. Bn.
Ft. Bragg, NC

Material Management Center
Ft. Bragg, NC

Naval Special Warfare Group One
Coronado, CA

Naval Special Warfare Unit 1 NAVSTA
Guam

SEAL Team One
Coronado, CA

SEAL Team Three
Coronado, CA

SEAL Team Five
Coronado, CA

SEAL Del Veh Team 1
Pearl Harbor, HI

Detachment Kodiak
Kodiak, AK

Naval Special Warfare Group Two
Little Creek, VA

Naval Special Warfare Unit 2
Stuttgart, Germany

Naval Special Warfare Unit 4 NAVSTA Roosevelt Roads, Puerto Rico

Naval Special Warfare Unit 8 NAVSTA Rodman, Panama

Naval Special Warfare Unit 10 NAVSTA Rota, Spain

SEAL Team Two
Little Creek, VA

SEAL Team Four
Little Creek, VA

SEAL Team Eight
Little Creek, VA

SEAL Del Veh Team 2
Little Creek, VA

Naval Special Warfare Dev. Group
Dam Neck, VA

Naval Special Warfare Center
Coronado, CA

Special Boat Squadron 1
Coronado, CA
Special Boat Unit 12
PC 3 USS Hurricane
PC 4 USS Monsoon
PC 7 USS Squall
PC 8 USS Zephyr

Special Boat Squadron 2
Little Creek, VA
Special Boat Unit 20
Special Boat Unit 22#
New Orleans, LA
Special Boat Unit 20
Panama
PC 1 USS Cyclone
PC 2 USS Tempest
PC 5 USS Typhoon
PC 6 USS Sirocco
PC 9 USS Chinook
PC 10 USS Firebolt
PC 11 USS Whirlwind
PC 12 USS Thunderbolt
PC 13 USS Shamal

16th Special Operations Wg
Hurlburt Field, FL
4th Sp Ops Squadron (AC-130U)
6th Sp Ops Squadron (UH-1)
8th Sp Ops Squadron (MC-130E)
9th Sp Ops Sq (MC-130P)
Eglin Air Force Base, FL
15th Sp Ops Squadron (MC-130H)
16th Sp Ops Squadron (AC-130H)
19th Sp Ops Squadron (TRNG)
20th Sp Ops Squadron (MH-53J)
55th Sp Ops Squadron (MH-60G)

352nd Sp Ops Group
Mildenhall, UK
7th Sp Ops Squadron (MC-130H)
21st Sp Ops Squadron (MH-53J)
67th Sp Ops Squadron (MC-130P)
321st Special Tactic Squadron

353rd Sp Ops Group
Kadena Air Base, Japan
1st Sp Ops Squadron (MC-130H)
17th Sp Ops Squadron (MC-130P)
31st Sp Ops Squadron (MH-53J)
Osan Air Base, Korea
320th Special Tactics Squadron

720th Special Tactics Group
Hurlburt Field, FL
10th Combat Weather Squadron
23rd Special Tactics Squadron
21st Special Tactics Squadron
24th Special Tactics Squadron
Pope Air Force Base, NC
22nd Special Tactics Squadron
McChord Air Force Base, WA

193rd Sp Ops Wing*
EC-130E
Harrisburg IAP, PA

919th Special Operations Wing #
Duke Field, FL
5th Sp Ops Squadron (MC-130P)
711th Sp Ops Squadron (MC-130E)

USAF Special Operations School
Hurlburt Field, FL

18th Flight Test Squadron
Hurlburt Field, FL

Air Force Sp Ops Command ASOS
Ft. Bragg, NC

* *Denotes National Guard Unit*
# *Denotes Reserve Unit*

Current as of May 1998

161

Pararescue specialists check their gear before boarding their MH-60G Pave Hawk helicopter for a mission during a joint Army-Air Force exercise conducted by the U.S. Special Operations Command, at Pope Air Force Base, North Carolina. (U.S. Air Force)

During Operation Enduring Freedom Navy SEALs disembark an MC-130E Combat Talon from the 16th Special Operations Wing, Hurlburt Field, Florida, to provide perimeter security for a maintenance team performing critical repairs to a MH-53J Pave Low Helicopter at a forward deployed airfield. (U.S. Special Operations Command)

SOCOM OVERSEAS DEPLOYMENTS BY TYPE OF UNIT
(in 1998)

	PERSONNEL STRENGTH	TOTAL MAN-WEEKS SPENT OUTSIDE CONTINENTAL U.S.	TOTAL COUNTRIES INVOLVED
ARMY UNITS			
Special Forces	8,781	53,555	129
Civil Affairs	5,112	16,030	82
Psychological Operations	3,863	12,568	78
Rangers	1,895	5,309	5
Special Operations Aviation	1,666	2,799	10
ARMY SUBTOTAL	21,317		
AIR FORCE UNITS			
AFSOC Wings	10,122	32,395	58
Special Tactics	450	1,987	24
AIR FORCE SUBTOTAL	10,572		
NAVY UNITS			
SEALs	2,707	22,199	77
Special Boats	2,455	13,086	38
NAVY SUBTOTAL	5,162		
SOF Headquarters and Special Operations Commands	2,006	8,373	66
SOCOM Total	39,057	168,202	146

HIGH DEMAND-LOW DENSITY SPECIAL OPERATIONS UNITS AND EQUIPMENT

ARMY

Special Forces Teams

75th Ranger Regiment

Active Duty Civil Affairs Battalions

Active Duty Psychological Operations Units

112th Special Operations Signal Battalion

160th Special Operations Aviation Regiment

NAVY

SEAL Platoons

Patrol Coastal (PC) Ships

Rigid Inflatable Boat (RIB) Detachments

Mark V Special Operations Craft (SOC)

SEAL Delivery Vehicle Task Units

AIR FORCE

Special Tactics Squadrons

AC-130H (Combat Talon) Aircraft

AC-130U (Spectre gunship) Squadrons

EC-130E (Commando Solo) Aircraft

*9th Special Operations Squadron
(MC-130P Aircraft)*

*MC-53J/M Pave Low Special Operations
Squadrons*

HH-60G Pave Hawk Rescue Helicopters

worldwide listing thirty-one so-called "low-density, high-demand" units and weapons systems in such short supply that requests for their deployment far outstripped the assets available; eighteen of the units or equipments mentioned—58 percent of the total—were from U.S. Special Operations Command. Thus, 3 percent of the nation's military strength represented almost three-fifths of its most valued resources. Those units are shown in the box above along with the unique special operations hardware in shortest supply.

The location of land mines is marked with a sign near Brus, Bosnia-Herzegovina. Most of the six million mines in the former Yugoslavia are not marked with a sign. As part of Operation Joint Endeavor, the U.S. Army's 10th Special Forces Group . . . working with the State Department and former warring factions . . . embarked on a mission of humanitarian de-mining training. The training included leadership, planning, mine detection, mine disposal, and medical triage, and was accomplished at four different sites for Bosnia-Herzegovina nationals. (U.S. Special Operations Command)

U.S. SOCOM Heraldry

The first patch designed as the emblem for U.S. Special Operations Command featured a Sea Griffin, a mythical monster with the body and hind legs of a lion, the head, wings, and claws of an eagle, and the fins and gills of an early dinosaur and a fish. It symbolized the land, air, and sea environments in which SOCOM's three service-oriented component commands operate and thus also embodied their joint work. In 1987, the year in which SOCOM formally stood up, General James J. Lindsay, its first commander in chief, was given an "unofficial" Office of Strategic Services patch from World War II. He decided to refashion SOCOM's emblem after it to strengthen SOCOM's ties with its lineal predecessors and to signify SOCOM's role as the "tip of America's spear."

The spearhead not only represents the initial forces of attack, but is a traditional emblem that has topped military unit colors dating back to antiquity. The black background represents special operations clandestine activities under the cover of darkness. The three gold rings surrounding the shaft of the spear symbolize the forces assigned to SOCOM from the Army, Navy, and Air Force. The four stars represent the four points of the compass and emphasize the command's global mission. Finally, the braided cord encircling the shield symbolizes SOCOM's strength through jointness.

 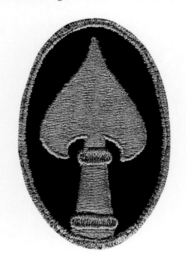 

Oddly, there was no mention whatsoever of any steps taken by the Department of Defense to correct this force-resource mismatch in either of its next two annual Posture Statements, required annually by Congress and submitted by then Defense Secretary William Cohen. Nor was the problem even mentioned in the September 2001 Quadrennial Defense Review mandated by Congress, a seventy-one-page study that, like its vacuous predecessors, was overwritten and void of substance or details. But it was pending early in Cohen's tenure and he kept referring to its forthcoming release whenever he wanted to dodge a question from the press. Yet Cohen had been the prime mover, along with Senator Sam Nunn, of the 1986 legislation that created U.S. Special Operations Command over the vehement objections of the Joint Chiefs of Staff and the Defense Department's civilian hierarchy.

In late January 2002, Defense Secretary Donald Rumsfeld remarked, almost as an aside during a speech at the National Defense University, that the Pentagon needed to take a look at "low density-high demand capabilities," explaining only that this was a euphemism meaning that "our priorities were wrong and we didn't buy enough." He acknowledged, however, that the department had known for some time that it did not have enough of "certain types of special operations forces." But all his subsequent Posture Statement said of the issue was a vague charge that the Pentagon

Opposite: U.S. Navy SEALs search the passageways of the USNS Leroy Grumman *for an intruder during a search and seizure exercise. (U.S. Navy)*

165

Joint Special Operations Command

The Joint Special Operations Command was established in 1980 and is located at Fort Bragg, North Carolina. JSOC is a joint headquarters designed to study special operations requirements and techniques; ensure interoperability and equipment standardization; plan and conduct joint special operations exercises and training; and develop joint special operations tactics.

needed to "better address requirements for low density-high demand assets." His report said nothing of the special operations shortages.

Belatedly, fixes finally appeared in the Pentagon's Fiscal Year 2004 budget request, which included an unprecedented 22 percent in funding for U.S. Special Operations Command following the stunning successes of its forces in Afghanistan late in 2001 and early in 2002. SOCOM's funding would increase from $4.9-billion in Fiscal Year 2003 to close to $6-billion of the Pentagon's $379.9-billion new budget, a dramatic contrast to the average annual increases of 3.4 percent (ones that barely covered inflation) during the preceding ten years for which Congress had given the command budget authority independent of the Army, Navy, and Air Force. Over a six-year period, moreover, SOCOM's budget would grow by a total about $7-billion and 4,000 personnel.

The first year of that buildup included 1,890 more personnel, bringing SOCOM's strength to over 48,500 military men and women. Most all of those initial new personnel, however, would be intelligence specialists and planners rather than operators (or "shooters," as core personnel are sometimes known), since no one joins SOF *per se* and because the command has long had difficulty finding seasoned soldiers, sailors, and airmen who could meet the stringent qualification requirements of its units. The additional personnel, Defense Secretary Rumsfeld said on 7 January 2003, would be used to beef up operational planning at SOCOM's MacDill Air Force Base, Florida, headquarters as well as throughout its six regional or theater special operations component commands, in line with SOCOM's expanded charter to function as a supported—not just "supporting"—command in the war on terrorism. Under that construct, for instance, the European Special Operations Command could call on Marine units in its area of operations as well as conventional Army, Navy, and Air Force assets to help execute operations directed by SOCOM rather than by U.S. European Command.

In addition, some of the new personnel billets would increase the manning of the Army's 160th Special Operations Aviation Regiment, one of SOCOM's most critical "high-demand, low-density" units. With a 129 percent increase in SOCOM's procurement budget (to almost $2-billion), that unit was to get more MH-47E helicopters while Air Force Special Operations Command would get additional MC-130 Combat Talons, largely to offset losses over the preceding eighteen months, and the first of its long-awaited, new CV-22 tilt-rotor aircraft.

A SEAL team fast ropes from the back of an Army CH-47 Chinook helicopter during a joint training exercise. (U.S. Special Operations Command)

Whatever the details, the new budget signaled that America's special operations forces had finally come into their own following the decades of neglect that had characterized SOF fortunes in the years following the Vietnam War.

USAF Senior Airman Dean Unger, from Pope Air Force Base, North Carolina, calls in wind conditions to the STARS (Special Tactics and Rescue Specialists) team members preparing to jump. The team is doing practice jumps at Naval Air Station, Key West, Florida. (U.S. Special Operations Command)

A U.S. Army soldier armed with a Beretta runs across an opening while another covers him. The soldiers are participating in a joint United States and United Kingdom Special Forces exercise. (U.S. Special Operations Command)

167

Army
Special
Operations
Command
1992-2002

Army Special Operations Command (USASOC)

Colonel John M. Collins, USA (Ret)

Only one can be the best.

Others cannot pass that test.

They indeed may huff and puff,

But only one is skilled enough

To clearly outclass all the rest.

—JACK SWIFT, *UNPUBLISHED POEM*

Army Special Operations Forces encountered rocks aplenty along the way from outcast to acceptance to center stage, as previous chapters confirm, until Secretary of Defense Donald Rumsfeld on 31 January 2002 told students and faculty at the National Defense University, "In Afghanistan we saw composite teams of U.S. [Army] Special Forces on the ground, working with Navy, Air Force, and Marine pilots in the sky to identify targets, communicate targeting information and coordinate the timing of strikes with devastating consequences for the enemy. . . . Precision-guided bombs from the sky did not achieve their effectiveness until we had boots and eyes on the ground to tell the bombers exactly where to aim."

U.S. Army
Special Operations Command
Structural Snapshot

U.S. Army Special Operations Command (USASOC) was activated at Fort Bragg, North Carolina, on 1 December 1989 as an Army Major Command. It controls all Active and Army Reserve SOF in the Continental United States, transmits guidance to Army National Guard SOF through state adjutants general, and provides a rotation base for all Army Special Operations Forces overseas.

Organization	Commander	Headquarters Location	Personnel Strength (Approx)	Primary Area of Responsibility
USASOC	Lieutenant General	Fort Bragg, NC	24,200	Global
Special Forces Command	Major General	Fort Bragg, NC	9,100	Global
Active Groups				
1st SFG	Colonel	Fort Lewis, WA	1,300	East Asia, Pacific
3d SFG	Colonel	Fort Bragg, NC	1,300	Africa
5th SFG	Colonel	Fort Campbell, KY	1,300	Southwest Asia
7th SFG	Colonel	Fort Bragg, NC	1,300	Latin America
10th SFG	Colonel	Fort Carson, CO	1,300	Europe
ARNG Groups				
19th SFG	Colonel	Draper, UT	1,300	Southwest Asia, Pacific
20th SFG	Colonel	Birmingham, AL	1,300	Latin America
Civil Affairs and PSYOP Command	Major General	Fort Bragg, NC	9,900	Global
CA Battalions				
1 Active	Colonel	Fort Bragg, NC	200+	Global
24 USAR	Colonel	Widely Scattered	200+ each	Assorted
PSYOP Groups				
1 Active	Colonel	Fort Bragg, NC	1,100+	Global
3 USAR	Colonel	Widely Scattered	1,100+ each	Assorted
75th Ranger Regiment	Colonel	Fort Benning. GA	1,800	Global
160th SOAR	Colonel	Fort Campbell, KY	1,500	Global
Special Operations Support Command	Colonel	Fort Bragg, NC	1,000	Global
JFK Special Warfare Center and School	Major General	Fort Bragg, NC	1,000	N/A

Source: U.S. Army Special Operations Command

Incomparable Capabilities

U.S. Army Special Operations Command, headquartered at Fort Bragg, North Carolina, is the largest of USSOCOM's components. The three-star general at its apex heads the world's finest Army Special Operations Forces (ARSOF). Few other nations possess comparable capabilities in any regard and none can perform the full range of roles, functions, and missions that versatile Green Berets, Rangers, aviators, PSYOP, and Civil Affairs professionals fulfill every day as a matter of course.

There is no close foreign counterpart of area-oriented, linguistically qualified, culturally attuned U.S. Army Special Forces, which are designed primarily to develop, organize, equip, train, and direct indigenous military and paramilitary forces for designated purposes anywhere in the world. Green Berets are superbly prepared to perform many other functions, but force multiplication is their forte.

Whether U.S. Army Rangers are better man-for-man than foreign analogues that specialize in short-fuse, short-duration, direct-action missions is open to dispute, but such foreign assets are comparatively small. Not even the cream of the crop in other countries consequently is as well prepared to conduct battalion-sized or larger operations.

The 160th Special Operations Aviation Regiment acknowledges no peer, because its short- and medium-range helicopters feature high-tech capabilities that aspirants do not possess, while "Night Stalker" crews, in collaboration with Special Forces, Rangers, Delta Force, and Air Force SOF, incessantly create cutting-edge tactics and techniques that keep them ahead of contenders.

U.S. Army psychological operations battalions provide multifaceted, large-scale military PSYOP capabilities on a global basis that no nation other than the United States has needed since the Soviet Union collapsed in 1991. Civil Affairs battalions, which perform administrative and humanitarian functions that helpless foreign governments cannot handle themselves, are unique for identical reasons.

Center and above: *Ranger training builds on a foundation that teamwork is key to overcoming obstacles.* (Soldiers *magazine*)

173

The John F. Kennedy Special Warfare Center and School (JFKSWCS) at Fort Bragg, North Carolina, develops Army Special Operations doctrines and conducts individual as well as unit training that promote preparedness within each component command. JFKSWCS additionally ties dissimilar ARSOF together, then links the lot with the entire U.S. SOF community and traditional forces.

Military Operations Other Than War

President George H. W. Bush's *National Security Strategy of the United States*, dated August 1991, envisioned a New World Order that implicitly paid unprecedented attention to military operations other than war (MOOTW) along with perennial deterrent and defense responsibilities. Army SOF were well represented during the first two following years, when USSOCOM conducted thirty contingency opera-

tions and performed various functions in forty-five other countries on four continents plus seventeen islands. The *National Security Strategy of Engagement and Enlargement* that President William J. Clinton signed in July 1994 multiplied ARSOF tasks immeasurably. Resultant trends, accompanied by rapid operational tempos, continued unabated in 2002.

Extreme versatility accordingly has become an indispensable virtue. Peacekeeping, humanitarian assistance, model demining programs, and counternarcotics activities cover just a small segment of the MOOTW spectrum, but adequately exemplify "peacetime" challenges that ARSOF have faced since Desert Storm subsided in 1991.

Peacekeeping in Bosnia

Josip Broz, better known as Tito, in 1946 laced together a fragile federation called the Socialist Federal People's Republic of Yugoslavia, which

USASOC hand-to-hand combat courses still dispense advice much like British Major William Fairbairn and his apprentice Rex Applegate gave OSS students during World War II. Markets indeed remain for Applegate's 1943 book entitled Kill or Get Killed. *Fairbairn's* Lessons in Ungentlemanly Warfare *recently reached open print. (Robert Bruce Military Photos)*

175

Army Special Operations Liaison Control Elements (LCEs) attached to NATO and other non-U.S. brigades/battalions in Bosnia performed a wide range of functions analogous to services that Coalition Support Teams rendered during Operations Desert Shield and Desert Storm. LCE members shown here confer with an officer from the Russian brigade. (U.S. Special Operations Command)

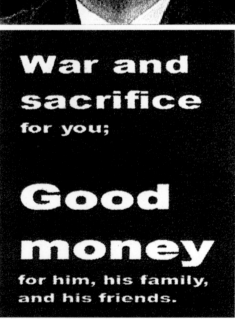

The 4th Psychological Operations Group distributed more than 100 million leaflets (like this one, but printed in Serbo-Croatian, Slovene, Macedonian, Albanian, or Hungarian) throughout Serbia and Kosovo during Operation Allied Force in March 1999. Many messages castigated Serbian President Slobodan Milosevic for genocidal practices and skullduggery that lined his pockets at the expense of common people. (U.S. Special Operations Command)

amalgamated Serbia, Croatia, Slovenia, Macedonia, Montenegro, and Bosnia-Herzegovina. Tito kept a tight lid on that kettle until his death in 1980, but it bubbled over before 1990 because Serbian President Slobodan Milosevic sought to replace him atop most (maybe all) of former Yugoslavia.

Bloodletting in Bosnia began in May 1992 when Serbian residents backed by Belgrade seized three-fourths of that nominally independent nation from its Croat and Muslim citizens, besieged its capital city at Sarajevo, and commenced "ethnic cleansing," a gentlemanly term for genocide. Brutal assaults that generated a tidal wave of refugees continued until 25 November 1995, when U.N., U.S., and NATO arm twisters in Dayton, Ohio, convinced belligerents it was time to call it quits. The NATO-led Implementation Force (IFOR) that commenced peacekeeping duties the following month delegated most Special Operations responsibilities down the chain of command to a U.S. headquarters with Special Forces, Civil Affairs, and PSYOP components.

Eighteen of NATO's nineteen members plus eighteen other polyglot countries with dissimilar customs and military doctrines contributed peacekeepers. The main mission of linguistically adroit, diplomatically attuned Army Special Forces, as during Operations Desert Shield and Desert Storm five years before, was to ensure that all participants consistently sang off the same sheet of music. Elements of the 10th Special Forces Group accordingly installed secure, reliable communications between IFOR's three multinational divisions and higher headquarters to ensure that each subordinate not only received and understood instructions but could respond intelligibly. Division teams in turn tacked a small liaison cell onto every brigade and battalion, where they installed tactical communication channels, conducted route reconnaissance missions, patrolled with "foster parents," laid figurative fingers on the public pulse, kept sharp eyes on potential troublemakers, and acted as go-betweens that local ethnic leaders came to trust. SOF further prepared to call for fire support, designate targets, and furnish localized quick-reaction forces if combat reerupted.

More than 500 U.N., governmental, and nongovernmental organizations shared responsibilities for repatriation, relief, and reconstruction in Bosnia. A Combined Joint Civil Military Operations Center, which attached U.S. Civil Affairs units to every multinational division, helped coordinate efforts that ranged from simple to complex. Some hearties, for example, chopped wood to keep geriatric citizens warm during wicked Balkan winters, while others strove to reestablish grass roots governments, public transportation, utilities, and medical services. Common people as a direct result soon began to see foreign armed forces in Bosnia as benefactors rather than trespassers.

Psychological operations forces solicited popular support for programs that IFOR and its successors promulgated as situations evolved. *The Herald of Peace*, a weekly newspaper, reached audiences whose adherents variously favored Latin or Cyrillic letters. PSYOP specialists similarly tailored posters, handbills, and other literature as well as radio and television broadcasts.

Farsighted PSYOP specialists, whose aim was willing cooperation at every level of Bosnian society, began to distribute informational newsletters to children as well as adults throughout the U.S. area of responsibility soon after NATO-led peacekeepers commenced operations in December 1995. (As the twig is bent, so the tree inclines). (U.S. Army Special Operations Command)

Peacemaking in Kosovo

Peacekeepers had barely stabilized Bosnia before the situation deteriorated between Islamic Albanians and Orthodox Christian Serbs in Kosovo. Hyper-nationalistic Milosevic launched ethnic cleansing campaigns on preposterous scales in 1998 and continued despite U.N. pleas to stop until relentless aerial bombardments that U.S.-led NATO forces began on 24 March 1999 made him change his mind on 19 June. NATO's Kosovo Force (KFOR) immediately subdivided that shattered province into U.S., British, French, German, and Italian areas of responsibility, each of which contained contributions from other nations.

A Civil Affairs Task Force assigned to each multinational division in Bosnia during Operation Joint Endeavor (December 1995- December 1996) helped restore devastated civilian infrastructure and essential services, much like predecessors did in Kuwait five years earlier. Construction specialists here confer with a Romanian military engineer. (U.S. Army Special Operations Command)

177

Green Berets, who entered the U.S. occupation zone first, reconnoitered situations for follow-on forces, then posted liaison parties with Russian and Polish participants. Special Forces patrols thereafter monitored the withdrawal of Serb troops, assessed the flow of returning refugees, searched for illegal weapons caches, helped war crimes investigators ferret out massacre sites, incarcerated troublemakers, otherwise defused tensions, and continually kept higher authorities informed.

Monumental relief efforts actually began before NATO intervened. U.S. Reserve Component Civil Affairs experts, like fictional Clark Kent, almost literally swapped civilian clothes for Superman's cape, then helped international groups provide desperately needed food, shelter, and medical

Above: *The 10th Special Forces Group constantly kept a finger on the public pulse throughout southeastern Kosovo. Captain Don Redd, Commander of A-Detachment 093, got the low down from this highly-placed Serbian contact in Strpce, then tapped sources whose opinions differed significantly to obtain balanced observations. (U.S. Army Special Operations Command)*

Right: *Civil Affairs specialists depicted in war-ravaged rural Kosovo conducted an open air conference circa 1999 outside makeshift hovels where comfortable homes once stood. Top priority requirements included shelter, reliable food supplies, potable water, fuel, and clothing, followed by early restoration of damaged utilities and lines of communication. (U.S. Army Special Operations Command)*

care to nearly a million refugees who inundated nearby nations. Compassionate activities quickened as soon as shooting ceased, because several hundred thousand more charity cases within Kosovo required similar attention. Civil Affairs annals contain no prouder chapter than its practitioners wrote under such stressful conditions.

Humanitarian Assistance Around the World

Humanitarian assistance by U.S. Armed Forces primarily attempts to improve the quality of life in foreign countries. *Title 10, United States Code* legally confines related Department of Defense activities to medical, dental, and veterinary care in rural areas; rudimentary surface transportation, well drilling, and basic sanitation projects; simple construction and repair of public facilities; and the delivery of relief supplies. Commanders in Chief of U.S. Special Operations Command, however, approve broader interpretations that subsume limited scope and duration responses to natural and man-made disasters as well as efforts to alleviate endemic human pain, disease, hunger, and privation that afflicted countries cannot provide alone.

Air Force Special Operations Forces that deliver essential supplies to desperate populations in remote regions on a moment's notice receive most plaudits, but Army Special Forces, PSYOP, and Civil Affairs unob-

Opposite, top: U.S. Armed Forces occupied Kosovo in June 1999. The 10th Special Forces Group's A Detachment 092 in January 2002 posed with Russian counterparts, who shared their potentially explosive southeastern sector near Kamenica, along the border between Kosovo Province and Serbia proper. (U.S. Army Special Operations Command)

Rangers and Special Operations Aviation Regiment (SOAR) helicopters aboard the aircraft carrier America *prepared to invade Haiti in September 1994 before former President Jimmy Carter, Senator Sam Nunn, and retired General Colin Powell brokered a deal with Haitian strongman Raoul Cedras that nullified needs for forcible entry. (U.S. Army Special Operations Command)*

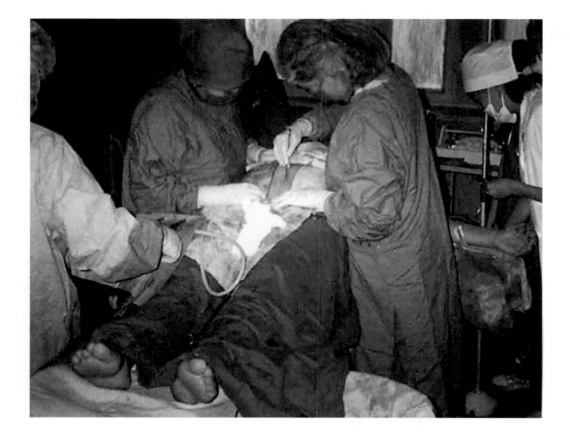

trusively perform equally useful services. Examples below scarcely scratch the surface of good deeds galore during the last decade.

Civil Affairs teams early in 1993 established centers from which they coordinated relief efforts by more than forty U.N. and nongovernmental organizations throughout famine afflicted Somalia. Psychological operations campaigns concurrently reinforced humanitarian efforts.

Green Berets comprised the only source of law and order outside Haiti's capital city of Port-au-Prince, and Civil Affairs detachments restored essential utilities countrywide in autumn 1994 during U.S. actions to stabilize Haiti after a military coup left that poverty-stricken nation in disarray.

Four doctors, three nurses, and one medic inoculated 60,000 Cameroon citizens in ten days during a meningitis epidemic. The cost was minuscule because a U.S. pharmaceutical company donated vaccines that otherwise would have expired.

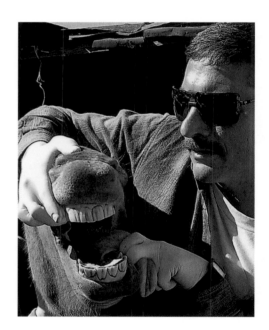

Special Forces in East Africa during the early 1990s taught game wardens how to reduce poaching, which discouraged tourists who wanted to see wild beasts in their natural habitats and thereby deprived troubled countries of hard currency.

Noncombatant evacuation operations invariably have humanitarian overtones. When riots racked Albania in March 1997 one Special Forces sergeant first class personally helped the U.S. ambassador revise emergency evacuation plans, selected the most appropriate helicopter landing zone, prepared manifests, vectored in the first chopper with his flashlight, then assisted the embassy staff and rescuers for two weeks until nearly 900 civilians escaped.

Humanitarian Demining

It's hard to imagine any military mission that is more humanitarian than demining, which benefits more people every day in more places than any other "peacetime" operation. Needs are Homeric, because more than

181

110 million unmarked antipersonnel land mines await unwary footfalls in at least sixty-eight countries, according to United Nations estimates. Afghanistan, Angola, and Cambodia account for more casualties than all other nations combined, but deaths and disablement (mainly leg amputations) are commonplace in Vietnam, El Salvador, Kurdistan, and a flock of African states. Booby traps and live munitions strewn helter skelter frequently complicate disposal problems.

Resourceful, linguistically competent members of the 5th Special Forces Group made demining history between 1988 and 1991 when they developed previously nonexistent doctrine and then, in concert with countless private organizations, taught millions of Afghan citizens how to identify, mark, and report more than forty different versions of mines that departing Soviet invaders left unattended. Several thousand more Afghani civilians learned how to disarm tricky (sometimes booby-trapped) mines, which wait patiently, never sleep, and never miss when they detonate. Best of all, Green Berets progressively lightened their own loads by training indigenous trainers to whom they gradually transferred responsibilities.

Those pilot projects became models for demining elsewhere. PSYOP and Civil Affairs forces initiated highly effective, country-specific education programs that sharpened public awareness and simultaneously reduced public risks. SOF deployments doubled from fourteen to twenty-eight countries soon after October 1997, when President Clinton put demining high on his priority list. Graduates of schools that taught students how to

183

Top left, above, and top right: *Decades of civil war by the early 1990s blanketed Yemen with maybe 100,000 unmarked landmines that took an endless toll in human lives and inhibited economic development. Indigenous deminers, organized, equipped, and trained by SOF assigned to U.S. Central Command, since then have "sanitized" the Port of Aden and countless pastoral acres. (U.S. Special Operations Command)*

NCOs seldom attract the attention of potentates, but Swaziland's King Mswati in 2000 applauded the demining skills of Green Beret Sergeant First Class Scott Stockdale, while related correspondence from U.S. Ambassador Gregory L. Johnson to Secretary of State Madeleine Albright praised his "reputation for professionalism and initiative." (U.S. Special Operations Command)

measure and dismantle minefields enabled farmers to plow thousands of previously lethal acres. All five active Special Forces groups, all six active PSYOP battalions, the only active Civil Affairs battalion, and selected Reserve Components still participate.

Positive results bring plaudits from grateful beneficiaries, great and small. Demining sharpie Sergeant First Class Scott Stockdale not only received heartfelt gratitude from all ranks in the Umbutfo Swaziland Defense Force, but from His Majesty King Mswati, who personally expressed appreciation at Army Day celebrations in April 2000. Positive results, perhaps more importantly, continue to bring great credit on Army Special Operations Forces at large and on the United States of America.

Counternarcotics Activities

Helping friends help themselves so they can help the United States is an important ARSOF mission. Related activities include individual and small unit training programs that better enable foreign narcs to detect, monitor, and disrupt the cultivation, production, and distribution of illicit drugs intended for U.S. markets.

Special Forces Mobile Training Teams (MTTs) currently conduct counterdrug missions in response to country-specific plans that regional commanders in chief and ambassadors approve. Bolivia, Colombia, Peru, and Venezuela have been perennial centers of attention, but other recent Latin American recipients include Barbados, Belize, Costa Rica, the Dominican Republic, Ecuador, El Salvador, Guatemala, and Jamaica. Packages in each case include elemental tactics, marksmanship, tactical

The Special Forces A Team at Chimore, Bolivia, in 1987 longed to help neophyte DEA agent Kevin Tamez and his indigenous narcs, but restrictive rules of engagement forbade counter-drug operations By 2002, Tamez was a big wheel in DEA's New York Division. (Drug Enforcement Agency Special Agent Kevin Tamez)

communications, seizure and control of evidence, laws of land warfare, and respect for human rights.

Military efforts alone obviously cannot solve all drug-related problems, but Army Special Forces and psychological operations professionals clearly play crucial roles. Best results pertain to Bolivia, where many (by no means all) Quechua Indians now are "going bananas" instead of growing coca, which previously was their predominant crop. The first of three battalions subordinate to a Colombian Counterdrug Brigade that ARSOF developed graduated in December 1999 and immediately opened operations in concert with gendarmeries in outlying areas. Two more replete with hand-picked volunteers soon followed.

Administrative restrictions that U.S. policy-makers impose for political reasons sometimes reduce ARSOF abilities to help U.S. counternarcotic units perform to best advantage and unnecessarily amplify risks that brave young men encounter daily in an exceedingly dangerous trade. Consider, for example, Kevin Tamez, an apprentice special agent with the Drug Enforcement Administration (DEA), who operated exclusively in urban environments from autumn 1985 until 1987, when superiors reassigned him to the Bolivian outback. Meager preparations featured Marine Corps Officer Candidate School courses in land navigation, small arms, and demolition techniques, followed by a quick and dirty introduction to jungle warfare at Fort Sherman, Panama, before he took charge of rough-cut indigenous narcs for three brief months.

Kevin set up shop near isolated Chimore (360 miles southeast of La Paz), where a Special Forces MTT was schooling Bolivian counternarcotic police. Collaboration could have made his mission immeasurably more productive because those consummate professionals were fully familiar with local situations long before he arrived, but prevailing policies forbade them to participate in drug busts unless life-threatening crises arose. They consequently chomped at the bit while he sallied forth to do battle with bad guys who turned coca leaves into cocaine. No such restrictions, however, applied to retirees. Thomas South, a former Special Forces medic on the DEA team that Kevin relieved in 1990, received the Attorney General's Medal of Valor for bravery under fire. Stringent constraints on relationships between ARSOF and DEA prevailed until 11 September 2001, when unreasonable rules of engagement started to relax.

Colombia's counterdrug battalions, the first of which opened operations in 1999, all received intensive instruction from U.S. Army Special Operations Forces. Curricula not only included ways to deal with illicit narcotic traffickers, but with insurgent forces that shield them, because dissimilar requirements demand different tactics and techniques. (U.S. Special Operations Command)

Fictional Major Warden, a British Commando in The Bridge on the River Kwai, *was fond of saying, "There's always the unexpected." Special Forces counterdrug teams coped well with the unexpected on 3 May 1999 when their convoy hit an ambush on a narrow, dark road in the Ecuadorian Andes. Conditioned reflexes kept casualties low while they seized the initiative, then routed bandits who were looting two civilian buses. ("Ecuador Firefight," Dan Peterschmidt)*

185

Combat Operations

Two widely-separated collisions gave Army Special Operations Forces dissimilar opportunities to put combat principles into practice during the decade between 1992 and 2002. The shootout in Somalia was, as British philosopher Thomas Hobbes might have phrased it, "nasty, brutish, and short," whereas finesse outweighed force during ARSOF's finest hours in Afghanistan.

ARSOF in Somalia

Mark Bowden's book entitled *Black Hawk Down* vividly describes Task Force Ranger's trials and tribulations in Somalia between 1545 hours on 3 October 1993 and 0630 the following morning. The sequence of events, key actions, and consequences nevertheless bear brief recital.

Outraged U.N. authorities offered to pay $25,000 for Somali warlord Mohammed Farah Aideed's head soon after his militia slaughtered twenty-four Pakistani "peacekeepers" and wounded fifty-three others on 5 July 1993. Task Force Ranger, which primarily contained elements of the 75th Ranger Regiment, Delta Force, and the 160th Special Operations Aviation Regiment (SOAR), conducted six search and seizure missions during late August and throughout September in fruitless efforts to capture that crafty kingpin along with lesser chieftains, then deliver them to U.N. officials for further disposition.

Foray number seven on 3 October started out more favorably because Task Force Ranger easily captured twenty-four of Aideed's trusted

Members of Task Force Ranger practice assaults within their sandy compound at Mogadishu Airport on the outskirts of the city. (Army Major Larry Perino)

160th Special Operations Regiment (SOAR) Night Stalkers in Somalia possessed awesome firepower that included 20mm rotary cannons aboard sturdy, state-of-the-art MH-60 Black Hawk helicopters. Those pictured here skirt the Indian Ocean coast en route to nearby Mogadishu, which is visible in the background. (Army Major Larry Perino)

henchmen during a daring daylight raid in downtown Mogadishu, loaded them aboard trucks, and prepared to depart. Problems began immediately thereafter when ragtag warriors armed with automatic weapons and rocket propelled grenades (RPGs) came swarming out of the woodwork like swarthy killer bees. Countless civilians, combative by nature and battle-

Psychological operations played pivotal roles in Somalia when humanitarian missions aimed to alleviate privation during Operation Restore Hope (December 1992–May 1993). Newspapers, leaflets, handbills, posters, and broadcasts influenced target audiences favorably. PSYOP in support of Task Force Ranger's operations subsequently flopped. (U.S. Army Special Operations Command)

Task Force Ranger's thin-skinned, lightly-armed High Mobility Multipurpose Wheeled Vehicles (HUMVEEs or HUMMERS), which generally mounted a .50 caliber machine gun or a Mark 19 automatic grenade launcher in an open turret, were much better suited for combat along open roads like the one depicted than in Mogadishu's rabbit warrens. (U.S. Army Special Operations Command)

187

Above: *Lethal struggles between Task Force Ranger's grunts and Somali warlord Aideed's militiamen transpired in Mogadishu's seedy shooting galleries, where buildings on both sides of narrow streets became enemy bee-hives and armed mobs blocked every intersection. Superlative training kept U.S. casualties relatively low despite those desperate conditions. (U.S. Special Operations Command)*

Left: *Somali Warlord Mohammed Farah Aideed's clan stronghold centered on Bakara Market in central Mogadishu. The three-story, flat-roofed, whitewashed stone structure partly visible in the upper right hand corner of this photo was Task Force Ranger's Target Building several blocks to the east, where bloody dramas began to unfold on 3 October 1993. (Army Major Larry Perino)*

188

Top, left: *First Lieutenant Larry Perino, shown here on the left with two NCOs in his Ranger platoon, was barely three years out of West Point when he got his baptism of fire with B Company in Mogadishu (Corporal Jaime Smith on the right was KIA). Horrific experiences during those frantic hours taught Perino more about urban combat than book learning could ever impart. He was an active duty major in 2002. (Army Major Larry Perino)*

Center left and right: *Ranger Sergeants Dominick Pilla and Lorenzo Ruiz were killed in Mogadishu, along with fourteen comrades and two members of the 10th Mountain Division. (Army Major Larry Perino)*

Bottom, left: *Chief Warrant Officer Mike Durant's Black Hawk hit the ground several blocks south of Cliff Wolcott. He survived, badly battered, after Somalis overran the site, killed Sergeants Gordon and Shughart plus injured members of his crew, and held him for ransom. Red Cross stretcher bearers carried him to a medevac aircraft eleven days later. (Army Major Larry Perino)*

Above: *SEAL snipers aboard thin-skinned humvees received little public credit for their role in efforts to extract trapped Task Force Ranger from Mogadishu, but each of the four enlisted men pictured here received a Silver Star for heroic actions. The SEAL captain on the right was similarly decorated for valor while leading an international armored relief column. (U.S. Special Operations Command)*

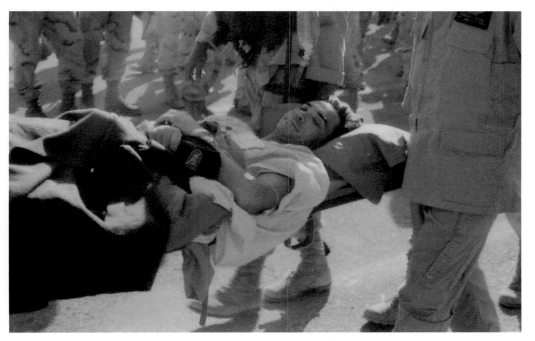

Above: *Operation United Shield, the withdrawl from Somalia, was completed on 3 March 1995. SEAL teams maintained security on the evacuation routes. (U.S. Special Operations Command)*

189

Right: *Short-range but heavily-armed A/MH-6 Mission Enhancement Little Bird (MELB) helicopters, like the Strawberry Roan bucking horse of Old Western fame, could "spin on a dime and leave you some change." (U.S. Army)*

Opposite, top: *Master Sergeant Gary L. Gordon and Sergeant First Class Randall D. Shughart, voluntarily inserted into the thick of a critical firefight, and lost their lives trying to save Chief Warrant Officer Mike Durant and his downed Black Hawk helicopter crew during the ferocious battle in Mogadishu on 3–4 October 1993. Both posthumously received the Medal of Honor for their valor. (Association of the United States Army)*

Above and oppposite, bottom: *Medal of Honor recipients Sniper Team Leader Gary Gordon and teammate Randall Shughart aboard a Black Hawk helicopter under intense enemy fire volunteered three times before they received permission to protect wounded comrades at a crash site in Mogadishu. They did so against impossible odds at the risk of certain death. (U.S. Army)*

190

hardened by ceaseless clan feuding, joyously joined the fray. ARSOF participants, outnumbered 100 to 1, instantaneously switched from offense to defense, then struggled to survive the fiercest urban firefight any U.S. forces had faced since North Vietnamese regulars and Viet Cong guerrillas assaulted Saigon, Hué, and other cities in South Vietnam during the Tet Offensive two decades earlier.

One well-aimed RPG downed Chief Warrant Officer (CWO) "Elvis" Wolcott's MH-60 Black Hawk helicopter three blocks from the target building, killing him on contact. Ground fire in quick succession crippled two more Black Hawks and dropped CWO Mike Durant's bird a few blocks farther south, where Somalis who hoped for a handsome ransom spared him but savaged his crew. Desperate street fights followed in Mogadishu's warrens while defenders, with splendid SOAR support, held Somalis at bay.

The multinational "quick reaction" force that finally linked up about 0200 on 4 October after ten harrowing hours freed Wolcott's body from twisted wreckage, loaded the worst wounded onto armored personnel carriers, and at daybreak headed for home, providing as much cover as they could to all others who ran a gauntlet called the Mogadishu Mile, while Little Bird helicopters rode shotgun. The cost on both sides was heavy: Task Force Ranger counted nearly 100 battle casualties, including sixteen dead (two 10th Mountain Division fatalities increased the total to eighteen). Mangled Somalis numbered maybe 1,500 (nobody ever tried to calculate property damage). President Clinton, in response to adverse public opinion at home and abroad, withdrew all U.S. forces in March 1994, which thereafter left Somali warlords alone to do as they wished without foreign interference.

Contrary to popular belief, there may be atheists in foxholes, but Task Force Ranger contained no cowards during its agony in Mogadishu.

Acts of heroism were routine. The first Medals of Honor since the Vietnam War went to Master Sergeant Gary L. Gordon and Sergeant First Class Randall D. Shughart, both Delta Force snipers, who sacrificed their lives to save Mike Durant and thereby posthumously joined what former Secretary of the Army Jack Marsh called "a tiny fraternity whose common bond is uncommon valor." Both hopped from a hovering helicopter into a hornet's nest 100 meters south of Durant's crash site. Both, armed with nothing more than a sniper's rife plus a pistol, fought their way to the crash site. Both pulled Mike and critically wounded crew members from remains of the aircraft, then established a two-man perimeter (a military oxymoron). Both fought with no chance of relief until fatally wounded. "Greater love hath no man than this, that a man lay down his life for his friends" fit perfectly in both cases (John 15:13).

ARSOF in Afghanistan

Innovative actions in Afghanistan put jewels in ARSOF's crown. Rangers, Delta, Night Stalker air crews, PSYOP, and Civil Affairs units all participated, but the most brilliant stars clearly were very special Army Special Forces, which equipped, supplied, directed the activities of and, in tandem

with Air Force Special Tactics troops, provided aerial fire support for uncoordinated Northern Alliance freedom fighters, who sought to oust the oppressive Taliban regime. Their mission, in short, was classical unconventional warfare with high-tech twists.

The curtain rose on Act 1, Scene 1 of *Hairy Meets Hercules* when four Special Forces A Teams of junior officers and NCOs touched down in Afghanistan after dark on 19 October 2001. They made contact with CIA reception parties that put them in touch with hairy Alliance leaders, some of whom spoke obscure dialects, but linguistically agile Green Berets

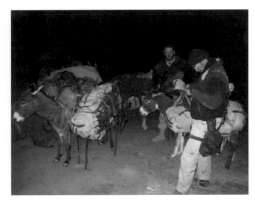

quickly closed communication gaps by trying English, French, Arabic, Russian, even Chinese until they found a tongue that fit.

The term "Northern Alliance" was a misnomer, because winner-take-all Uzbek, Tajik, Hazara, and Pastun generals not only competed with each other for power, but distrusted strangers of any ilk, especially pale-faced foreigners. Tiny Special Forces A Teams, which normally total twelve men apiece (but in Afghanistan often consisted of only four to six men) plus one or two embedded AFSOC combat controllers, occupied the latter category. However, they won early welcomes when precise air strikes plus woolies, footwear, blankets, food, and ammo summoned at their beck and call replenished skimpy Alliance supplies. First aid and field expedient surgery for casualties solidified relationships.

Special Forces reconnaissance parties acquired real-time intelligence as soon as they went to work, used Global Positioning Systems (GPS) to pinpoint Taliban target coordinates, figuratively painted bullseyes thereon with laser designators, then passed essential info to U.S. Air Force and Navy aircraft armed with precision-guided munitions. Results outstripped all expectations, the most optimistic of which predicted victory (however defined) no earlier than summer 2002. Devastating aerial firepower instead made demoralized enemy troops abandon Mazar-e-Sharif on 9 November, which opened the way to the capital city at Kabul and to

Above: *Barren Afghan terrain leaves large paramilitary formations few places to hide. Army and Air Force SOF in close collaboration consequently were able to acquire lucrative targets easily during autumn 2001, then direct devastating air strikes that turned previously victorious Taliban battalions into clouds of debris and dust.* (U.S. Army Special Operations Command)

193

Top, left: *Compact, easily portable laser designators, like this one manned by a casually clad Army Special Forces captain at an observation post on commanding terrain, "painted" targets in Afghanistan for Air Force and Navy bombers and attack aircraft, which plastered Taliban positions with surgical precision. (U.S. Army Special Operations Command)*

Top, right: *Army SOF benefit immensely from mobile satellite communication terminals with built-in laptop computers that one man can transport across mountainous Afghanistan and install in a few minutes. Users can collect, process, and rapidly disseminate information wherever needed and receive messages from higher, lower, and adjacent headquarters. (U.S. Army Special Operations Command)*

Right: *A Special Forces soldier prepares his .50 caliber machinegun for an assault on Taliban forces during Operation Enduring Freedom, 2002. (Robert Bruce Military Photos)*

Above: *Bearded Air Force Special Tactics and Green Beret horsemen clad in scruffy Afghan attire accompanied Northern Alliance allies in late autumn 2001 as they bounded from one barren terrain spur to another, then attacked Taliban strong points and severed escape routes. Rudyard Kipling's verses likely would have lauded such versatility if he were still alive. (U.S. Air Force Special Operations Command)*

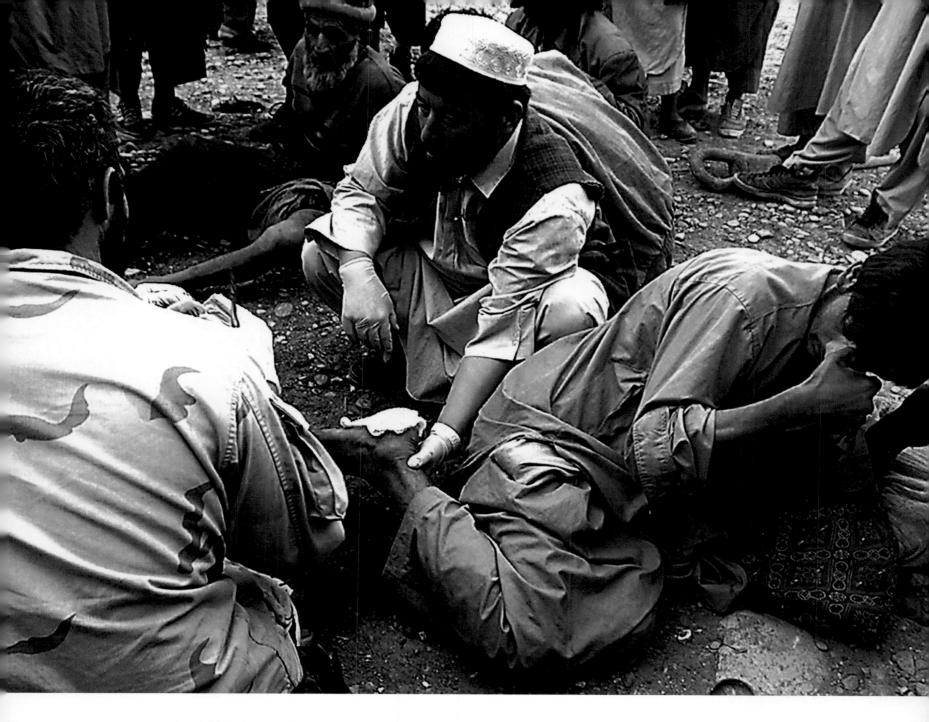

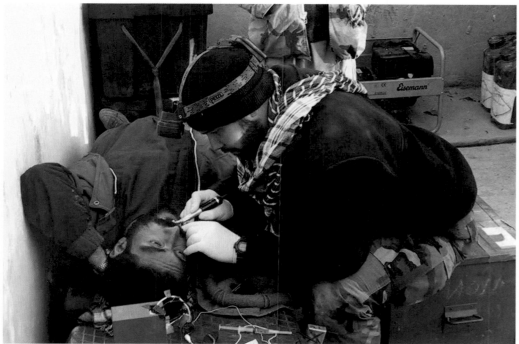

Taliban's Kandahar redoubt. Organized military opposition collapsed on 5 December, just forty-nine days after the first A Team arrived.

The termination date of continuing combat in Afghanistan is impossible to predict. Facetious recruiters on the Internet offer "Career Opportunities in Armed Anthropology" for adventurous young men who crave "interesting careers fighting evil, promoting civilization, and liberating the

Above: Compassion when warranted has always been a laudable Army Special Forces characteristic. The medic shown here ministered to a wounded Taliban soldier captured during the battle for Mazar-e-Sharif in early November 2001, while indiscriminate looting and killing by indigenous troops on both sides continued nearby. (U.S. Army Special Operations Command)

Left: This 5th Special Forces Group NCO, who filled, extracted, and cleaned indigenous teeth without benefit of an office, plied his trade on Afghan streets wherever grateful "customers" congregated. Services rendered in fact were an active form of psychological warfare, because they gave U.S. armed forces a good name. (U.S. Army Special Operations Command)

Page 196–197: Enhanced techonogies only increase the lethality and effectiveness of individual Special Forces members. The U.S. Army Night Vision Laboratory has greatly improved on these capabilities since its advent during Vietnam. This specially fitted weapon carries a Target Location and Observation System (TLOS) that employs a near infrared low-energy laser. (Gary L Kieffer)

Page 197: The Land Warrior System (LWS) is an integrated fighting system for infantry and Special Forces. This is the true line where technology and warrior meet. (Robert Bruce Military Photos)

oppressed." They promise open-ended opportunities to use the latest in lasers; observe soon-to-be-extinct Al-Qaeda terrorists; enjoy combat spelunking; practice medicine without a license; visit modern ruins; and have a real impact on important people. One conclusion even so seems certain: U.S. military operations in Afghanistan became anticlimactic on 5 December 2001. Mop-ups, which include perilous searches for Osama bin Ladin and other hard-core holdouts, may continue for many more months (perhaps years), but standards that 200 highly professional Green Berets set during Act 1 of *Hairy Meets Hercules* will be hard to surpass.

Outlook

The outlook for Army Special Operations Forces is more favorable than ever before. Flawless performance in Afghanistan, for the moment at least, turned the Secretary of Defense and many previously skeptical senior flag officers into true believers. Budgetary bonanzas that transnational terrorists triggered on 11 September 2001 make it possible to purchase required quantities of cutting-edge technologies already in production, to accelerate state-of-the-art items under development, and to initiate promising research programs that could multiply ARSOF abilities to accomplish emergent as well as perennial missions.

Readers, however, should constantly bear in mind that the more things change, the more they *really are* the same. Superlative human beings always have been, are now, and always will be what makes Army Special Operations Forces truly special. They stand alone, in a class by themselves, able to perform feats that no competitor, foreign or domestic, can accomplish equally well if at all, mainly because the best brains in the business prepare creative plans and outstanding operators implement them.

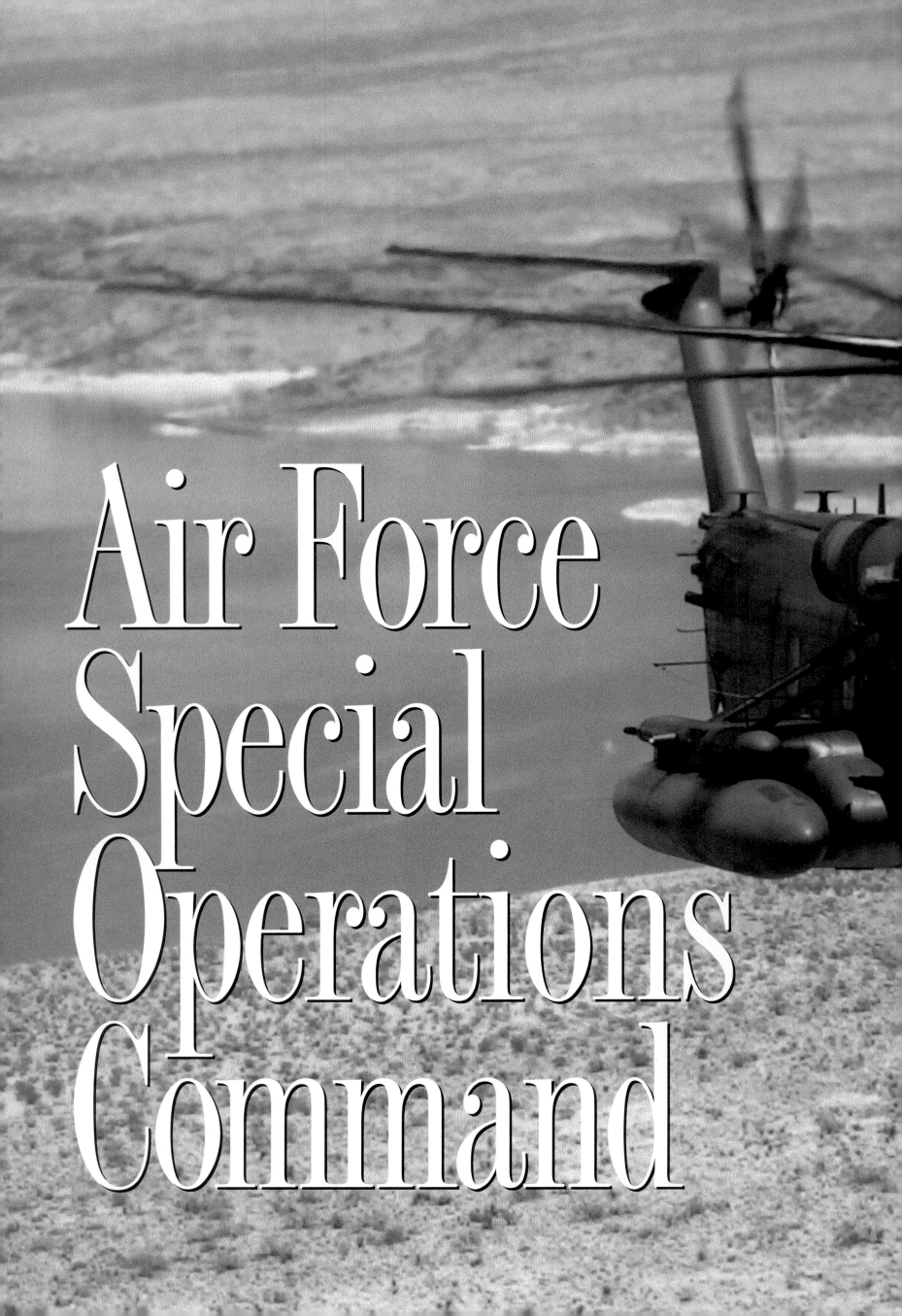

Air Force Special Operations Command

Air Force Special Operations Command (AFSOC)

Colonel John Gargus, USAF (Ret)

Establishment and Mission

Establishment of AFSOC on 20 May 1990 was a memorable event for Air Commandos of all ages. Finally, after forty-seven years of ad hoc existence that was marked by repeated activation, deactivation, and shuffling of special operations units among various Air Force major commands, they were grouped into a major command of their own. With it came a clearly defined role in the U.S. military doctrine to provide readily deployable unconventional warfare forces for the regional unified commands. AFSOC's commanders would be three-star generals. The sustainability of their new command would no longer be a worrisome problem because under the equally new budgetary process they would not have to compete with other Air Force commands for scarce resources. They would receive their share of resources to forge a well-trained and well-equipped special operations air force that could support all challenges to the U.S. national interests in joint military operations, not only in war, but also in peace and in all levels of conflict in between, at "any time, any place."

Home Base

Hurlburt Field, formerly Auxiliary Field No. 9 of the sprawling 724-square-mile Eglin Air Force Base complex in the Florida panhandle, is the home of AFSOC. It is an ideal location for a busy command that requires extensive ground and air space to conduct its rigorous training. This part of Florida is rich in Commando heritage. It has been the starting point of many memorable unconventional warfare operations, such as Doolittle's

Above: *Four special tactics team members make a hasty nighttime exfiltration rendezvous with a Pave Hawk helicopter that will fly them back to their forward operating location. (USAF)*

Pages 198–199: *Pave Low crews receive their initial training from the 58th SOW at Kirtland AFB in New Mexico. This is a low-level training flight over the southwestern United States. (USAF)*

Opposite: *This MC-130 version of Combat Talon I, seen here firing its anti-heat-seeking flares, requires only nine crewmembers. It has vastly improved precision navigational capabilities with terrain-following/terrain-avoidance and mapping radar that is integrated with inertial and global positioning satellite navigation systems and is augmented by infrared sensor with TV quality displays. Its passive ECM has kept up to date with enemy airborne and ground-based threats. It costs about $45.2 million. (USAF)*

This is an aerial view of Hurlburt Field looking north from the Gulf of Mexico. The wooded area beyond the Field is the Eglin AFB training area that stretches all the way to where the horizon meets the sky. (AFSOC)

carrier-based bombing raid on Tokyo and the 1970 Son Tay prisoner of war (POW) rescue raid in Vietnam. Many old Air Commandos have chosen to retire there. They honor their fallen comrades with a very attractive Memorial Park at the main entrance to the field, whose streets bear the names of deserving Commandos. Two retirement communities for senior citizen widows and widowers of Air Force enlisted personnel

This is the entrance to the Bob Hope Village, one of the two retirement communities for surviving spouses of Air Force enlisted personnel that is operated by the Air Force enlisted Men's Widows and Dependents Home Foundation, Inc. The other community is called Teresa Village. (Courtesy photo of the Foundation.)

were constructed between Eglin AFB and Hurlburt Field. The whole area is a favorite site for reunions of air commando and other military veteran organizations and is a permanent home base for large, organized special operations groups such as the Air Commando Association and the Stray Goose International.

AFSOC's Organization

AFSOC's main force consists of the 16th Special Operations Wing (SOW) at Hurlburt Field. Its motto—"Any Time, Any Place"—dates back to the original World War II Air Commandos in Burma. The wing maintains a high combat readiness posture and provides much of the rigorous training for personnel that staff the command's stateside and overseas components. In England, the 352nd Special Operations Group (SOG) at Mildenhall Royal Air Force Station forms the air component of the Special Operations Command Europe (SOCEUR), and at Kadena Air Base in Okinawa, Japan, the 353rd SOG does the same for the Special Operations Command Pacific (SOCPAC).

In addition, AFSOC has two nonactive duty wings. These are the Air Force Reserve Command's (AFRC) 919th SOW at Duke Field in Florida and the Air National Guard's (ANG) 193rd SOW at Harrisburg International Airport in Pennsylvania. Both have been tasked repeatedly to augment active duty forces in major special operations.

The command's present organization, weaponry, and geographical dispersal of forces are optimally suited to support U.S. national objectives anywhere in the world.

Many old Air Commandos stay fit and wear their uniforms while attending annual October reunions at Hurlburt Field. Retired Technical Sergeant Joe Sotuyo talks to Second Lieutenant Kim Miller from the 15th SOS at the Memorial Park after a memorial service honoring the Hmong allies of the Vietnam War. (AFSOC)

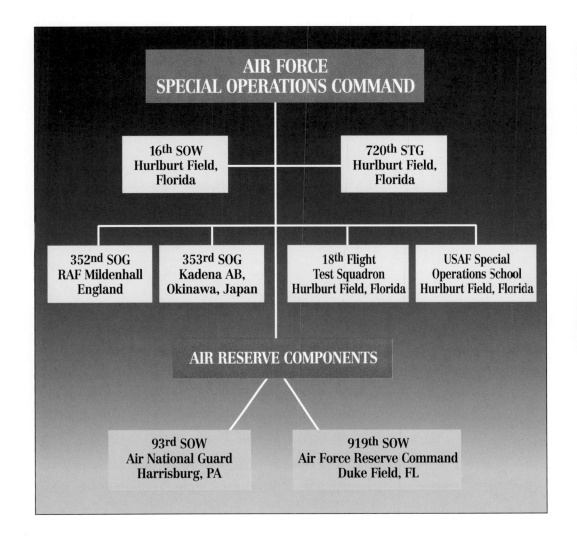

Above: *An MH-53J Pave Low III crew chief from the 16th Special Operations Wing inspects the exterior of a helicopter during Operation Enduring Freedom, 2002. (USAF)*

Left: *The AFSOC Organizational Chart shows major AFSOC components as of 2002.*

203

Lieutenant Colonel Paul Harmon, Commander of the 21st SOS from Mildenhall, UK, assists the natives of Xai-Xai, Mozambique, with the offloading of donated clothing that he flew in on his unit's Pave Low helicopter. During Operation Atlas Response the 352nd SOG airlifted over 700 tons of relief cargo. (Ron Jensen, Stars & Stripes.)

Staff Sergeant Billy Wince from the Air Force Reserve 919th Medical Squadron assists Guatemalan families during a humanitarian civic action training mission in the summer of 1999. During a two-week visit, forty-five medical and support reservists saw more than 8,000 patients. (AFRC)

Opposite, bottom left: *Philippine and U.S. paratroopers are ready to execute a high-altitude, low-opening (HALO) jump from a Combat Talon II aircraft during a joint exercise called Balikatan 2000. The purpose of this exercise was to improve the U.S./Philippines combined planning, combat readiness, and interoperability. (USAF)*

Opposite, bottom right *The first paratrooper is off the MC-130H tail ramp at 10,000 feet over Balikatan, Philippines. Floating backwards, he will count the members of his team as they jump after him and direct their free fall reassembly before their parachutes open at a predetermined lower altitude. (USAF)*

AFSOC and U.S. National Policies

Many nations have incorporated special operations into their military establishments, but none have elevated them to the level of proficiency of U.S. Special Operations Forces. As today's leading superpower with worldwide geopolitical interests, the U.S. needs to maintain close diplomatic and military ties with many nations. We opt to be an active participant in the molding of the international environment and hope to avoid responding to uncontrollable crises that spring up among contesting nations. In such a global setting, the Air Force Special Operations Command has become a very useful instrument of international diplomacy. As a vital component of U.S. air power, it is poised for employment under regional commander-in-chiefs of our unified commands. It can be effectively employed as a humanitarian relief provider, peacekeeper, nation builder, and whenever required, as a powerful adversary in hostilities ranging from low-intensity conflicts up to all-out wars.

Above: *The extent of devastation caused by flooding in Mozambique is seen in this photograph of a Pave Low from the 352nd SOG as it approaches a Combat Shadow for refueling. Humanitarian relief for Mozambique in 2000 was so extensive that it became an international effort with its own code name, Atlas Response. (USAF)*

Left: *The eruption of Mount Mayon in the Philippines in March 2000 brought a quick 12-hour response from the 353rd SOG in what became the Operation Fiery Relief. This Combat Talon flew into Legaspi with 36,000 pounds of emergency supplies that included electrical generators, plastic sheeting, and water jugs. (USAF)*

AFSOC rose to the challenge of international terrorism whose perpetrators do not respect international boundaries and who may not be claimed as their own by any recognized sovereign nation. Its Pave Low helicopters responded promptly to the 2001 terrorist attack on the World Trade Center. Staging from nearby McGuire AFB in New Jersey, they provided critically needed relief operations to Lower Manhattan after 11 September. (USAF)

Night vision goggles (NVGs) are now a part of each crewmember's personal equipment. (USAF photo.)

An Electronic Warfare Officer (EWO), seated to the right of the navigator in this nighttime NVG Combat Talon II photograph, is an indispensable crewmember in hostile environments. His electronic countermeasures (ECM) equipment can detect and identify enemy ground-based and airborne radars that target his aircraft. He can counter by electronic jamming, dispensing cloud-producing chaff, and dropping flares to decoy heat-seeking missiles fired at his aircraft. (352 SOG)

Maintenance mechanics service the hub of a Pave Low helicopter. Each of its six blades is shaped like a wing. Rapid rotation of the blades causes swift movement of air over their surfaces and provides the same lifting force for a helicopter like the stream of air flowing over a fixed wing of a forward-moving conventional aircraft. This aircraft can lift up to 50,000 lbs. (USAF)

AFSOC Aircraft

AFSOC's fixed-wing aircraft are the very reliable Lockheed Hercules C-130 transports. Equally reliable and battle-tested Sikorsky HH-53 Super Jolly Green Giant helicopters serve as the command's rotary-wing aircraft. All have been extensively modified for their specific unconventional warfare missions. All can be refueled in-flight and, if required, they can fly non-stop from their home bases to any location in the world. Crew endurance is the only limitation to their operational ranges.

Today's AFSOC aircraft are no longer recycled machines rigged up for the conflict of the moment. Even though they are aged, they have been expensively equipped with the latest in navigational and electronic equipment, and instrumentation. Their uniqueness challenges the airmanship skills of their all-volunteer crews, and aviators world-wide admire and respect their capabilities for unconventional warfare. Those that conduct clandestine operations, MC-130E/H Combat Talons and MH-53 J/M Pave Low helicopters, can fly with unprecedented precision using the latest inertial navigation and global positioning systems that do not depend on any

ground-based electronic transmissions. For deep penetrations into hostile territory, they rely on all-weather, terrain-following, and terrain-avoidance radars that permit them to fly safely at low terrain clearances to make their intruding night flights difficult to detect by enemy surveillance radars. They have forward-looking infrared (FLIR) systems that provide daytime TV-quality presentation of terrain even in complete darkness and assist them with positive identification of targets and checkpoints along their routes. In addition, their aircrews wear night vision goggles (NVGs) that permit them to take off, fly, work, and land in total darkness. Aircraft landing lights are equipped with infrared filters that make their light visible only to the NVG-wearing personnel.

Combat Talons

Lockheed C-130s will probably be remembered as the aviation's cargo-carrying workhorses of the Cold War era. Almost every nation that was not affiliated with the Soviet Union acquired some of its many production

A Combat Talon I with the Y-shaped Fulton Recovery System on its nose refuels from a KC-135 tanker. Combat Talons and other AFSOC C-130s have the same refueling capability that gives them a true global range. (USAF)

This MC-130E, Stray Goose is the first version of the frequently modified Combat Talon that was used in Vietnam. It had terrain-following and terrain-avoidance radar integrated with Doppler and up-to-date passive electronic countermeasures systems (ECMs). Its most unique feature was the ground-to-air Fulton Recovery System. It had a crew of eleven. (8th SOS)

Vietnam-era Stray Goose MC-130Es were modified in the 1970s with vastly improved terrain-following and mapping radar that was integrated with an inertial navigation system and Loran C. Other modifications included reinforcement of the ramp and tail sections of the aircraft that would permit cargo drops at normal operational airspeeds. (USAF)

models. Of all the existing models, none can match the special warfare capabilities of the two Combat Talons in AFSOC's inventory. The Combat Talon I is an expensively modified MC-130E and the newer one, Combat Talon II, is the MC-130H.

Gunships

The AC-130H Spectre and AC-130U Spooky gunships do not fly clandestine missions; consequently, they do not have the low-level navigational capability of Combat Talons. They are tremendous offensive weapons

used to interdict enemy forces and to provide protection for friendly forces with very accurate close air support. They have demonstrated their accurate and devastating firepower in all hostile actions involving U.S. forces since the Vietnam War and especially in Afghanistan. Because of that, they became effective as persuasive deterrents just by circling over contested areas. This deterrent factor was well exploited in Haiti, Somalia, and in the Balkans. No other nation possesses this kind of airborne firepower capability. None of the gunships are based at AFSOC's overseas locations. Their permanent home base is at Hurlburt Field.

Combat Shadows

The third type of Hercules, MC-130P, is called Combat Shadow. These models are modified as tankers to provide in-flight refueling for AFSOC helicopters and for refuelable helicopters of other services at extremely low altitudes and in total darkness. Such conditions are beyond the capabilities of other U.S. tankers. Most of the Combat Shadows are modified to

Above: *This MC-130P tanker is uniquely suited to support other AFSOC aircraft that must refuel at night and in hostile air space. It has sophisticated navigational equipment similar to Combat Talons. It can refuel two like aircraft at the same time and take on fuel from any other U.S. tanker to extend its global range. Eight crewmembers fly in this 75-million dollar aircraft. (USAF)*

210

receive fuel from other airborne tankers. Combat Shadows provide other AFSOC units with needed airlift and are also capable of taking on some of the missions normally assigned to Combat Talons.

Commando Solos

Finally there are uniquely configured EC-130E/Js called Commando Solos that belong to the Air National Guard component of the Air Force Special Operations Command. Their mission is to conduct psychological operations by airborne radio and TV broadcasts anywhere in the world. During Desert Storm they both wooed and frightened many Iraqi soldiers into surrendering by making attractive offers to those who would give up and promised certain devastation by 15,000-pound "Daisy Cutter" bombs delivered by Combat Talons to those that continued opposing coalition forces. They also provided morale-boosting broadcasts to friendly forces. Known as the "Voice of the Gulf," they brought news, sports, and other stateside entertainment programs to our troops. During Operation Just Cause, they warned people of Panama to stay off the streets and explained the limited intentions of our invading forces. Who knows how many noncombatant lives were saved by such advisory broadcasts in this and other operations in which our forces had to fire on nearby targets?

The MH-53J/M, Pave Low III/IV is a much-modified version of Vietnam-War-era Super Jolly Green Giant rescue helicopter, which flew a Special Forces team 337.7 miles from Udorn, Thailand, to San Tay prison, 23 miles west of Hanoi in North Vietnam in November 1970 trying to rescue 61 American POWs. The current version is equipped with a terrain-following/terrain-avoidance radar, infrared sensor, and a global positioning system that allows it to fly at night and in adverse weather with unprecedented precision. With a range of 550 nautical miles, it often requires refueling support from Combat Shadow tankers. The aircraft costs about $25-million; it takes two pilots, two flight engineers, and two aerial gunners to fly it in combat. (USAF)

Pave Lows

Sikorsky's Super Jolly Green Giant helicopters, modified for special warfare missions as MH-53J/Ms, are AFSOC's rotary-wing workhorses. They are called Pave Lows. "PAVE" is an acronym for Precision Avionics Vectoring Equipment, which makes them the most technologically advanced helicopters in the world. Their wartime mission is to carry out long-range, low-level insertions of personnel and equipment into hostile objective areas and to conduct search and rescue operations for friendly combat personnel.

Pave Lows carry any combination of three 7.62 miniguns and .50 caliber machine guns that are useful in conducting rescue operations in hostile environments. Two aerial gunners and one flight engineer operate these weapons. This photo shows a tail gunner with a ramp-mounted 7.62 minigun on an over-water, low-level training flight. (USAF)

212

One must pause and wonder how our history would have been altered if we had possessed today's Combat Talons, Combat Shadows, and Pave Lows when we attempted to rescue our prisoners of war from North Vietnam in 1970, or Pave Lows when we attempted to free the hostages from our embassy in Iran ten years later in 1980.

It took about six months from the initial proposal to the early morning hour when our specially trained-for-the-occasion "Joint Contingency Task Force" found the Son Tay prison camp empty. With today's trained ground forces and mission capable aircraft in the same command, so much time could have been saved that the raiders might have arrived there before the prisoners were relocated.

The story of the Iranian hostages also might have been different if the air operation could have been conducted with today's AFSOC aircraft. That would have solved many of this operation's problems, especially the helicopter refueling in the desert that resulted in the disastrous collision between one U.S. Marine helicopter and an Air Force C-130.

Pave Hawks MH-60G

Pave Hawks, flown by the 55th Special Operations Squadron, were in the AFSOC inventory until September 1999 when the squadron was deactivated and its helicopters turned over to the Tactical Air Command. It was a sad event to see them deactivated because they had compiled such a distinguished combat and live-saving record in every campaign in which they participated. Their nostalgic departure was a part of carefully planned replacement and renovation of the command's aging aircraft fleet.

MH-60G Pave Hawks could carry only eight to ten combat troops, but had the same special operations mission capability as the larger Pave Lows. They were equipped with an all-weather radar, personnel rescue hoist, and two crew-served 7.62mm mini-guns. (USAF)

A relatively small helicopter, the HH-60G Pave Hawk could get into tight landing zones for exfiltration of personnel. A personnel rescue hoist with a 200-foot cable and a 600-pound lift capacity was installed in its side doors. (USAF)

Other AFSOC Aircraft

The 6th SOS of the 16th Special Operations Wing at Hurlburt Field, Florida, is the AFSOC unit to watch into the future. It is the best airpower ambassador in the U.S. military. Composed of enthusiastic aviation experts, it is organized into teams much like those of the U.S. Army Special Forces. Their primary mission is to assess, train, advise, and assist air forces of allied and friendly nations in air operations that are within the capabilities of aircraft in their inventories. They build valuable alliances with foreign nations that should reap beneficial dividends in U.S. foreign relations. This unique squadron flies the twin-engine UH-1N Bell helicopters, Spanish-made CASA 212-200 transports, and other aircraft, even including some Soviet-made helicopters.

Above: *This Spanish-built transport aircraft, CASA-212, is used by the 6th SOS in its expanding role as a provider of aviation expertise to other nations in support of their internal defense and development efforts. (USAF)*

The first of four MacKay Trophies went to this 16th SOS Spectre crew for extraordinary combat performance in Panama during Operation Just Cause in 1990. The third MacKay Trophy was awarded to the 7th SOS from Mildenhall for a heroic Combat Talon rescue of fifty-six people from the Republic of the Congo in 1997. (USAF)

AFSOC's Human Resources

The U.S. Special Operations Command claims as one of its enduring truths that people are more important than the hardware. This is plainly visible to any visitor to Hurlburt Field. People are enthusiastic about their work and proud of their airmen, many of whom are always deployed on some operation or an exercise. Enduring Freedom's offensive in the fall of 2001 coincided with the Air Commando Association's annual reunion. The 16th SOW was not able to provide the traditional aircraft static displays because so many of its aircraft had deployed to Afghanistan. Dedication of a memorial for a Combat Talon aircrew lost in the Philippines had to be moved from the Memorial Park to the beachfront because access to Hurlburt Field was restricted for heightened security reasons. Then, just at the start of the ceremony, it was announced that the bombing in Afghanistan had begun. Solemnly assembled commandos and families erupted in loud cheers and applause that, for many, turned to tears and silent prayers. Everyone there was keenly aware that the "quiet professionals" from the base across the street were now in harm's way.

The second and the fourth MacKay Trophies were awarded to the 20th SOS. The second one in 1991 for rescuing Navy Lt Devon Johnson, whose aircraft was shot down by an Iraqi missile on the first day of Operation Desert Storm. The most recent trophy went to this jubilant Pave Low crew and the Special Tactics team that rescued another downed helicopter from the 20th SOS on 2 November 2001 in Afghanistan. In the same heroic rescue operation, the 8th SOS Combat Talon I crew received the Brigadier General Ross Hoyt Award from the Air Mobility Command for being the most outstanding air refueling aircrew of 2001. (USAF)

Air Crews

All aircrew members are enthusiastic volunteers, many with backgrounds in other flying commands. Most of the officers are career-minded individuals and almost all special operations trained enlisted personnel are on repeat reenlistments. They are all volunteers who have gone that extra mile by submitting to continuous, rigorous, and specialized training. They have the can-do attitude of their air commando predecessors as shown by their prestigious awards. They won four MacKay Trophies in eleven years for the "most meritorious flights of the year by either an Air Force military member or an aircrew."

Strain and intensity show on the face of this 23rd Special Tactics Squadron competitor from Hurlburt Field, gathering his parachute and equipment after a successful HALO jump. Now he must navigate a four-kilometer compass course before he can set up a helicopter landing zone. This is just one of Ft. Bragg Rodeo 2000 events that attracted competitors from seventeen nations. (USAF)

Maintenance and Logistics Personnel

Maintenance and support personnel are just as well trained and motivated as the aircrews. They understand the importance of their unit's mission and carry it out with dedicated enthusiasm. They are the best in the Air Force and have a long string of excellence awards they could show off at the risk of compromising their status as the quiet professionals. AFSOC

attained the highest mission capable and readiness rates in over thirty years. The 16th Logistics Group won the Deadalian Trophy in 1999 for being the best logistics group in the Air Force and followed it up in 2000 by winning the Secretary of Defense Maintenance Excellence Award. This shows that the flying and combat ready crews are not the only ones who are in top-notch readiness; they have a sound and equally superior maintenance and logistics base to keep them mission-capable anytime anywhere.

Reserve and Guard Personnel

The same excellence applies to the Air Force Reserve and Air National Guard members. Unlike their active duty counterparts that move periodically from one base to another, they remain at the same post for years and get to know the idiosyncrasies of each aircraft and piece of equipment they service. This leads to some tender loving maintenance care that has its obvious rewards.

Reservists and National Guard personnel have civilian jobs and experience deployment problems that do not confront their active duty

Top, left: In a jubilant display of "non-quiet professional" behavior, these members of the 16th Logistics Group celebrate their 1999 award of the coveted Daedalian Trophy for being the best logistics group in the United States Air Force. (USAF)

Top, right: Senior Airman Thomas Kown from the 919th Maintenance Squadron works on a Combat Talon I engine. He began his reservist career as a student working extra days at engine maintenance. That effort lead to his promotion to staff sergeant and full time work in the engine shop as an Air Reserve Technician. (AFRC)

Above: *Staff Sergeant "Michael," a hydraulics specialist from the 16th SOW, uses only his first name while on duty in Operation Enduring Freedom. He is seen here checking the blades of an MH-53J Pave Low helicopter. (USAF)*

Left: *Technical Sergeant Ronnie Sims from the 353rd Maintenance Squadron, Kadena AB, Okinawa removes the radome of an MC-130 Combat Talon II during a routine inspection. (USAF)*

counterparts. Fortunately, their employers are very reasonable and the command has established lenient rules that ease this problem.

Because the Commando Solos are in such heavy demand, their crews and support personnel have been called to deploy as many as ten times a year. This is the highest deployment rate of any Air National Guard unit. Retention of personnel is very good and there are several positions within the wing that have fathers, sons, mothers, and daughters on the same teams.

Personnel of the AF Reserve's 919th SOW have a special "associate" relationship with the active duty 16th SOW at Hurlburt Field, only seventeen road miles away. They mix and share operations and maintenance for Combat Talon I's that now belong to the Reserve and for the Combat Shadows that are owned by the 16th SOW. In this associate arrangement the active duty and reserve squadrons maintain their own identity and work side-by-side on one common mission. Almost 600 members of the Wing were activated for deployment in October 2001 for Operation Enduring Freedom.

The 919th Medical Squadron is a very special Reserve unit that provides personnel for a fifty-bed air transportable hospital as well as flight surgeons and medical technicians who can deploy as needed with other flying squadrons. The squadron has been supporting humanitarian and civic action programs with regular two-week training deployments to South America.

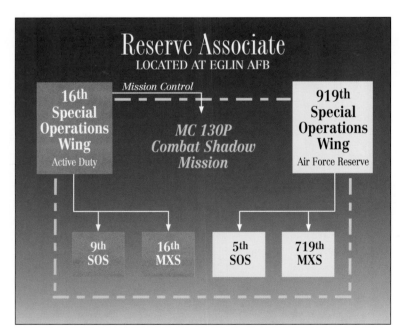

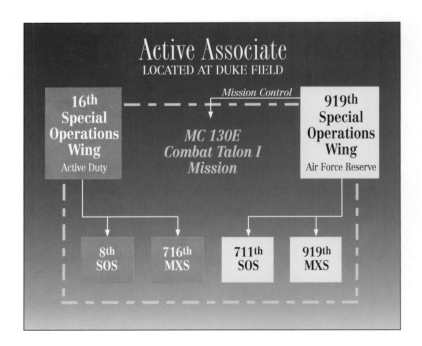

720th Special Tactics Group

The 720th Special Tactics Group provides AFSOC with versatile ground combat forces that form the link for effective joint operations with other U.S. and friendly forces. Its members are combat controllers, pararescuemen (PJs), and weather personnel. They must undergo arduous Air Force training in air traffic control, radio communications, small unit tactics, demolition, personnel recovery, battlefield trauma care, and weather observation and processing. In addition, they must be graduates of specialized courses of combat training schools of other services where they acquire combat training and qualifications in SCUBA and HALO. Many speak foreign languages and are culturally oriented toward specific regions of the world. Physically, they measure up to the standards of professional athletes.

Members of Special Tactics teams (SSTs) are the most convincing ambassadors of the command, and are usually the first ones on the scene of conflicts. Using their covert infiltration skills, they often arrive unnoticed. Once on target, they blend in with friendly forces and prepare drop and landing zones, open up forward operating bases for air landing of combat and support forces, and direct close air support attacks against the enemy. These men are entrusted with critical on-the-scene authority that is out of proportion to their enlisted ranks. Because they interact with indigenous forces, they often find themselves behind the enemy lines. They may be out of direct contact with higher authorities, yet they have to make critical and timely decisions. Their judgment must always be in step with the objectives of their mission and with the intent of our national policy. They have proven their vital role in joint forces operations during the initial phases of Enduring Freedom in Afghanistan. Their valiant efforts raised the ageless principles of war to a newer level.

18th Flight Test Squadron

There has always been a great need for new ways of doing things in special operations. The 18th Flight Test Squadron evaluates new ideas and explores new frontiers to ensure that the command exploits all available technology pertinent to special operations.

Top, left: *This combat controller is setting up his satellite communications antenna for radio contact with support aircraft. (USAF)*

Top, right: *Combat controllers are the true "quiet professionals" who do not brag about their successes. They are the "eyes and boots" on the ground who give our attacking aircraft fresh and precise target coordinates and make excellent fighter pilots out of otherwise pretty good pilots. (USAF)*

Lieutenant General Maxwell C. Bailey, AFSOC Commander, pins a Purple Heart on Staff Sergeant "Mike," a combat controller, who was injured during the 2001 fight for Mozar-e-Sharif in northern Afghanistan. Mike suffered ruptured eardrums and a scratched cornea when a U.S. bomb struck too close to his concealed position. (USAF)

219

Professional Education

An important feature of AFSOC is its well-established Special Operations School in a new building named after one of the first Commando legendary leaders, Major General John R. Alison. The school provides over twenty-five professional education courses that are based on real-time intelligence and range in scope from regional affairs and cross-cultural communications to special operations planning, psychological operations and antiterrorism. Attendees are individuals from all military services, members of government agencies, and officials from allied nations.

Training

Training for all AFSOC personnel is intensive and never-ending. Because of frequent deployments to many parts of the world, AFSOC's flying units cannot provide initial qualification training for incoming personnel. Another Special Operations Wing, the 58th at Kirtland AFB in New Mexico, that belongs to the Air Education and Training Command, provides this flying and flight simulator crew training as well as training for combat controllers and pararescuemen.

Joint Training and Exercises

AFSOC forces train extensively with counterparts of other US services in various scenarios on responses to probable contingencies. Much of joint training occurs with armed forces of our allies and friendly nations. Members of the 352nd Special Operations Group from Mildenhall Royal Air Force base in England train regularly and extensively with the forces of our NATO allies. They also conducted joint training exercises with units from nine of the now-friendly nations of the former Warsaw Pact. Lessons

Top: *A quick ramp exit from the rear of any AFSOC aircraft remains the safest way to deliver troops to their destinations. This normally happens only after an AFSOC Special Tactics team or other friendly forces secure a suitable landing field. (USAF)*

Above: *High-altitude, low-opening jumps have many advantages over the standard low-altitude jump that has soldiers landing in a long line. HALO jumpers can regroup during freefall before their special maneuverable chutes open. After opening, they can control their descent toward the drop zone with steerable chutes and land in a relatively small area. (USAF)*

learned from these exchanges have born fruit during the hostilities in the Persian Gulf, in the civil war conflicts among the nationalities of former Yugoslavia, and in the most recent liberation of Afghanistan from its oppressive Taliban and Al-Qaeda terrorist-dominated regime.

Members of the 353rd Special Operations Group from Kadena air Base in Okinawa train regularly with our allies and friends in the Far East. The group, which at that time was the 353rd SOW, was forced to evacuate from its prior home at Clark Air Base in the Philippines when the nearby volcano Pinatubo erupted and made the base unusable. Its temporary relocation to Okinawa became a permanent one, but its Pave Low helicopters in the 31st Special Operations Squadron were settled at Osan Air Base in Korea.

Right: *Members of the Army's 1st Special Forces Group and a Special Tactics Team from the Air Force's 353rd Special Operations Group load onto an MH-47 helicopter to participate in Operation Enduring Freedom—Philippines. This joint U.S. effort trains and advises the armed forces of the Philippines in their efforts to combat terrorism by the insurgent Abu Sayyaf organization. (USAF)*

Above: *When the State Department requested airlift support for more than 150,000 Vietnamese families that were displaced from their homes by November 1999 floods, the 353rd SOG responded within thirty hours. Vietnamese soldiers and policemen are seen here helping Technical Sergeant Porche and Staff Sergeant Splinter to arrange pallets that contained eagerly offloaded relief supplies. (353rd SOG)*

Civil unrest in Liberia in 1996 caused an evacuation of noncombatants from that country as part of Operation Assured Response. Pave Lows from the 352nd SOG were used to bring evacuees to safe airports such as this one for further flights to safety in other U.S. fixed wing aircraft. (USAF)

Operations

It is a standard practice to give operational code names to significant engagements of our military forces. AFSOC squadrons proudly display on their hallway walls photographs and memorabilia that document their participation in them.

Because the special operations forces were the first ones to respond to our fight to counter terrorism, there is a tendency to conclude that they were designed for use as aggressive offensive forces. This is far from the truth. AFSOC's resources have always been effectively employed as America's force of choice in a variety of peacetime scenarios where they were able to advance our national goals and help to shape the future environment of recipient nations. On visits to foreign nations, AFSOC's personnel act for the State Department with the guidance of the U.S. ambassadors as instruments of our national policy.

Humanitarian and Civic Assistance

Because AFSOC units are ready to deploy on a short notice, they are the first ones to be called for responses to humanitarian needs of nations when

Above: *The 352nd SOG delivered more than forty tons of food, water, medicine, shelter equipment, and other urgently needed supplies to Kosovar refugees who were stranded in isolated camps in the mountains of Albania. This 1998 humanitarian relief was carried out under the code name of Operation Shining Hope. (USAF)*

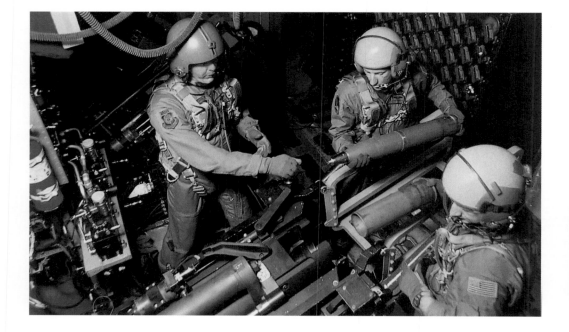

natural- or local-conflict-generated disasters strike. These may include emergency evacuations of populations from areas threatened by civil unrest, food delivery to refugees from wars, or periodic medical assistance to people in remote regions that do not have access to normal medical care.

Low Intensity Conflicts and War

Gunships were first employed in the Vietnam War. Their firepower and accuracy surprised the military tacticians and changed the nature of close air support in a conflict where air supremacy can be maintained. Today's technologically advanced Spectre and Spooky aircraft are vastly superior in performance to their Vietnam predecessors and have been effectively used in all our conflicts since.

Jolly Green Giants belonged to the Military Airlift Command during the Vietnam War, when they proved their worth in recovering downed aircrew members from hostile environments. Now, modified as MH-53J/M Pave Lows, they have been performing similar life-saving missions by recovering downed fighter pilots from Iraq, Kosovo, and Afghanistan.

Above: *Even though an MH-53J/M Pave Hawk can reach any destination in the world with multiple air refuelings, often the quickest and the best way to get it to its forward operating base is to fly there inside of a C-5 aircraft. (352nd SOG)*

Right: *Tightly secured inside of a C-5 with its rotor blades tucked in, the Pave Low will arrive where it is needed with a well-rested crew and a full complement of maintenance supplies and support personnel. (USAF)*

During Operation Desert Storm, Pave Hawks provided combat rescue for allied forces in Iraq, Saudi Arabia, Kuwait, and the Persian Gulf. Two Pave Hawks are seen here in their low level training over desert terrain. (USAF)

Because the Pave Lows are equipped with precision low-level navigational aids comparable to the Combat Talons, they can execute shorter-range clandestine operations. They demonstrated this capability when they escorted U.S. Army Apache attack helicopters to destroy two early warning radar sites that triggered the start of Operation Desert Storm.

Combat Talons saw their first combat employment in Vietnam where they operated successfully over North Vietnam's night sky that at that time was the most heavily defended airspace in the world. In carefully planned covert flights they airdropped native infiltrators and resupplies into strategic areas. Climbing to high altitudes over North Vietnam, they dispensed millions of psychological leaflets all over the country. Two Combat Talons provided precision low level navigation and escort for A-1Es and Jolly Greens during the attempted 1970 POW rescue from Son Tay, a prison compound twenty-three miles from downtown Hanoi. More recently, these aircraft delivered psychological operations material and combat personnel to other world trouble spots such as Grenada, Panama, the Persian Gulf, and Afghanistan.

Master Sergeant Bart Decker, an eighteen-year combat control veteran from the 720th Special Operations Group, joins the first cavalry charge of the twenty-first century in Afghanistan. Prior to this adventure he and his team opened up the first U.S. forward operating base on an austere field in Uzbekistan. (USAF)

Enduring Freedom

Employment of AFSOC's assets in concert with other U.S. military forces was aptly documented for the whole world in 2001 during the early stages of Operation Enduring Freedom in Afghanistan. Among the first Americans on the scene, the Special Tactics Teams provided accurate and real-time intelligence to orbiting bombers that were able to deliver smart bombs on well-concealed cave complexes with unprecedented precision. It was the first use of heavy strategic Air Combat Command's bombers in close tactical support of ground forces. Such coordinated employment of combat controllers and cutting edge technology ensured President Bush's promise to Al-Qaeda and its Taliban supporters: "You can run, but you can't hide." The Taliban's strike-and-hide tactics that were so effective against the USSR two decades before, became obsolete. They were killed or forced to run.

AFSOC's aircraft were employed to their maximum capabilities. Combat Shadows became reliable airborne gasoline stations that extended operational ranges of Pave Low helicopters, keeping them airborne for long missions. They surprised and harassed the enemy with unprecedented mobility by bringing troops to locations that were impossible to

Bottom, left: Pennsylvania Air National Guardsmen are busy at work in the suite of their Commando Solo aircraft somewhere over Afghanistan. Radio and TV programs they broadcast are prepared for them by the 4th Psychological Operations Group at Fort Bragg, North Carolina, and can be fed via satellite directly to the aircraft's roof-mounted, phased-array antenna. (USAF)

Bottom, right: The ramp of an MC-130H Combat Talon II became a hospital emergency room at Bagram Air Base in Afghanistan. Staff Sergeant Frederick Hutchinson and a team of Special Operations Forces medics: First Lieutenant Charlie Thomas, a senior flight nurse; Captain Mark Bieniarz, a flight surgeon; and Major (Dr.) Richard Conte operated to save the life of a soldier brought in from the scene of battle. (USAF)

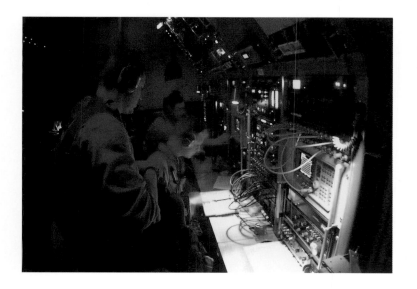

225

reach by foot. They evacuated wounded and provided timely airlift for special operations teams. Spectre and Spooky gunships dominated the nighttime skies. They denied the enemy mobility over his familiar mountain trails and provided precise fire support to ground troops. Combat Talons stayed busy day and night providing long-range airlift for personnel and supplies and flew every type of special operations mission within their capability. They infiltrated and resupplied highly mobile teams that could live off the land but had to rely on accurate and timely delivery of batteries for their high tech equipment. In psychological operations they dropped leaflets to the enemy forces and to the Afghans that were often printed in their tribal dialects. They also delivered some surprising and devastating blows to hiding Taliban and Al-Qaeda soldiers with their oversized Daisy Cutter bombs. Sense of mission accomplishment of aircrews and their support personnel at forward operating bases ran high. They were challenged by the successes of their missions and were eager to do their very best. Not to be outdone, the "never seen, always heard" Commando Solos continued challenging their prior record-setting aircraft-in-commission rates and broadcast-hour achievements. They reintroduced Afghanistan to television and entertaining music that had been outlawed by the Taliban regime.

Many aspects of AFSOC's participation in the Operation Enduring Freedom are classified and will not be available to the public for years. The quiet professionals are good at keeping secrets for security considerations. The extent of their involvement can be assessed by their aircraft losses during the first nine months in Afghanistan. They lost one Pave Low in November of 2001, one Combat Shadow in February, and one Combat Talon II in June of 2002. None of these losses was attributed to hostile enemy fire. Even though several crew members sustained various injuries, only two Combat Talon crew members and one passenger lost their lives.

Assessment of AFSOC

What a big difference a few years can make! There was significant reluctance to exploit the full capabilities of special warfare forces during the Gulf war against Iraq. At that time the United States Special Operations Command was still a new command and conventional forces and their leaders had a lingering distrust of all special operations warriors. In addition, adequate liaison between all the participating forces in the theater had not yet been refined. However, the subsequent motivational efforts of USSOCOM's commanders, combined with continued streamlining of interservice command channels, and successful employment of special forces in Somalia, Haiti, former Yugoslavia, and Afghanistan helped to change skeptical views of unconventional warfare forces.

AFSOC has stepped up magnificently to meet all of its challenges. Its Special Tactics Teams proved to be a vital ingredient in forging the necessary liaisons with other U.S. and allied forces before the well-coordinated Enduring Freedom offensive started. From its onset, all deployed aircraft exercised the full range of their capabilities. The net effect was not only the surprisingly rapid collapse of the well-entrenched Taliban forces, but also a very rewarding low casualty rate for all U.S. forces.

Opposite: *Afghan Northern Alliance soldiers witness a new employment of U.S. air power. Air Force, Navy, and Marine fighter-bombers paint contrails in the clear morning sky and are ready to release their "smart bombs" on targets identified by Special Tactics combat controllers who are observing enemy activity on the ground. (A.P. Wide World)*

This B-52 will soon launch against targets in Afghanistan. The weapons load team loads a Multiple Ejector Rack with Mk-84 2000lb general purpose bombs equipped with Joint Direct Attack Munition kits. The fins or strakes attached to the bomb double the range of a normal Mk-84. When dropped from 40,000 ft, it will fly about fifteen miles. The tail kit contains a GPS receiver and three steerable fins to guide the bomb to the target. (USAF)

This huge 15,000 lb. BLU-82 bomb is fastened to a specially-rigged pallet and ready to be dropped from high altitude by either model of Combat Talon. Nicknamed the "Daisy Cutter," the bomb was first used in Vietnam to clear helicopter landing zones in the jungle. It was used very effectively to clear Iraqi mines during Desert Storm and to decimate Taliban and Al-Qaeda forces in Afghanistan. (USAF)

227

Three of the fifty Ospreys that will be operational in AFSOC units by 2009 are being assembled in the Bell Helicopter plant in Amarillo, Texas. (Bell Helicopter Textron Company)

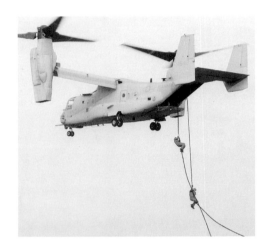

Quick deploying by rope is not likely to go out of style. There will be many locations where Ospreys will not be able to land because of their size or unsuitable terrain. (USAF)

AFSOC's Outlook

The future of AFSOC is promising. Since its establishment in 1990, the command has proven its value to the Department of Defense and its frequent calls to duty are likely to continue in this new turbulent century. No longer dependent on the Air Force for its budgetary needs, AFSOC is assured of adequate resources apportioned to it by the United States Special Operations Command under a special 1987 Congressional mandate that gave it its own budget authority equivalent to that of the Army, Navy, and Air Force. With that, AFSOC will keep in step with technology that will upgrade the capabilities of its aircraft and ensure the best possible training for its quiet professionals.

Every two years, the command initiates a twenty-month-long planning process to modernize its aging assets. On immediate horizon is a new tilt-rotor aircraft, the VC-22 Osprey, that is scheduled to replace the Pave Low helicopters. This revolutionary aircraft will have a 15 percent

It is not likely that AFSOC's Ospreys will be transported on ships because they will be able to fly anywhere with more frequent refuelings at the same speeds as Combat Talons. This U.S. Marine Corps Osprey is shown in a patented, blade-folding wing stow (BFWS) configuration that allows its wings to parallel the fuselage and the propeller blades to fold for stowage on board ships. (Bell Helicopter Textron Company)

228

This revolutionary tilt rotor aircraft, the CV-22 Osprey, will replace AFSOC's Pave Low helicopter fleet. It will have the hover capability of the MH-53M/J and fly with eighteen combat troops without refueling for 500 miles at 265 mph. It will have a nose mounted .50-caliber gun and require a crew of four: pilot, co-pilot, and two flight engineers. (USAF)

AFSOC CREDO

The "quiet professionals" of today's AFSOC live by this credo that honors their Air Commando predecessors and pledges to perpetuate their proud heritage.

I am a Commando

As my brothers before me, I am proud

to step into history as a member of the

Air Force Special Operations Command.

I will walk with pride with my head held high,

my heart and attitude will show my allegiance

to God, country and comrades. When unable to

walk another step, I will walk another mile.

With freedom my goal, I will step into destiny

with pride in the Air Force Special Operations Command.

greater vertical take-off payload than the MH-53J and, in its fixed-wing configuration, will be able to cruise at 265 miles per hour, or one hundred miles faster than the Pave Low. Its operational range will also be greater, and with its refueling capabilities, it will be limited only by the endurance of its four-man crew. It will have the best of precision navigational equipment and terrain following radar for conducting clandestine penetrations into hostile environments and will be protected against hostile threats by up-to-date ECM countermeasures.

Combat Talon C-130s need to be replaced by smaller, faster, and more maneuverable aircraft that will be harder to detect by hostile radars and sensors. Already in conceptual stage of development, these MC-X replacements should be phased in by 2017.

Replacement AC-X gunships will be introduced in 2018. They too will be smaller and more maneuverable and will have the capability to operate in more lethal environments than today's Spectres and Spookies.

Commando Solo aircraft will see somewhat earlier replacement. Currently available heavier payload aircraft, such as Boeing 767, will meet the command's requirements for added and improved electronic equipment.

Equipment used by the Special Tactics Teams will keep up with the innovations in technology and with future updates to the command and control systems used by the U.S. forces. This will include new vehicles for improved mobility on the ground, sophisticated communications equipment, more precise target identification and marking methodology, advanced personnel protection, combat enhancement tools, and use of unmanned aircraft for observation, targeting, and secure relaying of battlefield intelligence data.

Finally, the brightest spot must be the people serving in the command. Their careers will be exciting, promising, and promotion rewarding. There will be no shortage of dedicated Americans who will volunteer and compete for challenging positions in Air Force Special Operations. The old Air Commando spirit will continue to thrive and will no doubt soar to even greater heights.

A CV-22 is seen here after a short field take off from a small unprepared clearance in a wooded area. (USAF)

Naval Special Warfare Command

Naval Special Warfare Command

Rear Admiral George R. Worthington, USN (Ret)

From the islands and atolls of the Pacific Campaign to the Normandy beaches in France; from the beaches at Inchon in Korea to the Rung Sat Special Zone of Vietnam's Mekong Delta; from Grenada in the Caribbean to Panama in Central America; from Liberia and Mogadishu in Africa to the Persian Gulf, the Balkans and Afghanistan. Naval Special Warfare (NSW) forces have participated in every major American test of arms since their founding at Fort Pierce, Florida, in 1943. The U.S. Navy SEAL (SEa-Air-Land) and Special Warfare Combatant-craft Crewmen (SWCC) have a proud combat history. These maritime commandos form one of the Navy's foremost combat communities that serves today under the United States Special Operations Command (USSOCOM) based at MacDill Air Force Base, Tampa, Florida.

Naval Special Warfare boat operator drives a Special Warfare Craft, Light—SEAFOX, a twin-engine, fiberglass-hull boat. These high-speed craft were first used in 1981 to support SEAL operations. Today's primary Naval Special Warfare surface platforms include the Combat Rubber Raiding Craft; eleven-meter Rigid-hull Inflatable Boats; MK V Special Operations Craft; and riverine craft. Special Boat Teams are located in San Diego, California; Norfolk, Virginia; and Stennis, Mississippi. (Gary L. Keiffer, Arms Communications)

Pages 230–231: *SEAL combat swimmers emerge from the water in a training evolution off Coronado, California, home of the Naval Special Warfare Command and subordinate SEAL and Special Boat Teams. (David Bassett, Arms Communications)*

Opposite: *An underwater demolition team (UDT) pulls a 300-pound rubber landing boat ashore at Wonsan, Korea, on 26 October 1950. The UDT members destroyed a North Korean minefield in advance support of the Wonsan invasion. (Naval Historical Center)*

Naval Special Warfare operator mans a .50 caliber machine gun on a SEAFOX, Special Warfare Craft, Light, during an interdiction patrol. This boat operator was the precursor of today's Special Warfare Combatant-craft Crewman (SWCC). Focusing on clandestine infiltration and exfiltration of SEALs and other special operations forces, SWCC provide dedicated rapid mobility in shallow water areas where larger ships cannot operate. (Gary L. Keiffer, Arms Communications)

233

Right: *A typical combatant craft anchorage in Suisun Bay, Carguinez Straits, California. Similar bases of operations have been used since Vietnam, where "ammie barges" were used as support platforms in the rivers. The Riverine Forces in Vietnam migrated to Special Boat Squadrons under later reorganizations. Maintenance and supply personnel assisted in the upkeep of craft. (Richard Benne, Arms Communications)*

Above: *SEALs insert in a ZODIAC Combat Rubber Raiding Craft (CRRC). These craft are used throughout Special Operations. (Robert Genat, Arms Communications)*

Operating in small numbers, U.S. Navy SEALs' ability to conduct clandestine, high risk missions and provide real-time intelligence and eyes on target, offer decision makers immediate and virtually unlimited options in the face of rapidly changing wartime situations. (U.S. Navy photo by Ken Jacques)

234

NAVAL SPECIAL WARFARE COMMAND STRUCTURAL SNAPSHOT

The U.S. Naval Special Warfare Command (NAVSPECWARCOM), established 16 April 1987 at the Naval Amphibious Base in Coronado, California, organizes, equips, trains, and deploys combat-ready maritime special operations forces in support of fleet and joint operations worldwide.

ORGANIZATION	COMMANDER	HEADQUARTERS LOCATION	PRIMARY AREA OF RESPONSIBILITY
NAVSPECWARCOM	RADM	Coronado, CA	Global
NSWG-1	Captain	Coronado, CA	PACOM, CENTCOM
SEAL Team 1	Commander	Coronado, CA	
SEAL Team 3	Commander	Coronado, CA	
SEAL Team 5	Commander	Coronado, CA	
SEAL Team 7	Commander	Coronado, CA	
NSWU 1	Commander	Guam	
NSWU 3	Commander	Bahrain	
NSWG-2	Captain	Little Creek, VA	EUCOM, SOUTHCOM
SEAL Team 2	Commander	Little Creek, VA	
SEAL Team 4	Commander	Little Creek, VA	
SEAL Team 8	Commander	Little Creek, VA	
SEAL Team 10	Commander	Little Creek, VA	
NSWU 2	Commander	Germany	
NSWU-4	Commander	Puerto Rico	
NSWU 10	Commander	Spain	
NSWG-3	Captain	Coronado, CA	PACOM, CENTCOM
SBT-12	Commander	Coronado, CA	
SDVT-1 (ASDS)	Commander	Hawaii	
NSWG-4	Captain	Little Creek, VA	EUCOM, SOUTHCOM
SBT-20	Commander	Little Creek, VA	
SBT-22	Commander	Stennis, MS	
SDVT-2	Commander	Little Creek, VA	
NSWC	Captain	Coronado, CA	Not Applicable

Abbreviations: *NSWG is Naval Special Warfare Group; NSWU is Naval Special Warfare Unit; SBT is Special Boat Team; SDVT is SEAL Delivery Vehicle Team; ASDS is Advanced SEAL Delivery Team System; NSWC is Naval Special Warfare Center; CENTCOM is Central Command; EUCOM is European Command; PACOM is Pacific Command; SOUTHCOM is Southern Command.*

Above: *BUD/S trainees undergo "up close and personal" demolition exposure. Although not personally dangerous, the disorientation caused simulates the shock of combat situations. (Gary L. Keiffer, Arms Communications)*

Left: *A Naval Special Warfare Center SEAL training officer barks orders to the Basic Underwater Demolition/SEAL (BUD/S) trainees. BUD/S training is long and hard, and students remain wet and cold throughout the course. Instructors push the students to go beyond their own perceived limits. Those who endure the seven-plus months of intense physical and mental conditioning come to realize it's only the start to becoming a Navy SEAL. (Gary L. Keiffer, Arms Communications)*

"The Only Easy Day Was Yesterday"

SEa-Air-Land (SEAL) teams make up about 44 percent of the roughly 4,950 men (and a few women) in Naval Special Warfare Command, organized in April 1987 as the smallest component of U.S. Special Operations Command. The community has about 850 officers and 4,100 enlisted ranks; 1,200 of the total are members of the Navy's Individual Ready Reserve who have served at least four years on active duty.

Eight SEAL teams, which contain forty-eight 16-man platoons, total 2,800 operators, including SEAL-qualified medical corpsmen, 2,000 fleet support technicians, and fewer than 200 administrative personnel. The command also includes SEAL Delivery-Vehicle or dry dock shelter-qualified personnel, 500 Special Warfare Combatant-craft Crewmen.

Trainees "play" in the mud pits during Hell Week while instructors thwart their attempts to stay dry. (Gary L. Keiffer, Arms Communications)

235

Right: *BUD/S Third Phase concentrates on teaching students the basics of individual infantry: weapons, explosives, land navigation, patrolling techniques and small unit tactics. (Naval Special Warfare Command)*

Opposite: *Log PT is another form of physical conditioning used to teach trainees the need for teamwork. (Gary L. Keiffer, Arms Communications)*

Bottom, left and right: *Basic Underwater Demolition/SEAL (BUD/S) trainees get a break during this rock portage evolution due to the fact that the sun is still up. Surf passage evolutions and the task of negotiating the IBS (Inflatable Boat, Small) over rocks become increasingly treacherous when they are conducted in the dark of night. For a warfare community that comes from and returns to the sea, this training is an important tool used during BUD/S First Phase to build teamwork among the boat crews and to teach students how to get their boat and gear across a rocky shoreline. (Left photo: Naval Special Warfare Command; right photo: Elizabeth Schemmer)*

Hydrographic reconnaissance, other intelligence collection, underwater demolition, raids, sabotage, counter-terrorist direct action missions, and riverine operations are traditional Naval Special Warfare roles.

SEAL warriors are molded by stringent physical and mental screening, five weeks of indoctrination, and a brutal seven-month Basic Underwater Demolition/SEAL (BUD/S) course at Coronado, California, that weeds out all but the most highly motivated at the onset. "Hit the surf!" is a command every SEAL will remember as long as he lives. Instructors, who have served on teams and later will rejoin them with new graduates, impose sky-high standards that become progressively more demanding—hence the adage: "The only easy day was yesterday."

Phase One of BUD/S, thirteen weeks long, instills camaraderie as each class bonds in the face of constant pressure from instructors during the weeks of calisthenics, running, swimming, and strength work. The goal is to develop teamwork, tenacity, endurance, and self-confidence. Candidates burdened by boots swim competitively in a pool and mimic fish in San Diego Bay or the adjacent Pacific Ocean, where water temperatures average 62 degrees Fahrenheit. They "dump" (capsize) seven-man inflatable boats beyond the breakers, right them, reembark, ride ashore

Above: *"Up boat!" An IBS is hoisted in
the air by its trainee crew. The boats are
carried everywhere during First Phase of
BUD/S training. (Gary L. Keiffer, Arms
Communications)*

through surf seven or eight feet high, then manhandle those heavy hunks
of slippery rubber across huge rocks in front of the historic Hotel del
Coranado. Mini-marathons in soft sand are routine. Every event is a
race—including one of five miles in the ocean paddling the inflatable
rubber boats—so "it pays to be a winner."

The capstone, called "Hell Week," runs nonstop from Sunday
evening through noon Friday, during which time trainees enjoy about
fours hours of sleep. It is the ultimate test of motivation and, as Naval
Special Warfare Command summarizes the ordeal, proves to those who
make it through that the human body can do ten times the amount of
work the average man thinks possible.

Phase Two is an eight-week-long diving regimen that combines physical training with classroom courses that expect commissioned officers to
score at least 80 percent on exams and accept no less than 70 percent
from enlisted men. Open- and closed-circuit Self Contained Underwater
Breathing Apparatus (SCUBA) instruction starts in the pool, then switches
to San Diego Bay during daylight hours and after dark until swimmers can
cover 2,000 yards without excessive stress. Faculty members rigorously
enforce a two-man buddy system for safety reasons. If any "frogman's"
buddy surfaces before the finish line, he follows suit to ensure that his
partner is okay. Candidates learn, "Never leave your buddy."

BUD/S culminates in a ten-week land warfare course at San
Clemente Island, seventy miles off the California coast, where aspiring
SEALs learn to handle small arms, live ammunition, and demolitions.
Physical training and classroom exercises continue. Night combat hikes

are frequent and long. The longest swim, with fins and back in San Diego Bay, exceeds five miles against strong currents. Duty days normally terminate around midnight.

About two-thirds of all entrants drop out during BUD/S. Those that survive all ordeals without breaking justifiably stand tall on graduation day, having proved to themselves as well as observers that they can endure grueling conditions and think straight despite exhaustion.

BUD/S by no means fully qualifies graduates to be SEALs. Alumni first take three weeks of parachute training at Fort Benning, Georgia. The Naval Special Warfare Center at Coronado then subjects all officers and men to its SEAL Basic Indoctrination Course, which lasts twelve weeks. Stalwarts who pass those practical tests, then, and not until then, proudly pin on coveted trident and anchor insignia of an exclusive sea-air-land fraternity and join a genuine SEAL or SEAL Delivery Vehicle team for six to twelve months of operational training before they can become fully fledged members of U.S. Special Operations Forces.

Top, left and right: Basic SCUBA diving is taught in Second Phase of BUD/S. Here two trainees with open circuit (compressed air) SCUBA bottles (left) and Draeger closed-circuit SCUBA gear. (right) jump into San Diego Bay for an underwater orientation swim. (Gary L. Keiffer, Arms Communications)

Above: Hell Week trainees negotiate a mock battlefield. Tired, gritty, wet and cold, students get up to four hours sleep the entire week and still have to perform "under fire." Hell Week is not for everyone. It is specifically designed to test the physical and mental fortitude of those who want to join the ranks of the Navy's most elite special warfare operators. (Gary L. Keiffer, Arms Communications)

Left: BUD/S graduates receive three weeks of basic parachute training at Army Airborne School, Fort Benning, Georgia, prior to returning to the Naval Special Warfare Center for fifteen weeks of SEAL Qualification Training (SQT). (Naval Special Warfare Command)

Opposite, bottom: Drown proofing instruction teaches the BUD/S trainee to be comfortable in the water. Here a trainee, hands tied, dives to retrieve his face mask in twelve feet of water. During First Phase, trainees learn how to free dive holding their breath and loading obstacles with demolitions. (Robert Genat, Arms Communications)

NSW personnel on board a MK V Special Operations Craft monitor a mock attack during a Fourth of July Demonstration in Coronado's Glorietta Bay. The MK V SOC is a medium-range vessel used for inserting and extracting special operations forces, conducting maritime interdictions, escort and tactical swimmer operations, reconnaissance and coastal patrols. The eighty-two-foot craft is capable of sustained speeds of more than 40 knots. The MK V has a five-man crew, seats an additional sixteen passengers, can support up to four Combat Rubber Raiding Crafts and tow two Rigid-hull Inflatable Boats. (Naval Special Warfare Command)

Swim Fins, Special Boats, and Submarines

SEALs rely on assorted delivery systems to deposit them at proper times and places, then rendezvous and recover. Fixed-wing aircraft and helicopters play important roles, but special boats, unique submarines modified for NSW missions, parachutes, strong legs, and swim fins provide most SEAL mobility.

Roughly 500 incomparable boat crews, many of whom possess diplomas from a nine-week course at Coronado, not only transport and support SEALs along littorals and inland waterways, but perform coastal patrol, surveillance, harassment, armed escort, interdiction, deception, and search/rescue missions on their own. Featured craft include:

- Thirteen Cyclone-class 170-foot long Coastal Patrol Ships (PCs) displace 331 tons when fully loaded; have open ocean capabilities, but are best suited for littoral operations; and are employed on homeland security missions jointly with the Coast Guard to protect the nation's coastline, ports, and waterways from terrorist attack.

- Medium-range, adverse-weather Mark V Special Operations Craft (Mk V SOCs) can sustain speeds faster than 40 knots under favorable conditions.

- Light counterdrug patrol boats (PBL-CDs) help narcs conduct riverine warfare.

- Rigid-hull Inflatable Boats (RHIBs) crewed by three men simplify ship-to-shore insertions.

- Short-range, outboard-motor-propelled Combat Rubber Raiding Craft (CRRCs) are perennial workhorses.

A Rigid-hull Inflatable Boat (RIHB) is operated by Special Boat Teams to insert SEALs over hostile beaches. A Navy warship is seen in the background. (Naval Special Warfare Command)

Naval Special Warfare operators employ Rigid-hull Inflatable Boats to conduct maritime interdiction operations in the Persian Gulf. Special Boat Teams insert SEAL elements onto merchant ships to inspect cargo for contraband. Throughout Operation Enduring Freedom, NSW operators and coalition forces have also conducted at-sea Leadership Interdiction Operations (LIO) in the search for terrorists attempting to escape by sea. (Naval Special Warfare Command)

An RHIB makes a high-speed training approach on a target vessel. SEALs will board the vessel and rehearse take down procedures. (Naval Special Warfare Command)

SEALs frequently favor clandestine submarine transportation. Slightly more than 200 NSW personnel are qualified to operate Dry Deck Shelters (DDSs) or SEAL Delivery Vehicles (SDVs) embarked thereon.

Dry Deck Shelters, mounted behind the conning towers of SSGNs (former ballistic missile submarines converted for SOF operations), are large enough to accommodate one SDV or twenty SEALs with rubber raiding craft. Two shelters, for which some submarines are fitted, not only double capacity but amplify flexibility because they can carry dissimilar loads. Each DDS chamber fills with water when operators open valves; a massive rear door admits the sea after internal pressures equal those outside, and occupants then slip out. Submerged SDVs proceed unobserved to objectives, whereas SEALs with CRRCs float on the surface.

SEAL pilots and navigators man SDVs, which are free-flooding submersibles equipped with sophisticated electronic gear that facilitate navigation during trips that can last eight hours. First generation models could carry just four SCUBA-equipped combat swimmers plus a crew of two, but the Advanced SEAL Delivery System (ASDS), in final stages of operational testing, promises vastly improved capacity, range, diversified payloads, and stealth features. ASDS, unlike its predecessor, eliminates the need for Dry Deck Shelters because it departs parent submarines

under its own power. Dry interiors ensure that well-rested SEALs arrive in target areas ready to do business and, as a bonus, enable nonswimmers, such as civilian agents and land-loving SOF, to perform otherwise impossible deeds.

The Era of Violent Peace

The big battles of World War II are not thought to be on the military horizon. Rather, small wars of ethnic clashes, counterterrorism, and counterproliferation operations against weapons of mass destruction appear to make up the bulk of United States national security challenges in the twenty-first century. Special Operations Forces (SOF) offer the precise "weapons systems" to deal with today's threats. The war against terrorism has taken center stage since the attack on the World Trade Center, 11 September

Top: *Naval Special Warfare Command has seventy new, short-range Rigid-hull Inflatable Boats (RHIBs). Handled by a three-man crew, these thirty-six foot-boats carry eight combat-equipped special operations personnel and their cargo. Powered by twin 470-horsepower engines driving two waterjets, they have a full-load cruise speed of more than 30 knots and a range of more than 200 nautical miles. (Naval Special Warfare Command)*

Above, left: *SEALs are maritime, multi-purpose combat forces organized, trained, and equipped to conduct a variety of special missions in all operation environments and threat conditions. (U.S. Navy photo by Ken Jaques)*

Above: *Members of the Navy's Parachute Team, the Leap Frogs, rehearse a jump. The Leap Frogs deploy nationally on an annual basis performing in support of Navy recruiting. Navy personnel are assigned to the team for two to three years. After a Leap Frog tour, NSW personnel return to their team and are able to teach advanced freefall techniques to their fellow operators. (Naval Special Warfare Command)*

Above: *Small SEAL tactical elements employ the Combat Rubber Raiding Craft to reach an objective area. The CRRC can be employed from ships, boats, aircraft, and submarines. (U.S. Navy)*

Above: *Thirteen long-range, high-speed Cyclone Class Patrol Coastal (PC) ships—first used by NSW to conduct maritime special operations—are now employed in support of homeland defense. With a range of 2,680 nautical miles, a cruising speed of ten knots and a maximum speed of thirty-five knots, the ships have a crew of four officers and roughly twenty-five enlisted ranks. They support a twenty-five-man embarked SEAL detachment or berth a nine-man special operations team. Five of the thirteen PCs have a stern ramp that permits launch and recovery of Rigid-hull Inflatable Boats (with SEALs aboard) while underway. (Bollinger Shipyards)*

Right: *Navy SEALs conduct a fast-rope exercise from the cargo door of an SH-60H Seahawk launched from USS* Enterprise *onto the hull of the fast-attack submarine USS* Hampton *(SSN 767). (U.S. Navy)*

2001. Operations against Osama bin Laden's Al-Qaeda network and Afghan Taliban extremists called forth the multifaceted skills of NSW Special Operators as perhaps never before. This is the future of warfare, which the Navy SEALs and SWCC represent extraordinarily well owing in large measure to the unique training they receive. That training evolves from lessons learned in past encounters.

Most recently, Naval Special Warfare forces played prominent roles during Operation Restore Hope (1992–1995), the Somalia relief effort; Operation Support Democracy (1994–1995), relief from political repression in Haiti; and several operations in the Balkans from 1995 to the present—Operations Joint Endeavor, Joint Guard, Joint Forge, Allied Force, Joint Guardian; and Operation Assured Response (1996), the rescue of diplomats from the U.S. Embassy in Liberia. In this last operation, SEALs who deployed from Germany were the first U.S. forces available to assist the embassy evacuation. The platoon provided armed protection and deterred a rebel force from attacking the embassy. They later helped

Army Special Forces teams escort 436 American personnel and 1,677 foreign nationals to safety.

SEALs acquitted themselves admirably in each of the foregoing engagements. Another example is a combat swimmer operation conducted by Lieutenant Tom Dietz. He led the diversion operation off a Kuwaiti beach during preparations for Operation Desert Storm that tied down a sizeable portion of an Iraqi division and prevented the division's employment against the main allied attack far inland. Dietz led his swimmers into the shallows and planted explosive charges which, when detonated later, simulated the beginning of an amphibious landing—the diversion worked.

Naval Special Warfare forces were among the first U.S. Special Operations Forces to participate in Operation Enduring Freedom, in

Above: *SEAL combat swimmers risee from the depths. They were delivered close to shore for this training exercise from a SEAL Delivery Vehicle (SDV). (Robert Genat, Arms Communications)*

Left: *A SEAL combat swimmer emerges from the surf zone. He is wearing a Draeger closed-circuit SCUBA, a pure oxygen rig that emits no tale-tale bubbles. (Robert Genat, Arms Communications)*

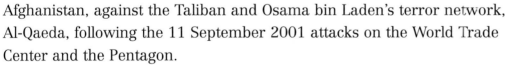

Above: *SEAL Team combat swimmers emerge from the surf zone. These swimmers could have exited a SEAL Delivery Vehicle (SDV); they will accomplish their mission and extract in a variety of ways. (Robert Genat, Arms Communications)*

Opposite: *SEALs skydive from the tailgate of a C-130 transport plane. Several military aircraft are available to Special Operations Forces for airborne insertions. SEAL Teams routinely practice static-line insertions and freefall techniques. The usual freefall mode is called "High Altitude, Low Opening," a technique used worldwide by skydivers. The jumper leaves an aircraft at altitude and freefalls to an opening altitude, then steers the parachute to a designated landing zone. Another technique involves jumping at a high altitude, opening the parachute immediately, and "flying" the descent a great horizontal distance before landing. This is called "HAHO," High Altitude High Opening. SEAL Teams practice all airborne techniques including jumping into water. (U.S. Navy)*

Afghanistan, against the Taliban and Osama bin Laden's terror network, Al-Qaeda, following the 11 September 2001 attacks on the World Trade Center and the Pentagon.

Navy SEALs operated entirely on land in mountainous regions in Afghanistan, often at elevations of 10,000 feet. A SEAL commander, for the first time, commanded forces from the U.S. Army, U.S. Air Force, Australia, Denmark, Germany, Norway, and Turkey. He also had tactical control of U.S. Marine Corps helicopter and fixed-wing crews. This tight control allowed friendly forces to compress the planning cycles necessary to attack identified targets before the defenders could escape. A large Al-Qaeda cave system—the Zhawar Kili complex—was identified, and

U.S. Navy SEALs exit a CH-53E Sea Stallion during a training exercise in an abandoned Federation of Bosnia sand pit in 1997. Developing dedicated maritime, ground, and air tactical mobility platforms for NSW forces throughout their training and deployment cycle has become especially important as the community looks to enhance its ability to carry out the myriad of complex SOF missions required in the war on terrorism. (U.S. Navy)

SEAL-led forces spent nine days cleaning out forty-three cave complexes with extensive tunnel structures, capturing and destroying huge stockpiles of ammunition and explosives, including surface-to-air missiles. They killed twelve Taliban fighters who had tried, unsuccessfully, to engage them. Later, at another remote, mountain location, SEALs operating for the first time in the field with a German SEAL Team attacked the Taghow-

Above: SEAL Team counter-terrorism elements rehearse take down procedures. Special teams are trained in elite counter-terrorism techniques, many of which remain classified. (David Bassett, Arms Communications)

stay compound, a suspected Taliban cave complex on the peak of a ridge at 9,000 feet. They landed in snow and proceeded to clear the village and caves. This operation was the first time since World War II that German forces had participated in offensive military operations. SEALs continue to perform in operations requiring their special skills and have proven their relevance to ongoing conflicts.

Opposite, top: Each SEAL Team Desert Patrol Vehicle (DPV) "dune buggy" configured vehicles packs a punch with its .50 caliber machine guns and rocket launchers. With a crew of three, the DPV was designed to patrol coastal areas for reconnaissance missions. They can also be employed to rescue downed pilots or other personnel behind enemy lines. (Robert Genat, Arms Communications)

Left: During a Sensitive Site Exploitation (SSE) mission, SEALs explore the entrance to one of forty-three cave complexes they discovered on the Zhawar Kili area of eastern Afghanistan in early 2002. Used by Al-Qaeda and Taliban forces, the caves and other above-ground complexes were subsequently destroyed either by Navy Explosive Ordnance Disposal (EOD) personnel or through air strikes called in by the SEALs. (U.S. Navy)

Opposite, bottom right: A SEAL swimmer jumps from a hovering helicopter during the Coronado Annual Fourth of July Demonstration. The limits on this type of exercise are twenty feet at twenty knots. Any higher or faster endangers the SEAL. (U.S. Navy)

SEALs on patrol approach a target. SEALs practice small unit tactics, and elements are mutually supporting. They can usually call in air support, if required, and on-call artillery may be assigned to a unit. (Robert Genat, Arms Communications)

Above: *SEALs prepare to commence a patrol in a jungle area. They operate in all terrain, including arctic and jungle extremes. (Robert Genat, Arms Communications)*

SEALs practice storming a stronghold. Urban warfare requires house-to-house search techniques, which are practiced by all SEAL Teams. (Gary L. Keiffer, Arms Communications)

Metamorphosis

Naval Special Warfare forces have been morphing at the speed of light since September 2001. Innovative organizational lash-ups, doctrines, tactics, techniques, arms, and equipment since then have responded expeditiously to accelerated operational tempos, new areas of responsibility far from blue, green, or brown water, and expanded missions that intensify attention to special reconnaissance, weapons of mass destruction, and counterterrorism.

Flexibility increased exponentially early in 2002 when NAVSPECWARCOM increased the number of SEAL teams from six to eight (each of which now sports six rather than eight platoons) without exceeding stipulated manpower authorizations and budgetary appropriations. Restructuring further

constituted Naval Special Warfare squadrons that unite SEAL teams with special boats, other delivery vehicles, mobile communications, logistical packets, and assorted support, such as cryptologists and explosive ordnance disposal experts. Those innovative formations standardize procedures, facilitate integrated training better than ever before, and simplify control.

The NSW Center in Coronado, which develops and validates creative concepts, supervises several specialized schools, where curriculum crafters struggle to keep pace with previously unexplored topics that unexpectedly compete with traditional subjects.

Eight widely dispersed detachments conduct sharply focused courses that similarly strive to keep pace. Students at Little Creek, Virginia, get "graduate degrees" in underwater demolitions. Instructors at Yuma, Arizona, and Hurlburt Air Force Base, Florida, impart fine points about joint air operations. Area orientations take place at Kodiak, Alaska (subarctic), Panama City (jungle warfare), and Key West (maritime subtropical). Hawaii handles the interface between SEALs and submarines. A Naval Small Craft Instruction and Technical Training School at Coronado is the fountainhead of all knowledge on such issues.

Cutting-edge technologies in the mill soon will enable naval SOF to shoot, move, and communicate far better than their predecessors, because USSOCOM's "acquisition executive," in tandem with the Naval Sea Systems Command and NSW advisors, is foreshortening times needed to research, develop, test, evaluate, procure, and put unbeatable hardware in the hands of unbeatable SEALs and boat crews. The future of Naval Special Warfare accordingly looks bright to all knowledgeable observers and promises a formidable foe to America's enemies.

A SEAL sniper sets up for a shot. Snipers normally work in pairs. One man spots for the shooter and maintains whatever communications are required. (U.S. Navy photo by Ken Jaques)

Naval Special Warfare forces train for contingencies in all environments, whether it is in the snow-capped mountains of Afghanistan, the jungles of the Philippines, or the waters of the Arabian Gulf. Pictured here, a Navy SEAL operator departs on a cold-weather Sensitive Site Exploitation (SSE) mission into the mountainous regions of Eastern Afghanistan to search for al-Qaeda leadership and recover any items of intelligence or evidentiary value. (U.S. Special Operations Command)

251

SOCOM's Theater Commands

SOCOM's Theater Commands

Benjamin F. Schemmer

Theater SOC

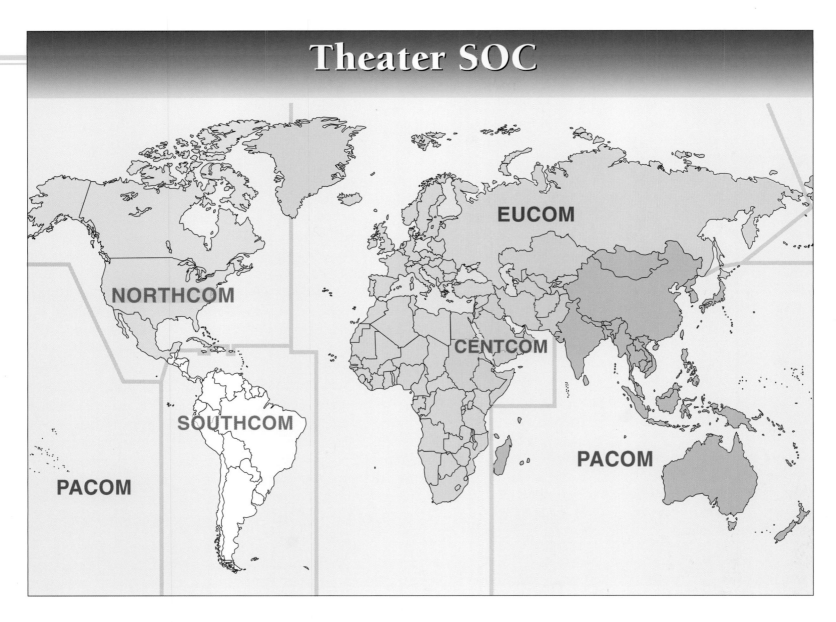

There are seven unified commands in the United States military structure, including U.S. Special Operations Command and the relatively new U.S. Northern Command, which became responsible for defense of the American homeland in 2002. The other five unified commands represent regional, war-fighting commands, each of which has its own Special Operations Command (SOC). By law, each is headed by a brigadier general or junior flag officer. The accompanying schematic map shows their geographic areas of responsibility.

The theater SOCs have small planning and operational staffs (varying from twenty-five to sixty people, but soon to increase) that can call upon the relatively small special operations units located within their theaters and quickly augment those forces—through U.S. Special Operations Command headquarters in Tampa, Florida—from the entire pool of SOF assets worldwide. Theater SOCs normally exercise operational control of all special operations forces (SOF)—except for civil affairs and psychological operations—within each geographic commander's area of responsibility. Additionally, the SOCs can provide a nucleus for the establishment of a larger joint special operations task force, as was done during Operation Enduring Freedom in Afghanistan in 2001 and 2002.

Under the expanded mission responsibilities announced for SOCOM in February of 2003, the theater SOCs may undertake missions directed by SOCOM headquarters in Tampa, FL and have access to a theater commander's conventional Army, Navy, and Air Force assets working under it's command and control.

Above: *Schematic map depicting the six regional warfighting commands of the U.S. military. Each area of operation has its own Special Operations component command: Pacific (SOCPAC), Europe (SOCEUR), Central (SOCCENT), Southern (SOCSOUTH), Joint Forces (SOCJFCOM), and Korea (SOCKOR). (Map by StyloGraphix)*

Pages 252–253: *A sniper from SEAL Team Eight of U.S. Atlantic Command's Special Operations Command (the forerunner of SOCJFCOM) trains his weapon on a ship during a 1999 visit, board, and search demonstration. (U.S. Special Operations Command)*

Opposite: *This air strike against Al-Qaeda and Taliban forces was designated by a team from the 5th Special Forces Group (Airborne), out of Fort Campbell, Kentucky, working with Air Force Tactics men during the initial ground drive on Mazar-e-Sharif soon after offensive operations began in Operation Enduring Freedom in Afghanistan in October of 2001. It took only forty-nine days from the insertion of the first U.S. special operations teams until the fall of Kandahar and the near total rout of Taliban forces. (U.S. Special Operations Command)*

The accompanying sidebar illustrates how SOCOM's missions are typically distributed throughout the unified commands. (The table is for 1997-1998, a relatively quiet period in terms of contingency operations and the last year for which such a breakout has been made available.)

The fifteen missions shown on the table for U.S. Special Operations Command apparently represent SOCOM training exercises, not "real world operations" since there were no notable contingency operations in 1997-1998. Some of them may have been full-up command post exercises designed to test the command's responsiveness, flexibility, and capabilities in a global challenge—such as the nearly simultaneous occurrence of two major theater conflicts—which has been the bedrock of American contin-

Navy SEALs search a village in Afghanistan
in support of Operation Enduring Freedom.
(U.S. Special Operations Command)

SOF AREAS OF OPERATION (1997–1998)

UNIFIED COMMAND	NUMBER OF SOF MISSIONS	NUMBER OF COUNTRIES
U.S. Pacific Command	699	34
U.S. European Command	766	67
U.S. Central Command	not available	
U.S. Southern Command	415	31
U.S. Atlantic Command*	261	15
U.S. Special Operations Command	15	2

*Redesignated as U.S. Joint Forces Command in October, 2000

gency planning since the Berlin Wall came down and is the basic scenario for which all U.S. forces are designed.

The missions shown for five of the six theater commands represent an average of more than four hundred SOF missions each, more than one every day—a heavy workload given the small size of each theater's Special Operations Command—and another indication of the degree to which America's military hierarchy has come to rely on Special Operations Forces to acquit the nation's worldwide responsibilities.

Following is how the five theater special operations commands break down, and what their respective areas of responsibility include, in addition to a sixth such sub-unified command under United Nations Forces in Korea.

Special Operations Command— Pacific (SOCPAC)

SOCPAC is headquartered at Oahu in Hawaii and covers the largest geographic area of any unified command—half the earth's surface, 105 million square miles, and 60 percent of the world's population living in forty-three countries and ten U.S. territories speaking seventy-five official languages and practicing twenty distinct religions.

Crisis response is Pacific Command's top priority and is provided by the rapidly deployable Joint Task Force 510, which has SOCPAC as its nucleus. In 1999, SOCPAC conducted thirty-seven Joint/Combined

Below: Schematic map depicting the area of operation of Special Operations Command Pacific (SOCPAC). From this global perspective, the massive geographical and political importance of the area are very apparent. (Map by StyloGraphix)

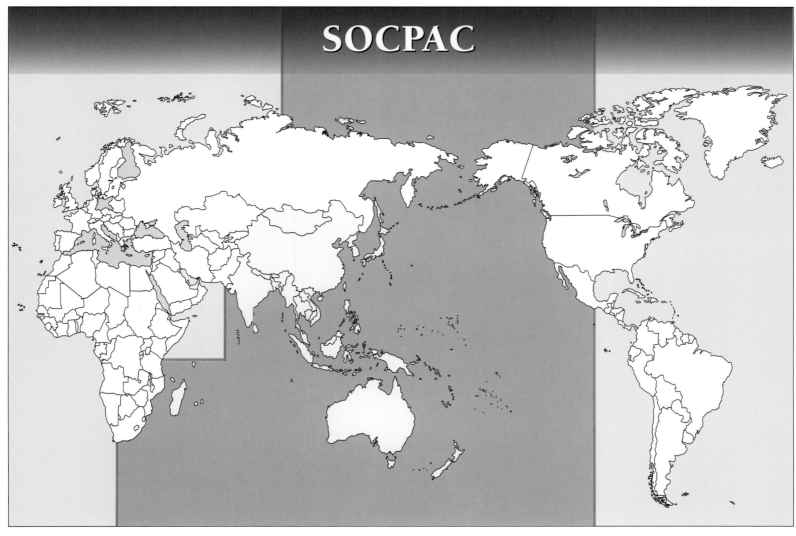

Above: *The 1st Special Forces Group, 2nd Battalion, Fort Lewis, Washington, and the Royal Thai Army Airborne preform a friendship static jump out of a CH-47 Chinook helicopter during Exercise Cobra Gold 2001 in Thailand. This multilateral exercise includes more than 10,000 participants, forty-five aircraft and nine ships from the United States military, the Royal Thai Armed Forces, and the Singaporean Armed Forces. (U.S. Army)*

Above: *Army Command Sergeant Major Hoopy Qualls, 1st Special Forces Group, Fort Lewis, Washington, presents Army parachutist wings to members of the Thai Armed Forces after participating in a joint-combined High Altitude Low Opening (HALO) jump at Phitsonulok, Thailand, in Exercise Cobra Gold. This regularly scheduled, joint combined exercise is designed to ensure regional peace and strengthen the ability of the Royal Thai Armed Forces to defend Thailand or respond to regional contingencies. (U.S. Army)*

Right: *U.S. Navy SEALs help the members of the Philippine Armed Forces recover an unmanned aerial vehicle from shallow waters after it crashed during a joint training exercise that was part of Operation Enduring Freedom–Philippines. (U.S. Special Operations Command)*

Exchange Training Exercises in twelve countries and hosted an annual week-long "theater engagement" conference with two hundred delegates attending from twenty-two countries, with twenty-six general and flag officers among them. The forum provides SOCPAC an "azimuth check" for peacetime engagement throughout its vast area of operations.

Humanitarian demining and counterdrug efforts represent the command's principal peacetime special operations missions. SOCPAC conducted four demining operations in Laos in 1998 and 1999 and two demining operations in Thailand in 1999. Four demining operations were undertaken in 2000.

Southeast Asia remains one of the world's biggest drug-producing areas. SOCPAC has been active in helping countries deal with this scourge and conducts regular training to help host nations improve planning, expertise, and small unit tactics among both military and law enforcement agencies to battle narco-criminals. Thailand and Malaysia participated in that training in 1999, and Laos and Cambodia joined those two countries in the program in 2000.

Special Operations Command— Korea (SOCKOR)

U.S. Forces, Korea have a unique theater Special Operations Command at Yongsan. It is the only theater SOC that is not a subordinate unified command, since the commander of U.S. Forces in Korea is not a unified commander, but commander in chief of the United Nations Command there. Instead, SOCKOR, established in 1988, is a functional component command of U.S. Forces, Korea. Whether in peacetime—more accurately, "Armistice time," since North and South Korea are still technically at war—or during contingencies and war, SOCKOR exercises operational control of the U.S. Army Special Forces Detachment Korea, the largest continuously serving Special Forces unit in Asia. Were hostilities with North Korea to erupt again, SOCKOR would join forces with the Republic of Korea to establish the Combined Unconventional Warfare Task Force.

South Korea's special operations capability is formidable, over fifteen thousand strong. Its warriors are well trained and physically conditioned in enviable shape. Typifying their spirit (and the country's economic constraints), virtually all of Korea's special operations forces would make their first-ever parachute jump into North Korea in actual wartime.

SOCKOR also functions as the Special Operations Command, United Nations Command, in which role it would integrate all third-country special operations forces committed to the Korean theater. When fully reinforced with U.S. troops, SOCKOR comprises the largest special operations task force in the world.

Besides the challenges facing U.S. and South Korean special operations forces should hostilities erupt, SOF members on the peninsula face a number of "wild card scenarios." These include North Korean terrorist actions, threats of the use of weapons of mass destruction, missile launches to provoke political and economic concessions, man-made as well as natural disasters, the outbreak of civil war in North Korea or the collapse of that state, and massive refugee flows that might well result.

This schematic map depicts the area of operations of Special Operations Command Korea (SOCKOR). While not a large geographical area, the strategic importance and current political atmosphere of this region commands a constant heightened sense of vigilance. (Map by StyloGraphix)

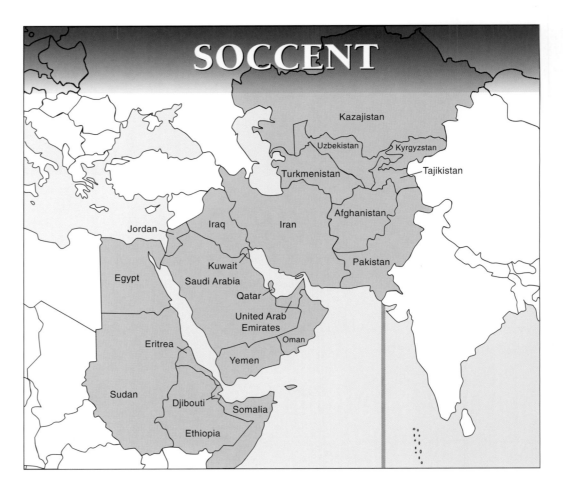

SOCCENT

Special Operations Command—
Central Command (SOCCENT)

Central Command's area of operations is the birthplace of three of the
world's major religions, has a population of over 400 million people com-
prising seventeen different ethnic groups speaking six major languages
with hundreds of dialects. The countries it works with have varied forms
of government, countless unique terrain features, and a wide range of
per capita incomes. The five "stans" of the former Soviet Union—Turkmenistan, Uzbekistan, Kasakhstan, Kyrgyzstan, and Tajikistan—were
recently added to CENTCOM's geographic responsibilities in central Asia.

While Central Command is headquartered at MacDill Air Force Base
in Tampa, Florida, like U.S. Special Operations Command, SOCCENT has
had a forward operating base in Bahrain for years and established a far
more sophisticated one in Qatar in 2002. It also has a forward operating
base in Kuwait to provide command and control for CENTCOM's annual
Desert Spring exercises, which provide combat support units to the
Kuwaiti Brigades and terminal guidance of close air support teams back-
ing the Combined Task Force Kuwait. Typically, up to nine Special Forces
teams and a Special Operations command and control element support
Desert Spring operations.

Operationally, SOCCENT has been heavily involved in humanitarian
demining work in Yemen, Jordan, Ethiopia, Eritrea, and Afghanistan.
As part of their counterdrug work, SOF units provided light infantry and
mountaineering training for Turkmenistan's state border service and
taught a course in warrant officer leadership and development. Similar
counterdrug work has recently begun in Egypt and Kenya.

SOCCENT teams also conduct regular Integrated Survey Programs, which evaluate security for embassies and consulates throughout the command's area of operations. These surveys support State Department emergency action plans and provide planning data for noncombatant evacuation operations. One such survey was underway in Nairobi, Kenya, in August of 1998, with SOF personnel from the survey team in the U.S. embassy when the terrorist bomb exploded there. The survey team quickly established a defensive perimeter to prevent pedestrian interference with rescue operations and a potential follow-on attack. Several members set up a first aid triage station, which initiated quick, decisive actions that were instrumental in saving additional lives. Nine Special Forces personnel and one Air Force Special Tactics airman were awarded the Soldier's Medal for heroic action to save human lives in a noncombat situation.

Central Command's Special Operations Command met its ultimate test in Operation Enduring Freedom soon after the 11 September 2001 terrorist attacks on the World Trade Center and the Pentagon. By 19 October Air Force Special Tactics men from the 720th Special Tactics Group parachuted into northern Afghanistan and Army Special Operations teams from the 5th Special Forces Group (Airborne) at Fort Campbell, Kentucky, were inserted by helicopter to link up with Afghan warlords who had been bribed by the CIA or persuaded to wipe out Al-Qaeda terrorists and evict the oppressive Taliban regime.

Immediately upon their arrival in Afghanistan, their commander split them into four separate teams, which traveled ten to thirty kilometers a day to four different locations to link up with General Rashid Abdul Dostum and other tribal leaders of the Northern Alliance. From mid-

Bearded Special Forces men from Operational Detachment Alpha of the 5th Special Forces Group (Airborne) stand with several USAF Special Tactics men, most all of them clad in the ragged battle dress of Afghan Mujahideen, on either side of Pashtun tribal leader Hamid Karzai, who was later voted Afghanistan's prime minister. (U.S. Special Operations Command)

October to 10 November, they coordinated an intensive close air support campaign, frequently calling in precision air strikes from horseback, to support a ground offensive that liberated six Northern provinces and fifty towns and cities, including the city of Mazar-e-Sharif, throughout 100 miles of the world's toughest terrain.

Within forty-nine days, their combined forces had liberated the entire country. By the time Kabul and Kandahar fell in December of 2001 and conventional Marine and Army forces began to arrive, fewer than two hundred U.S. Special Forces on the ground had confirmed that American special operations are indeed extraordinary force and diplomacy multipliers.

Nowhere was that better illustrated than special operations work with Hamid Karzai, the Pashtun tribal leader who on 8 October had infiltrated by motorcycle with eleven of his tribesmen back into the southern part of Afghanistan from exile in Pakistan. U.S. forces nicknamed his team "The Texas Twelve." Karzai barely escaped capture by the Taliban on 1 November when he convened a meeting of Pashtun elders in Oruzgan province near Kandahar, the center of Taliban power, but he was saved by U.S. special operations forces when they called in precision air strikes on about 500 Taliban fighters trying to overrun his position. A dozen Taliban were captured during one such engagement and revealed that their orders were to "make an example" by slaughtering all residents of a nearby town, including women and children. Karzai called it "the Taliban's last ditch attack."

Central Command's reliance on special operations forces during Operation Enduring Freedom under General Tommy Franks proved a dramatic contrast to the reluctance of CENTCOM commander General H. Norman Schwarzkopf to exploit SOF resources during his 1992 campaign to oust Iraqi forces from Kuwait. Schwarzkopf adamantly resisted suggestions that he use other, elite "special mission units" on direct action missions such as cross-border operations to sever Iraqi lines of communication and to hunt down the mobile Scud missiles with which Iraq was bombarding Israel in attacks that threatened to bring Israeli into the war with preemptive attacks and thus fracture the Pan Arab coalition. Schwarzkopf finally had to be ordered by Defense Secretary Dick Cheney and JCS Chairman General Colin Powell to deploy teams from Delta Force and Special Tactics to penetrate deep into Iraq and hunt down the Scuds. Once those teams began operating on 7 February—twenty-one days after the first coalition air strikes on Baghdad and in one case as far as 276

miles inside western Iraq. With as many as four SOF teams conducting such operations at a time, not one more Scud missile was launched against Israel. Special operations precluded Saddam Hussein from further use of his most effective terror weapon.

Helicopters from the Army's 160th Special Operations Aviation Regiment–the "Nightstalkers" out of Fort Campbell, Kentucky—braved not only blistering enemy fire, but thin air, freezing temperatures, unpredictable wind gusts, and near zero visibility at altitudes of 10,000 to 18,000 feet to insert, resupply, and extract Special Forces and Special Tactics teams throughout Afghanistan. They did it around the clock. One pilot said later, "The Taliban was our greatest threat, but the weather was our greatest challenge. Our motto is 'on target, plus or minus thirty seconds,' and we live by that motto even in the harshest weather and the harshest terrain."

Air Force MC-130 Combat Talon IIs and AC-130 gunships flew twenty-four hours a day for the first 100 days of Operation Enduring Freedom. The 352nd Special Operations Group out of Royal Air Force Mildenhall in the United Kingdom flew fourteen hours a day, logged 1,723 combat hours, and launched 130 combat sorties in that period. Its aircrews delivered 1.4-million pounds of war materiel to forces directly engaged with the enemy, often airdropping bundles of food and supplies on postage-stamp-size drop zones in inhospitable terrain.

EC-130E Commando Solo crews from the 193rd Special Operations Wing of the Pennsylvania National Guard soon began around-the-clock AM, FM, and short-wave radio broadcasts over Afghanistan with messages in Dari, Pashtun, and Arabic prepared by the Army's 4th Psychological Operations Group out of Fort Bragg, North Carolina. The aircraft also serves as an airborne TV station.

MH-47E "Nightstalker" helicopters negotiated foul weather in mountainous terrain throughout Operation Enduring Freedom. This photo was taken through the night vision or forward looking infrared equipment on all of the aircraft flown by the Army's 160th Special Operations Aviation Regiment. (U.S. Special Operations Command)

The wreckage of an MH-47E sits on the crest of a 10,000-foot mountain peak after being hit by intense small arms fire and a barrage of rocket propelled grenades from Al-Qaeda fighters. (U.S. Special Operations Command)

SOCEUR

Left: *Schematic map depciting the area of operation of Special Operations Command Europe (SOCEUR). This extensive theater covers some of the most stragically important regions on earth. (Map by StyloGraphix)*

A U.S. Army Special Forces officer conducts a tactical overview during staff training for officers of the Georgian military as part of Operation Silent Lance. (U.S. Special Operations Command)

Special Operations Command— Europe (SOCEUR)

U.S. European Command has the second largest area of operations in the unified combatant command structure—three continents and eighty-nine counties covering 13 million square miles with a total population of more than a billion people.

Key SOCEUR engagements include Joint/Combined Exchange Training (JCET) events, a combination of training and real world engagements that allows SOF to perform mission-essential tasks and regionally focussed training while simultaneously establishing U.S. presence and influence in priority countries, thus fulfilling their role as "global scouts"; the Joint Contact Team Program, to provide greater interaction with former Warsaw Pact countries and Soviet client states; the African Crisis Response Initiative to help select African countries to respond to regional crises with capable, professional, indigenous forces; and, finally, extensive humanitarian demining work. Within two years of the launching of the ACRI initiative, Special Forces teams from the 3rd Special Forces Group (Airborne) deployed from Fort Bragg, North Carolina, with elements of a civil affairs battalion, and

a psychological operations group had trained indigenous troops from Senegal, Malawi, Ghana, Benin, and the Ivory Coast.

The JCET program has helped new NATO countries from Central Europe develop more professional and better-trained noncommissioned officers, characteristics not often found in Soviet-modeled forces, and it has encouraged former Warsaw Pact countries to rely on special operations forces as a relatively inexpensive option for countries looking to make a viable but affordable contribution to NATO's force structure.

In the 1998–1999 Balkan conflicts, Central European SOF forces trained by the U.S. worked jointly with SOCEUR teams to rescue two American pilots downed by enemy fire over Serbia during Operation Allied Force.

SOCEUR's SOF teams are heavily engaged in Russia's New Independent States (NIS) as well, teaching their armed forces the role of the military in a democracy and assessing regional capabilities in an area where some countries are still under authoritarian rule, split by ethnic divisions, and

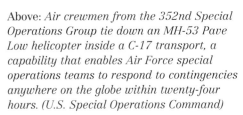

Above: *Air crewmen from the 352nd Special Operations Group tie down an MH-53 Pave Low helicopter inside a C-17 transport, a capability that enables Air Force special operations teams to respond to contingencies anywhere on the globe within twenty-four hours. (U.S. Special Operations Command)*

Above, right: *The wreckage of Commerce Secretary Ron Brown's aircraft entailed an arduous, four-day recovery effort in 1997 amidst foul weather in the rugged mountains of Croatia. No sooner had SOCEUR's recovery team returned to their home bases than they were dispatched to Liberia for an emergency noncombatant evacuation of U.S. embassy personnel and thousands of third-country civilians. (U.S. Special Operations Command)*

Evacuees from Liberia prepare to board a C-130 transport in Dakar, Senegal, for travel to safe haven after a special operations emergency noncombatant evacuation triggered by civil war. (U.S. Special Operations Command)

plagued by instability and uncertainty. In 1998, SOCEUR hosted the first NIS SOF conference in Stuttgart, Germany, with military personnel from Moldavia, Georgia, and the Ukraine attending. Demonstrations by various SOF units impressed them with U.S. SOF capabilities and prompted new opportunities for additional Joint/Combined Exchange Training. Operationally, SOCEUR's most notable events involved the recovery of bodies from the 1997 crash of Secretary of Commerce Ron Brown's plane in Croatia. Following that, the evacuation of embassy personnel and thousands of allied civilians from Monrovia, Liberia, 3,600 miles away; and the 1999 rescue of two American pilots downed over Serbia.

After Brown's T-43 hit a rugged mountainside in foul weather near Dubrovnik, killing everyone aboard, a SOCEUR team from the Air Force's 352nd Special Operations Group in England found the crash site and used two MH-53Js and an MC-130P refueling plane to begin recovering the victims in a remote area during gruesome weather conditions—cold, wind, rain, and snow. In time, crews from the 16th Special Operations Wing at Hurlburt Field, Florida, and from the 20th Special Operations Squadron had to be called in to assist in the four-day operation.

No sooner had SOCEUR finished its exhaustive work with Albanians finishing the recovery operation than the unit was dispatched to Monrovia, Liberia—within hours of when its personnel had redeployed from Dubrovnik to Stuttgart, Germany. Their new mission was a crisis response to help secure the American embassy, which had come under siege by wild mobs of armed militia forces, and then to evacuate its personnel plus 2,100 U.S. and foreign citizens from the city in MH-53Js and an MH-47E conducting dozens of flights. Although this was labeled a "Noncombatant Evacuation Operation," SOCEUR's teams often had to perform their missions under hostile fire and required precise overhead fire support from AC-130H Spectre side-firing gunships, which often had to guide friendly aircraft through small arms and rocket-propelled grenade fire. Both missions were personally led by then Brigadier General Michael A. Canavan, Commanding General of Special Operations Command

A soldier from the 3rd Special Forces Group (Airborne) out of Fort Benning, Georgia, trains two Rwandan People's Army men on proper placement of explosive charges. (U.S. Special Operations Command)

Europe. He next served (as a major general) as commander of Joint Special Operations Command, then (as a three-star general) as Chief of Staff of U.S. European Command in Germany, and later as Deputy Commander of U.S. Special Operations Command in Tampa.

The previous year, SOCEUR's special operations forces had been instrumental in the evacuation of noncombatants from Albania, Liberia, Central African Republic, the Congo, the Democratic Republic of Congo (formerly Zaire), and Sierra Leone.

Georgian President Eduard Shevardnadze shakes hands with Lieutenant Colonel Robert Waltemeyer, head of a U.S. military training team, in Tbilisi on 2 May 2002, as acting Ambassador to Georgia Philipp Rambler looks on. SOF trainers were sent to Georgia as part of Operation Enduring Freedom to help its military counter indigenous terrorist activities. (U.S. Special Operations Command)

267

SOCSOUTH

028°N

058°W

008°N

092°W

030°W

Special Operations Command— Southern Command (SOCSOUTH)

U.S. Southern Command covers the land mass and surrounding waters of Latin America south of Mexico, the Caribbean Sea, and the Gulf of Mexico. That area contains thirty-two independent countries and fifteen dependencies, including British, French, Dutch, and U.S. territories, and covers one-sixth of the globe's land area, 12.5 million square miles. Over 400 million inhabitants speak eight primary lanugages—English, Spanish, Dutch, Portuguese, French, Creole, Quechua, and Aymara. Extreme differences in geography, topography, prosperity, stability, and ethnicity characterize the theater.

Latin America has the most uneven distribution of income and wealth of any region in the world, and the poorest 40 percent of the population receives only 10 percent of the income. Widespread poverty, rapid population growth, proliferating transnational threats, environmental degradation, illegal immigration, ubiquitous land mines, and extra-legal paramilitary forces challenge stability throughout the region. Porous borders and the expanding influence of insurgent groups complicate the security equation, and counterdrug support has become a key SOCSOUTH mission.

SOCSOUTH manages over two hundred deployments annually, averaging forty-two missions in sixteen countries at any given time. SOUTHCOM is commonly called upon to respond to handle emergencies that require immediate military assistance, and SOCSOUTH usually leads those missions. When Hurricane George struck the Dominican Republic, for instance, SOF helicopters and soldiers were the first U.S. forces in the country. When Hurricane Mitch devastated Honduras, SOCSOUTH rescued over nine hundred people on the day of their arrival.

Special Operations Command— Joint Forces Command (SOCJFCOM)

Formerly known as U.S. Atlantic Command, Joint Forces Command— headquartered in Norfolk, Virginia—depicts the evolution of a geographic command with some functional roles to a functional unified command, charged largely with exercises to test and develop doctrinal development for joint operations and "transformation" of the U.S. military establishment for the twenty-first-century operations. It has no geographic responsibilities. Its principle focus is to train, integrate, and provide combat-ready conventional U.S. forces based in the continental United States to support the regional war-fighting commanders and to meet domestic requirements.

SOCJFCOM's mission is not only to conduct missions directed by the Commander, Joint Forces Command, but to integrate SOF operations with conventional U.S. and allied forces by joint, multilateral, and interagency training programs. It also assists U.S. SOCOM's training responsibilities through its joint Special Operations Psychological Operations Task Force and a joint Civil-Military Operations task force training center. SOCJFCOM is also tasked to conduct special operations that may be undertaken by

Above: *An American Special Forces soldier patrols the U.S. southwest border on horseback, assisting the U.S. Border Patrol and Customs Service to interdict the flow of narcotics and illegal immigration. (U.S. Special Operations Command)*

Page 270–271: *Air Force Combat controllers from the 22nd Special Tactics Squadron, McChord Air Force Base, Washington, on board an Air National Guard C-130 Hercules aircraft are being briefed ten minutes prior to actual jump time during Exercise Northern Edge 2001 in Alaska. (U.S. Air Force)*

Page 271: *Schematic map depicting the area of operations of Special Operations Northern Command (NORCOM). This new command is a direct response to the tragedies of September 11 and is responsible for the continental U.S. and Alaska, Canada, Mexico, Puerto Rico, U.S. Virgin islands, and includes a 500 mile buffer zone on all sea approaches. (Map by StyloGraphix)*

the new U.S. Northern Command in areas of operations once covered by the U.S. Atlantic Command. It is also tasked to be able to deploy a humanitarian assistance survey team within twenty-four hours.

There is considerable overlap between the responsibilities of the U.S. Joint Special Operations Command and SOCJFCOM, since both are charged to "ensure interoperability and plan and conduct joint special operations exercises and training and to develop joint special operations tactics," according to U.S. Special Operations Command. As JFFCOM undertakes more of those roles, presumably it will free the Joint Special Operations Command to focus on training for, planning, and executing high-risk vital missions by SOF special mission units such as Delta Force and SEAL Team Six that may be directed by the National Command Authorities.

Northern Command (NORTHCOM)

The special operations responsibilities and structure have yet to be delineated for the new United States Northern Command, formed in October of 2003 to provide for America's homeland defense. Unlike the other unified commands, however, there is no theater special operations command at Northern Command. Its headquarters in Colorado Springs, Colorado, has only a small special operations coordinating element. NORTHCOM's area of operations encompasses the continental United States, Alaska, Canada, Mexico, Puerto Rice, and the U.S. Virgin Islands and their air, land, and sea approaches out to five hundred miles. The defense of Hawaii and U.S. territories in the Pacific remains the responsibility of U.S. Pacific Command.

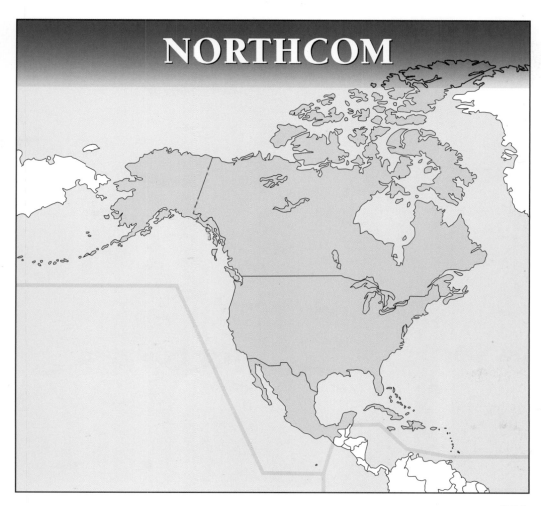

Special Tools
for Special
Operations

Special Tools for Special Operations

Colonel John T. Carney, Jr., USAF (Ret)

Left: *Combat operations require the Gentex helmet, bulletproof vests, camouflaged battle dress uniforms, and sturdy web harnesses carrying a myriad of ammunition, rations, and first aid equipment. (Fred J. Pushies)*

Above: *Air Force Special Tactics team members in Afghanistan (third and fourth from the left) use their foldable SATCOM communications antenna (bottom center) and a handset for secure communications with virtually limitless range. (U.S. Special Operations Command)*

Pages 272–273: *The Colt M-4 is a smaller, more compact version of the 5.56mm M-16A2 rifle used by conventional forces and incorporates a retractable buttstock with intermediate stops to add versatility in close quarters without compromising shooting capabilities. It has a muzzle velocity of about 3,000 feet per second and features selective fire controls for semi-automatic and full automatic fire, eliminating the three-round burst of the M-16. It has a redesigned barrel that can be fitted with the 3-pound M-203 40-mm grenade launcher shown here, which can also be operated as an independent weapon. SOCOM has begun fielding accessory kits that will tailor the M-4 carbine with a four-power day telescope, infrared and laser aiming devices, an improved night scope and visible light illuminator, signature suppressor, and a forward hand grip. (Fred J. Pushies)*

Opposite: *Members of SEAL Team Five pose with some of the equipment used for sea, air, and land operations around the world. This illustrates the range and diversity of special operations missions. (Robert Bruce Military Photos)*

T hroughout history, technological advancements have altered the course of warfare. From the cumbersome and heavy plated armor worn by knights of old to the lightweight, if uncomfortable, biological and chemical protective clothing worn by American forces today, and throughout the transition from longbows and crossbows to gunpowder and rifled weaponry, new technologies have provided critical advantages for the opponent that fielded them first. Just as it is the tip of America's spear, the special operations community has long taken pride in exploiting cutting edge technologies to give its quiet professionals decisive advantages over their adversaries. Yet no matter what leverage technology brings to the conflict, it will always be the training, skills, and resourcefulness of soldiers, seamen, and airmen standing behind new widgets that carry the day in harm's way.

Emphasizing that very point, Defense Secretary Donald Rumsfeld noted in his 2002 annual report to Congress: "In Afghanistan, precision-guided bombs dropped from the sky did not achieve operational

Special Tactics Equipment

Pictured are various equipment items used by Air Force Special Tactics members— their tools of the trade:

1. Twin 80s scuba tanks
2. Kawasaki, 250cc motorcycle
3. Rucksack
4. Kevlar helmet
5. SATCOM radio
6. KY-57 tactical radio
7. Assault vest
8. Laser range finder
9. Load bearing equipment/ running gear
10. Rucksack rigged for free fall parachute jump
11. PRC-112 multiban tactical radio
12. PRC-26
13. Gentex Jump helmet with oxygen mask attached
14. Altimeter for parachute operations
15. Bailout oxygen system for high altitude/low altitude freefall operations
16. Automatic opening device for freefall parachute operations
17. Compass board for tactical scuba and halo parachute operations
18. MT-1X Freefall parachute
19. Kawasaki 350cc motorcycle
20. Ak-47 assault rifle
21. M-4 rifle with night-vision scope attached
22. KNS-81 portable TACAN tactical air navigational system
23. Static line parachute system
24. MP-5 submachine gun
25. 45 Colt pistol

(Index courtesy of Chief Master Sergeant Wayne A. Norrad, USAF (Ret))

26. M-9 Beretta
27. Model 870 Remington shotgun
28. GAU-5 Sub-machine gun with 100-round magazine
29. Light Anti-armor Weapon (LAW)
30. Desert night jacket
31. PVS-7 Night vision goggles
32. Infrared Whalen assault zone lights
33. Overt assault zone markers
34. Runway beacons
35. Strobe lights
36. VS-17 Panels for Assault Zone Identification
37. Global Positioning System (GPS)
38. Fire Fly Lights for expedient assault zone marking
39. SATCOM Antenna
40. HST-4 Tactical Radio for satellite communication
41. PRC-104 High-Frequency (HF) Tactical Radio
42. SKY-515 Very-High-Frequency (VHF) Tactical Radio
43. Swim Fins
44. SPUD System
45. Camouflage Dry Dive Suit
46. Life Vest/Buoyancy Compensator
47. Kawasaki 4-Wheel All-Terrain Vehicle
48. TRN-41 Air Droppable Tactical Air Navigational System
49. Marine 40HP Outboard Motor System
50. Dive Mask & Snorkel
51. Rubber Dive Cloves
52. Dive tool with Mark-13 flare attached
53. Wet Suit
54. Deflated Rubber Raiding Craft with 40 HP outboard motor
55. Dive Knife
56. Snow Shoes

(Photo courtesy of Air Force Recruiting Service)

Above and opposite, top left: *Heckler and Koch Mark 23 Model 0 SOCOM .45-caliber pistol with sound suppressor and laser aiming module (LAM) with a white light, infrared, and laser sight. SOF troops never adopted the 9mm handgun issued to conventional forces and had originally preferred the old .45-caliber Colt M-1911 automatic because its low muzzle velocity let shooters actually see their bullet travel to the target. The Mk 23, which is far more accurate, was specifically designed for SOF in the early 1990s and is known as the Special Operations Forces Offensive Handgun. It features 40 percent less recoil than the old M-1911. It incorporates a threaded barrel for an integral sound and flash suppressor and has a grooved frame to accept the laser aiming module. Like the weapon itself, the latter two components were also designed by the United States Special Operations Command. The laser aiming module offers four modes of operation—visible laser only, visible laser/flashlight, infrared laser only, and infrared laser/illuminator. The weapon weighs 4.22 pounds loaded with a twelve-round magazine and one round in the chamber. (Fred J. Pushies)*

effectiveness until the United States placed old-fashioned boots on the ground." Given the proficiency, adaptability, innovativeness, self-reliance, and courage of the SOF warrior, mission success does depend equally on rugged, state-of-the-art equipment. The United States Special Operations Command emphasizes that synergy by framing its acquisition objective as "equipping the man, not manning the equipment"—the marriage of technology and the human dimension determines the survivability, lethality, and mobility of the SOF warrior.

Congress gave the U.S. Special Operations Command unprecedented acquisition authority to create and manage its own budget soon after it was activated, rather than having to depend on the military services for funds, personnel billets, and equipment. By "fencing" SOF money and extending to the command leeway over its structure and equippage, Congress assured that SOF's most innovative equipment would no longer be diverted to conventional U.S. forces, as it had been since the end of the Vietnam War. In 1992, Congress mandated that U.S. Special Operations Command establish its own Senior Acquisition Executive, with unique authority for developing and acquiring SOF-peculiar weapons and equipment.

Within one year, SOCOM's Special Operations Research Development and Acquisition Center (SORDAC) launched its first major acquisition

program, the high-speed (50 plus knots), 600-nautical mile range, 82-foot long, 57-ton Mark V Special Operations Craft. The first two boats were delivered only eighteen months later and won SOCOM the Defense Department's coveted David Packard Award for acquisition excellence.

As Operations Desert Shield and Desert Storm unfolded in 1991 and 1992, SOCOM exercised it special authority over SOF-peculiar equipment

Above: *The Heckler and Koch MP-5 9mm submachine gun is a high rate of fire weapon (800 rounds per minute) weighing 9.1 pounds loaded with dual thirty-round magazines. With the stock retracted, it is only 19.3 inches long. (Fred J. Pushies)*

Above, left: *MP-5-SD3: This is the same type of submachine gun as the MP-5, but with a shorter barrel and an integral sound suppressor for close-quarter battle when stealth and secrecy are paramount. It has a muzzle velocity of 1,312 feet per second and weighs 10.2 pounds. With the stock retracted, it is only twenty-four-inches long. (Fred J. Pushies)*

Left: *The Rescue All-Terrain Transporter (RATT) moves through the brush to search for wounded. It carries four litters. (Fred J. Pushies)*

Page 280, top: *An Air Force Special Tactics team member moves out on an airfield clearing mission on an M-4 motorcycle fitted with an M-203 grenade launcher. (Fred J. Pushies)*

Page 280, bottom and page 281: *The "Desert Patrol Vehicle," widely used by Navy SEALs during Operation Desert Storm in 1992 but since phased out of service, has a crew of three—driver, commander, and gunner—and can mount six different weapon systems. Most commonly, it mounts a 40mm grenade launcher and a .50-caliber machine gun facing forward and a 7.62mm machine gun covering the rear. (Hans Halberstadt)*

279

to respond to urgent new hardware needs of U.S. Central Command, validated twenty-three of its twenty-four special requirements, procured nineteen of the items, and placed them in the hands of SOF troops—with the needed equipment training—within thirty days.

Today, much of SOF equipment has become standard to their respective service counterparts; unfortunately, the equipment developed by the Army, Navy, and Air Force often fails to meet SOCOM's performance thresholds, and SORDAC is literally forced onto the leading edge of new technologies. Like all commands, of course, U.S. Special Operations Command is constrained by the finite resources made available to it. Thus, it has consciously decided to forego many product improvements of existing weapon systems in order to field leapfrog technologies that will give

SOF a distinctive edge over adversaries and operational advantages that distinguish them from America's conventional forces. The goal is equipment that is robust enough to withstand rough use but lightweight enough to let special operators move with agility and speed—differences that become life or death matters.

Right: *The simplicity, wide target area, and close-range stopping power of the shotgun still makes it the weapon of choice for special operators in many situations, especially close-quarters combat. (Hans Halberstadt)*

Right and bottom: *The superbly accurate Stoner SR-25 7.62mm semiautomatic sniper rifle, fitted here with the Tasco tactical scope, was designed by Eugene Stoner, the father of the AR-15 and standard-issue M-16. Made by Knight Manufacturing Company in Florida, 60 percent of its parts are common to the M-16 family, but it uses the barrel of the standard Army Remington M-24 bolt action sniper rifle. With a muzzle velocity of 2,766 feet per second, the 24-inch barrel is free floating so there is no interference with the barrel vibration, and the handguard is a special cantilevered design off the receiver so that any pressure on it will not affect the barrel. The 43-1/2-inch weapon can be fitted with a sound suppressor so that muzzle blast becomes negligible and the only sound will be the sonic crack of a round on its way to the target. The weapon can be broken down and transported in a smaller package for clandestine activities. (Fred J. Pushies)*

Opposite, top: *HMMWV's ("Humvees"—High Mobility Multipurpose Wheeled Vehicles) provide longer-range cross-country transport. (Fred J. Pushies)*

Opposite, bottom: *The four-wheel-drive Quad all-terrain vehicle with a left-hand infrared headlight and rifle racks. (Fred J. Pushies)*

282

Above: *Light 7.62mm machine gun. (Fred J. Pushies)*

Right: *The Heavy Sniper Rifle (HSR) is a .50-caliber anti-materiel weapon that weighs less than 27.5 lbs, is effective out to 1,500 meters and fires a variety of special ammunition. (Barrett Firearms)*

Opposite, top: *The SOF laser acquisition marker (SOFLAM) was widely used in Afghanistan to locate, range, and designate critical enemy targets using laser-guided precision munitions. (Fred J. Pushies)*

Opposite, bottom right: *The helmet-mounted ITT Enhanced Night-Vision Goggle is an improved third-generation system weighing less than two pounds. It combines a "thin-filmed" image-intensifier tube, roughly ten thousand times thinner than a human hair and yielding a green image, with an infrared thermal imaging sensor yielding a yellow image that registers body heat and virtually eliminates the "bloom" effect of previous night vision systems, which temporarily blinded operators wearing night vision goggles who suddenly saw bright flashes. The new technology eliminates fuzzy green blurs; can see through smoke, dust, haze, and adverse weather and at greater ranges than previous devices; operates under starlight conditions on moonless nights; and even provides some capability in overcast starlight conditions. It can distinguish a person from the tree he may be trying to hide behind. First fielded in 2001, the goggle sells for only about $2,500. A competing unfilmed tube developed by Northrop Grumman is being delivered to SOF under an August 2000 Navy contract and is used as the PVS-17 Mini Night Vision Sight on the M-4A1 carbine. (U.S. Special Operations Command)*

Future Equipment

The future promises to transform the application of force during special operations far more than the invention of the musket, the machine gun, and the radio affected land combat. Technological advances will transform the U.S. Special Operations Forces into a lethal, effective, and efficient force that will operate in new ways while serving at the tip of the spear well into the next century. New weaponry may include mini-, macro-, or even nano-weapons and platforms firing beams of tightly focused energy waves that could destroy anything from the brains of a computer to the electronics of aircraft and missiles. Since the human body is an electro-chemical system, such weapons could stun or kill enemy troops, attacking the electrical impulses of their nervous systems.

A whole new class of biological weapons and counter measures is also on the horizon, with robots ready to sniff out chemical, biological, or nuclear weapons in spaces too small or too dangerous for a human. In future conflicts, special operators will have instant access to live, three-dimensional images of the objective target displayed on their hand-held computers. The image will be generated by a network of sensors from

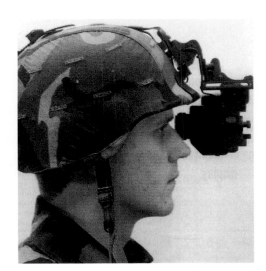

Left: *Robots being used by SOF are gaining increased tactical roles as they become more sophisticated. They can enter spaces too small or dangerous for personnel, such as bunkers and buildings that have been booby-trapped. They can also carry monitors to sniff out chemical, biological, and nuclear weapons. (U.S. Special Operations Command)*

Top, left: *The JBS TSC-135 V2 Aircraft Communications Package (ACP) is mounted on a single cargo pallet to provide en-route airborne satellite and line-of-sight radio, LAN, and intercom capability for eight work stations and two operator stations. (U.S. Special Operations Command)*

Top, right: *The Leaflet Delivery System (LDS) incorporates an autonomously guided powered ram-air parafoil that can deliver leaflets, radios, and supplies with pinpoint accuracy to targets in denied areas up to 750 kilometers away with a combined fuel and cargo payload of 1,000 pounds. A future variant uses a precision-guided canister bomb. (U.S. Special Operations Command)*

Above: *The Special Operations Media System B (SOMS B) mobile radio broadcast system (MRBS) in use here in Kandahar, Afghanistan, in March of 2002 and operated by the 4th Psychological Operations Group from Fort Bragg, North Carolina. The system can produce, broadcast, and record AM, FM, and SW messages twenty-four hours a day. (U.S. Navy)*

Center and left: *FOL—Aircraft is a family of loudspeakers with three variants. One can be mounted on the turret of an Humvee, or on Naval Special Warfare craft. A second variant, the FLO-AC, shown here mounted on a UH-60 helicopter, is a high-quality loudspeaker system used to broadcast recorded or live messages as well as to conduct acoustic deception or to perform harassment missions, such as the mind-numbing loud music that SOF forces played night and day to drive Panamanian dictator Manuel Noriega bonkers while he was holed up in the Papal Nuciatura in Panama City deciding which uniform to wear to his surrender. A third variant of this system is man portable. (U.S. Special Operations Command)*

Opposite: *High-altitude, low-opening parachute insertions require helmets and visors with oxygen masks, warm battle dress uniforms and gloves with the trigger finger free, and rugged web harnesses to carry equipment and rucksacks sometimes weighing up to 100 pounds. (Fred J. Pushies)*

287

Above: *The AN/PRC 126 short-range (3 to 5 kilometers) handheld VHF tactical radio transceiver, widely used for intrateam communications, can be carried in the pocket of a battle dress uniform. (Fred J. Pushies)*

Above: *40mm grenade launcher. (Fred J. Pushies)*

satellites, unmanned aerial and ground vehicles, and special operations personnel on the ground equipped with "do-everything" mobile sensors or robots. The SOF operator will be capable of engaging the enemy with volumetric explosives and shoulder-fired devices that use ultra- and infra-sonic waves that affect both living and inert materials. So-called mobility kills and soft kills may be achieved by super-slippery materials to fell a potential enemy on stairs or mountain trails and by odors so repulsive that just a whiff would render a person violently but temporarily ill.

Mobility may hinge on a new four-man hovercraft now being proto-typed by what SOCOM calls its "future concepts working group" that looks twenty-five years into the future. It will allow troops to skim over obsta-cles and have a higher platform during gun battles and would rely on wheels for landing but have a ducted fan beneath its body for propulsion.

Today's Weaponry

Special Operations Forces members rely on an array of high-tech, low-tech, and no-tech systems for an edge on the battlefield. The illustrations in this chapter depict many specialized weapons and pieces of equipment used by special operators—for instance the photo of SEAL Team Five on page 274 as well as the sidebar on pages 276–277 detailing the everyday equipment that Air Force Special Tactics team members use in order to lead other special operations units into and out of harm's way in denied territory. Also shown are the individual weapons used by SOF operators worldwide, who are generally permitted to use the weapons of their individual choice if that is the equipment that optimizes their proficiency.

Above: *The AN/PRC-138/150 is a fully integrated compact communications system with advanced HF-SSB/VHF-FM manpack radios for reliable, long range, and secure tactical communications. (U.S. Special Operations Command)*

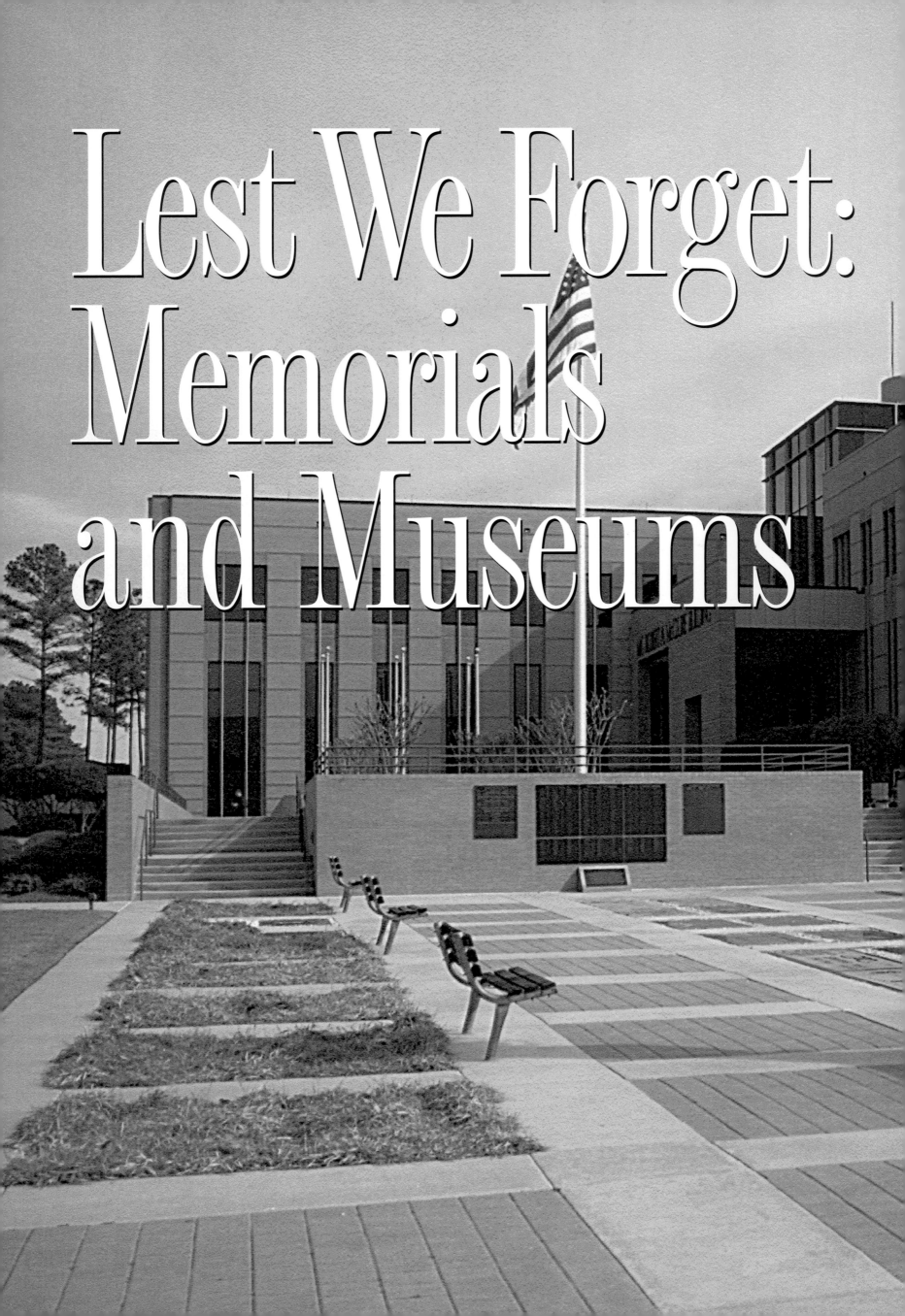

Lest We Forget: Memorials and Museums

Lest We Forget: Memorials and Museums

Roxanne Merritt

"The city is a center where, any day in any year, there may be a fresh encounter with a new talent, a keen mind or a gifted specialist—this is essential to the life of a country. To play this role in our lives a city must have a soul—a university, a great art or music school, a cathedral or a great mosque or temple, a great laboratory or scientific center, as well as the libraries and museums and galleries that bring past and present together.

—MARGARET MEAD,
U.S. ANTHROPOLOGIST, AUGUST 1978

The term "a city" is nonexclusive to an urban area. It can also be attributed to a military post or base. These "cities" are no less worthy to display their history, to honor their heroes, to pay tribute to their fallen comrades, or to proudly celebrate or mourn their recent past than a more traditional urban environment. Many of these bases or forts have a larger population than the towns they are near. Whereas many would view such monuments or museums as tributes to

Above: *OSS Detachment 101 was the first unit memorialized with a tablet in the U.S. Army Special Operations Command memorial plaza, which was laid in 1990. Behind it is the First Special Service Force tablet with the inlaid patch similar to those they mounted throughout Italy and Southern France. (JFK Special Warfare Museum)*

Pages 290–291: *The Special Warfare Memorial Statue (in the foreground) stands sentinel over the U.S. Army Special Operations Command memorial plaza at Fort Bragg, North Carolina. (United States Army Special Operations Command)*

Opposite: *Colonel Arthur D. "Bull" Simons statue dedication on 19 November 2000. Simons served with the 6th Ranger Battalion in World War II. After receiving his degree from the University of Missouri, he returned to active duty serving in various positions with Special Operations including the Ranger Training Brigade, the Military Assistance-Vietnam Studies and Observations Group, and as commander of 8th Special Forces Group (Airborne). Mr. Ross Perot donated this statue in tribute to Simons's rescue of eight of Perot's men held hostage in Iran in 1979. Shown in front of the statue, left to right: CSM Ron McCann, LTG Bryan D. Brown, MG Kenneth Bowra, Alan Brunstrom (Son Tay prisoner of war), H. Ross Perot, GEN Hugh Shelton, unidentified, and Larry Ludtke, sculptor. (JFK Special Warfare Museum)*

war or warlike ways, the community of a post or base maintains them as shrines to those who have fought to keep the peace. To some they serve as sanctuaries where memories can be revisited with pride and honor. To others they represent extensions of a schoolhouse where tenets and lessons can be graphically reinforced. And finally, to many they serve as a reminder that heroes are normal people who answered the call by doing extraordinary things when required. For those in Special Operations, memorials and museums take on an important, added dimension. They are its public face. Since most operations occur in the shadows, without cameras or fanfares, the soldiers as well as their family members may only see their lives remembered in a museum setting or memorial ceremony.

Memorials

Memorials allow reflection of those who have paid the ultimate price or, because of their lives, retain a presence that is greater than can be contained in the heart. They offer immortality to units and people who may otherwise easily be swept under the carpet of history, giving a name to a number, a value to a statistic. The Department of Defense regulations concerning memorialization offer little latitude toward those living. You won't see a street or parkway named in honor of someone who is still alive; military posts and bases reserve this right for those that have passed.

The memorials in this book spotlight those dedicated to, for, and by the Special Operations community in tribute to fallen comrades. Some are individual statues, while others encompass all those who have offered their lives in exchange for the dignity of those they left behind. One of the strongest underlying tenets of SOF can be found in this short passage found on the 160th Special Operations Aviation Regiment (SOAR) Association web page (http://www.nightstalkers.com). The attribute is unknown.

The U.S. Air Force's 801st/492d Bomb Group ("The Carpetbaggers") dropped agents and supplies behind enemy lines in World War II Europe. Before agents were inserted into their mission areas, their gear was thoroughly checked by both members of the Harrington OSS and Carpetbagger ground crew to ensure they were rigged properly. Also, all pockets were checked to remove any materials that may compromise their identities. The Carpetbagger Museum is discussed on page 311. (Stroud collection/ JFK Special Warfare Museum)

Montage of the Special Warfare Memorial Statue sculpted by Don DeLue and dedicated in 1969. (United States Army Special Operations Command)

294

"When a soldier was injured and could not get back to safety, his buddy went out to get him against his officer's orders. He returned mortally wounded, and his friend, whom he carried back, was dead. The officer was angry. 'I told you not to go,' he said. 'Now I lost both of you, it was not worth it.' The dying man replied, 'But it was, Sir, because when I got to him, he said "Jim, I knew you'd come".'"

United States Army Special Operations Command (USASOC) Plaza and Meadows Memorial Parade Field, Fort Bragg, North Carolina

The USASOC Major General Robert A. McClure headquarters building is relatively new, dedicated in December of 1994. The original tenants of the plaza—the U.S. Army Special Warfare soldier, eleven legacy unit tablets, and a memorial of those killed in action—were originally part of the JFK Special Warfare Plaza located two miles away, moved when the command moved to its new location.

The Special Warfare Soldier, fondly known as "Bronze Bruce," sculpted by Don DeLue and cast in Italy, was unveiled by Drew Dix, the first noncommissioned officer (NCO) Medal of Honor recipient, on 22 November 1969. The twelve-foot statue is one of the only statues, located on either civilian or military communities, dedicated to an NCO. The pose of the statue, often ridiculed for its stance and positioning of the arms,

Above: *The Special Warfare Memorial Statue, originally erected in 1969, now located at the U.S. Army Special Operations Command memorial plaza, Fort Bragg, North Carolina. (United States Army Special Operations Command)*

Left: *Mr. Ron Aman of the U.S. Army Special Operations Command Public Affairs Office tours Vice President Richard Cheney through the U.S. Army Special Operations Command Memorial Plaza on July 9, 2002. This stone they are discussing is one dedicated to the Ranger battalions from World War II. Behind it is the tablet dedicated by the Special Forces Association in 1982. (United States Army Special Operations Command)*

Top: *The Richard "Dick" Meadows Statue, sculpted by Larry Ludtke and dedicated in 1992. (United States Army Special Operations Command)*

Above: *Dick Meadows in Vietnam, 1969.*

was to evoke St. George slaying the dragon and the Archangel Michael delivering the final blow to Satan; an M-16 replaced the spear, and the hand was extended out in a gesture of assistance. It has been erroneously reported or believed that another statue of a woman and/or child was to be placed near the statue, but there is no evidence in any of the correspondence or conceptual drawings to validate the assumption. The snake under the rock upon which the right leg rests symbolizes hidden dangers that soldiers of Special Operations have to face during routine missions.

Twenty-two stone tablets are placed in front of the statue. The tradition, begun in 1992 by the Office of Strategic Services (OSS) Detachment 101 Association, provides legacy units a way to literally cement their bond with their present-day progeny. Some tablets were purchased through drives by individuals of former units, without the formal umbrella of an organization. Such was the case with tablets for the Mobile Strike Force (MIKE FORCE); 1st Special Forces Group; the Military Assistance Command—Vietnam—Studies and Observations Group (MACVSOG); Special Forces Panama; 10th Special Forces Group; and the United Nations Partisan Force—Korea.

A brass tabard with the names of those U.S. Army Special Operations soldiers who surrendered their lives is mounted on a wall at the head of the plaza. The original criterion, recognizing only those Special Operations killed in hostile action during the Vietnam War, has been expanded to include all Special Operations soldiers killed in operations since the inception of USASOC in 1994.

Away from the formal plaza stands the statue of Major Richard "Dick" Meadows. Donated by H. Ross Perot, the statue, unveiled in 1996, recognizes Dick Meadows's service to the U.S. Army Special Operations community. Sculpted by Larry Ludtke of Houston, Texas, the statue is depicted on patrol, advancing out of the tree line into the field also named in honor of Major Meadows.

The public is welcome to visit the plaza; however, access to the McClure headquarters building is restricted.

John F. Kennedy Special Warfare Plaza, Fort Bragg, North Carolina

The original home of the Special Warfare Soldier, the plaza was dedicated in 1969 as the first Vietnam War memorial in the United States. H. Ross Perot donated a monumental twelve-foot statue of Colonel Arthur D. "Bull" Simons leading a charge, also sculpted by Larry Ludtke in 1999, filling the void left by the move of the Special Warfare Statue to the USASOC headquarters building. The plaza is located adjacent to the JFK Special Warfare Museum, also memorialized for the legendary Colonel Simons.

The Special Operations Memorial, MacDill AFB, FL

The Special Operations Memorial, dedicated in 1998, is located near the main entrance of MacDill Air Force Base, Florida. The memorial, the first joint/all-service Special Operations memorial in the United

The Special Operations soldier stands at the ready at the United States Special Operations Memorial at MacDill, AFB, Florida. (The Special Operations Memorial Association)

States, pays tribute to all Special Operations personnel, military and civilian, men and women, regardless of the branch of service, who have made the supreme sacrifice in service to our nation, whether in combat or training. In total, over eight hundred names are listed. The memorial, conceived by Richard Leandri, consists of three walls and a statue known as the "Quiet Professional," sculpted by Steve Dickey of Brandon, Florida.

The Ranger Memorial, Fort Benning, Georgia

The Ranger Memorial began as nothing more than a desire to commemorate U.S. Army Rangers, past, present, and future and a napkin holding a sketch of an arrow, evoking the cry "Rangers Lead The Way." Located outside the U.S. Army Infantry School (Building 4) in Fort Benning, Georgia, the dream for the memorial was realized in 1994. A walkway, paved with 2,456 polished pavers purchased for or in memory of individual Rangers, leads up to the twelve-foot Fairbairn-Sykes knife, four winged twelve-foot tablets, and eight black granite Era monuments.

Each year, the Ranger Training Brigade inducts former Rangers into its Hall of Fame. Eligibility for the Hall of Fame is limited to those persons who are deceased or have been separated, or retired from active military service for at least three years at the time of nomination. Nominees must have served in a Ranger unit in combat or be a successful

Seven Era monuments form the point of the Ranger Memorial at Fort Benning, Georgia. This memorial is dedicated to the Ranger Training Brigade, which is also responsible for maintaining the Ranger Hall of Fame. (75th Ranger Regiment)

graduate of the U.S. Army Ranger School. Selection is very judicious and considered the ultimate honor for a Ranger. (As of 2002 there were 170 inductees.) Not only are the new members' portraits and citations placed in the headquarters conference room and along the lobby wall of the Ranger Training Brigade Headquarters, their names are etched on the black wings flanking the Fairbairn-Sykes knife of the Ranger Memorial as well.

Visitors to the Ranger Memorial first walk under an oversize Ranger Tab and then enter the Ranger Memorial. (75th Ranger Regiment)

The 160th Special Operations Aviation Regiment (SOAR) "Nightstalkers" Memorial, Fort Campbell, Kentucky

Although the 160th Special Operation Aviation Regiment (Airborne), nicknamed "The Night Stalkers," was activated in 1986, the unit was first formed in 1981 as Task Force 160 from assets of the 101st Airborne Division and the Mississippi and Pennsylvania National Guards. Previously, modern U.S. Army Special Operations fighting units had to rely on outside sources for air support. Beginning with Operation Urgent Fury, the 160th has been instrumental in every operation, including, more recently, Operation Enduring Freedom.

In 1989, the Night Stalker Association erected an evocative tri-part ebony wall on which the names of those who have been killed while serving the Regiment since 1981 are etched. The Night Stalkers' logo with its ever present motto "Night Stalkers Don't Quit!" spotlights the middle

The Fairbairn-Sykes knife is the focal point of the Ranger Memorial standing tall at the point of the arrow "Rangers Lead The Way." (75th Ranger Regiment)

299

The tri-part black granite memorial to fallen 160th Special Operations Aviation "Night-stalkers" Regiment soldiers is a constant reminder to these highly trained aviators of the dangers that await them on their missions. "Night Stalkers Don't Quit!" (160th SOAR Association)

memorial tablet. When the unit moved to its new headquarters, the memorial was expanded with walkways and landscaping.

Hurlburt Memorial Park, Hurlburt Air Force Base, Florida

Hurlburt Field is the home of the U.S. Air Force Special Operations Command and the U.S. Air Force Special Operations University. Parked about its attractive Memorial Park, dedicated in 1991, are almost all aircraft flown in various special operations missions by air commandos

The aerial shot of the Hurlburt AFB air park spotlights the manicured setting for the display of the numerous aircraft utilized by Air Force Special Operations. (John Gargus)

as far back as World War II and as recently as in Somalia. Additionally, monuments have been erected in honor of the Air Commandoes who perished in the quest for freedom.

Enroque Versace Plaza, Alexandria, Virginia

On 6 July 2002, the privately funded memorial plaza at the Mount Vernon Recreation Center on Commonwealth Avenue was dedicated to Humbert Enroque "Roque" Versace. Roque was not only the last Vietnam soldier to be presented with the Medal of Honor (posthumously), he was also Vietnam's first American prisoner-of-war. Located in the Del Ray neighborhood where Versace grew up, the plaza also honors more than sixty other Alexandrians who were killed in Vietnam. The centerpiece of the plaza is a statue, sculpted by Antonio T. "Toby" Mendez, of Roque playing with two Vietnamese children, an activity he most

Above: *Captain Humberto Enroque Versace was captured on 29 October 1963, just days before he was to enter into the Maryknoll seminary. A West Point graduate, and Army "brat," Rocky was fluent in English, French and Vietnamese. When taken by his captors on tour, pulled by a rope around his neck, through local towns for their indoctrination sessions, he would use all three languages to openly rebut the enemy's propaganda and talk about how great America was. His open defiance only increased the ire of his captors. Versace, however, seemed to relish the fight for he knew if could direct his captors' anger on himself, they would ease up on his fellow prisoners. He lived by the credo "Duty, Honor, Country." He tried to escape four times, even though his leg injuries were severe, his head was swollen, and he was suffering from jaundice. CSM Danny Pitzer, one of Versace's fellow prisoners, said of Rocky, "He got a lot of pressure and torture, but he held his path. There was no other way." On 26 September 1965, after being held captive for just under two years, Rocky was executed. The last time his fellow prisoners heard from him, he was singing "God Bless America" at the top of his lungs. This photo shows Captain Versace during his first tour in Vietnam in 1962, with two local Vietnamese children. (Courtesy of the Versace family)*

Left: *Captain Enroque Humberto "Roque" Versace with two Vietnamese children. This statue is the focal point of one of the most recent memorials erected for Special Operations heroes. (U.S. Army Historical Association)*

enjoyed during his two tours as an advisor in the Republic of Vietnam prior to his capture and eventual execution by the Viet Cong.

First Special Service Force Memorial and Cenotaph, Helena, Montana

The origins of the First Special Service Force Memorial and Cenotaph epitomize this unique World War II unit. Although first organized for a suicide mission in Norway, the unit instead found itself on the way to the Aleutian Islands for its first mission against the Japanese. Upon hearing of the sinking of the U.S. cruiser *Helena* in the South Pacific, they decided right there and then that they would raise the money needed for a replacement. Taking a percentage of all the gambling pots and a portion of all profits made from the two Liberty Ships' stores, the Force members, upon their return from the Aleutians, sent the money to the Secretary of the Navy. Although he sent back the money noting that this was not only highly unusual, but also illegal, he assuaged their gesture by proposing the pot be used as seed money for a war bond–selling campaign in Montana. When the story of the Force's original intent was recounted during bond drives, the campaign exceeded all expectations.

After the war, when the veterans established their association, they voted to use the bonds to build a monument in memory of their fellow "Black Devils" killed during World War II. In 1947, at the first reunion, the memorial was dedicated on land donated by the City of Helena, located by what is now Carroll College. Features of the monument include two flags—U.S. and Canadian—flying at equal height, twenty-four hours a day, representing the full integration of the U.S. and Canadian members of the unit into one fighting unit, the Force. A cenotaph was added behind the original memorial in 1992. In 2002, the city passed a resolution dedicating the ground as hallowed and prohibiting any building within one thousand yards of the memorial area.

Museums

Museums offer a living memorial to the history and recent past of the Special Operations units. Marrying three-dimensional material with two-dimensional photographs, graphics, and text, museum displays offer "snapshots" of diverse activities, operations, and aspects of Special Operations not readily understood. They also offer something less tangible. They offer a prop to those who want to tell their story, but either do not know how to begin, or feel that it is too incredible a story for someone to believe. When visiting, one leaves the realm of Hollywood and enters the real world of this little-known military community. Often that history is less dramatic than that portrayed in the movies; however, as a whole, it is more fully modulated than can ever be depicted in print, on the screen, or in a newscast.

American Historical Foundation Marine Raider Museum, Richmond, Virginia

A joint venture of the U.S. Marine Raider Association and the American Historical Foundation, the museum is located on Monument Avenue in downtown Richmond. The Marine Raider Museum, opened in 1985, is housed in a famous Richmond landmark building known as "Columbia." The museum documents the exploits of the four Marine Raider battalions, about 4,000 men in all, who fought throughout World War II under the command of Colonel Evans F. Carlson in the Pacific Theater. Formed for hard-hitting, fast surprise assaults, the units were designed to strike from

USS George Clymer *moves in to unload U.S. Marine Raiders during Bougainville assault, 1 November 1943. One of the Raiders' lasting legacies is the term "Gung Ho," a term Colonel Carlson borrowed from the Chinese —meaning "to work together"—when he was studying guerilla warfare in the 1930s. (American Historical Foundation)*

Above and left: *The exhibits of the Marine Raider Museum focus on their exploits in World War II in the Pacific Theater, encompassing actions from Midway 4 June 1942 to the Bougainville Campaign in November 1943. (American Heritage Foundation)*

3d Raiders (M Company) man Browning light machinegun during enemy attack. Piva Trail, Bougainville, Solomon Islands. (American Historical Foundation)

submarines, destroyers, air or regular transports. Their most famous battle was the Makin Island Raid of 1942.

The museum collection evolved from the first Japanese flag captured in World War II as well as Japanese equipment taken from this raid. The memorabilia was married to Robert A. Buerlein's (the President of the American Historical Foundation) personal collection of over 500 knives, swords and bayonets and a large quantity of combat photography taken of the Marine Raiders in World War II, acquired by the American Historical Foundation in the early 1980s.

A duplicate museum to the Richmond site was placed on the West Coast in the Command Museum at the Recruit Depot, San Diego, and is known as the "Raider Room."

Central Intelligence Agency Display Area, McLean, Virginia

Although not open to the general public, this unique collection needs to be included in a chapter on Special Operations museums as it spotlights covert activities from the Revolutionary War until today. Of special interest to the Special Operations community are the personal effects of Major General William J. Donovan, the founder of the Office of Strategic Services (OSS), from which both the U.S. Army Special Forces and the Central Intelligence Agency (CIA) claim lineage.

John F. Kennedy Special Warfare Museum, Fort Bragg, North Carolina

Upon assuming command of the U.S. Army Special Warfare Center/ U.S. Army School for Special Warfare, Brigadier General William P. Yarborough pushed to establish a museum to preserve the history and reinforce the historical parallels of both the past and current U.S. Army Special Forces and Psychological Warfare units. The JFK Special Warfare Museum opened to the public in April 1963. Moved from its original location in 1978, the museum is located on Ardennes Street across from the U.S. Army John F. Kennedy Special Warfare Center and School.

Above: *Brigadier General Yarborough at Simmons airfield February 1961. (US Army)*

Right: *JFK Special Warfare Museum, Fort Bragg, North Carolina, supports the training of the U.S. Army John F. Kennedy Special Warfare Center and School, which is responsible for the training of all U.S. Army Special Forces, Civil Affairs, and Psychological Warfare training as well as being the proponent of the Special Forces branch. (JFK Special Warfare Museum)*

The museum illustrates the history of U.S. Army Special Operations units as well as serving as the branch museum for the U.S. Army Special Forces. Beginning primarily in World War II, the JFK Museum displays rare and one-of-a-kind items, such as the original Lambertsen Rebreather Unit (LARU) and the Little Joe crossbow, a rubber band–powered weapon of the OSS. Also available to the visitor are a gift shop and outdoor exhibits, including the Colonel Arthur D. "Bull" Simons statue located adjacent to the museum off of Marion Street. Across Ardennes Street, in the JFK Special Warfare Center, the museum maintains the Hall of Heroes, an area

Wayside exhibit, JFK Special Warfare Museum. The interactive exhibit, the first in the U.S. Army system that is solar powered and totally ADA accessible, utilizes the 82mm mortar pit to examine the construction of Special Forces A-camps. (JFK Special Warfare Museum)

Above: *First brochure of the JFK Special Warfare Museum published in 1968. The museum was located in a World War II wooden orderly building. When opened on 17 May 1963, Major General Yarborough said "It will constitute a living monument to those officers and men [and women] presently serving in the field of Special Warfare in the most remote areas where they are helping to preserve human dignity and to alleviate suffering and hardship among fellow human beings, while providing a measure of security to the Free World." (Photograph courtesy of JFK Special Warfare Museum)*

Left: *As part of the memorialization of Bryant Hall on 22 June 1973, Sergeant William M. Bryant's wife and Major General Michael Healey unveil the Medal of Honor recipient's portrait. William Maud Bryant was killed in action in 1969. A total of twenty-one Medals of Honor have been presented to Special Operations soldiers for their actions in Vietnam. (JFK Special Warfare Museum)*

Entering into the Mighty Eighth Museum, the visitor is struck by the Lewis E. Lyle Rotunda, named in honor of Major General Lewis E. Lyle, USAF (Ret). Although MG Lyle flew sixty-nine B-17 missions in World War II, a feat in itself, the rotunda bears his name in recognition of his vision, faith, and determination that brought the museum into existence. The rotunda features banners from the various individual bomber and fighter groups which have served under the Mighty Eighth during its sixty year existence. (Mighty Eighth Museum)

This airborne shot of the UDT/SEAL Museum gives an excellent overview of what awaits the visitor to this Fort Pierce, Florida, facility. The museum illustrates the history of the two units from World War II until the present. (UDT/SEAL Foundation)

dedicated to the Medal of Honor and Victoria Cross recipients from the U.S. Army Special Forces, U.S. Army Rangers, U.S. Army Special Operations Command, and the Australian Special Air Service (SAS).

Montana Military Museum, Fort William Henry Harrison, Montana

The Montana Military Museum evolved from a singular focus on the Montana National Guard to a wider scope including all units originating from Montana, or composed principally of Montanans, or which fought in the badlands now known as Montana. One of the larger exhibits is of the First Special Service Force, the joint American-Canadian commando unit that trained at Fort William Henry Harrison in 1942 prior to going to the Aleutian Islands, Italy, and Southern France.

The Mighty Eighth Air Force Heritage Museum, Savannah, Georgia

The Mighty Eighth Air Force Heritage Museum honors the courage, character, and patriotism embodied by the men and women of the Eighth Air Force from World War II to the present. During World War II, the Eighth Air Force "Carpetbagger" unit was the primary aviation asset used when the OSS inserted agents into Europe. They were also responsible for all propaganda leaflet drops during the war, which, according to General Eisenhower, helped save civilian lives and make the transition from war to peace easier. Integrated into the 90,000-square-foot facility are exhibit areas, gardens, a gift shop, and restaurant.

UDT/SEAL Museum, Fort Pierce, Florida

Dedicated in November 1984 and expanded in 1993, the UDT-SEAL Museum explores the interesting history of U.S. Naval Special Warfare. A statue of a Frogman greets the visitor at the entrance. The exhibits chronologically follow the history beginning with the earliest training of Naval Combat Demolition Units and Scouts and Raiders in Fort Pierce in 1943 to current exploits of the SEALs. An extensive manicured outside park displays the varied crafts used in the transport of these specialized units. Included are a Vietnam-era Seawolf helicopter and swimmer delivery vehicles, also known as SDVs. Also available to the visitor is a small theater offering action-packed videos of UDT/SEAL operations and training. A retail shop is also on the premises.

U.S. Army Airborne and Special Operations Museum, Fayetteville, North Carolina

The U.S. Army and Special Operations Museum, located in downtown Fayetteville, North Carolina, is operated via a unique partnership between the military community of Fort Bragg and the civilian community of Fayetteville. The visitor is immediately drawn into the history of airborne

Above: *Not only does the U.S. Army Airborne and Special Operations Museum display all airborne units, past and present, it also pays a salute to the 6,000 brave men of glider units. A portion of a C-4A glider, perfectly restored, is located in the World War II wing of the museum. American glider pilots, along with airborne forces, spearheaded all the major invasions, landing behind enemy lines in their unarmed gliders in Sicily, Normandy, Southern France, Holland, Bastogne, Rhine Crossing, Luzon in the Philippines, and Burma. (US Army Airborne and Special Operations Foundation)*

Left: *Two airborne soldiers—one from the past in a World War II canopy and one from the present in Military Free Fall gear—descend into the entrance of the U.S. Army Airborne and Special Operations Museum to welcome visitors to the downtown Fayetteville, North Carolina, facility. (US Army Airborne and Special Operations Foundation)*

307

The architectural feature of the entrance of the U.S. Army Airborne and Special Operations Museum evokes the lines of the aircraft used to transport airborne soldiers. (US Army Airborne and Special Operations Foundation)

Opposite, bottom: *The First Special Service Force memorial in Villeneuve-Loubet on the Avenue de la Liberte was one of the first dedicated. The first was in Rome in 1984. The plaque set in a small memorial area reads: "On August 26, 1944, the First Special Service Force composed of Americans and Canadians, took part in an audacious night attack. Aided by the courageous citizens of Villeneuve-Loubet, they liberated their town from the enemy. Later, in November, the Force returned for a different reason—for their dissolution on 5 December 1944. During the operations in Southern France, 66 men were killed and over 200 were wounded. It is to these valiant soldiers and the courageous citizens of Villeneuve-Loubet that this plaque is dedicated. First Special Service Force 27 May 1989." (Photograph courtesy of BG Edward Thomas, USAR (Ret))*

and special operations upon entering the five-story glass enclosed lobby, where two fully deployed parachutes are suspended. This history extends back to the Parachute Test Platoon where volunteers wearing old leather football helmets and modified jeaned fatigues first jumped in this newly created speciality. Continuing through World War II, in all theaters of operation; the Korean and Vietnam Wars up to the training and tactical concepts of the airborne and special operations soldier of the twenty-first century, the 23,000 square foot permanent gallery details legendary feats performed by these special men and women. Units, including glider-borne troops, no longer in existence, whose extraordinary sacrifices and service may have faded from memory are displayed, giving them the recognition they so richly deserve.

Special exhibitions are mounted quarterly in the temporary gallery. The Yarborough-Bank Theater features a fifteen-minute Vistascope film, "Descending from the Clouds." The film gives the visitor an introduction to modern airborne and special operations training. If a visitor wants to feel the virtual reality sensation of jumping from an airplane, the twenty-four-seat Pitch, Roll and Yaw Vista-Dome Motion Simulator will fit the bill by physically moving a specially designed seating area up to eighteen degrees in concert with a film. Located outside the museum on the six-acre site are memorial unit pedestal monuments as well as the Memorial Gardens, an area where individuals can purchase paver stones in recognition or in honor of a loved one.

Foreign Special Operations Forces Museums and Memorials

Above: *The Pointe du Hoe monument, dedicated to the 2d Ranger Battion, which assaulted the cliffs during the World War II Normandy Invasion in June 1944. (Normandy Visitor's Bureau, France)*

Foreign Memorials

First Special Service Force Tablets, Italy, and Southern France

Beginning in 1984, with the fortieth anniversary of the Force entering Rome, the First Special Service Force has been mounting tablets along its passage through Italy to France. In Italy, the Force memorials are located in Anzio, Artena, Cori, Mignano-Monte Lugo, and Rome. Nine tablets have been placed in France: Cagnes-sur-Mer, Castellar, Castillon, Grasse, La Turbie, Menton, Port Cros, Rocquebrune-cap-Martin, and Villeneuve-Loubet.

Above: *The First Special Force plaque at Grasse, France, was dedicated in 1991 by a Force delegation and members of the French resistance. It is located on a retaining wall on Route Napoleon above the city. (Photo courtesy of BG Edward Thomas, USAR (Ret))*

Pointe du Hoc Federal Monument, Normandy, France

Located on a cliff eight miles west of the Normandy American Cemetery overlooking Omaha Beach, this monument was erected by France to honor elements of the 2d Ranger Battalion, commanded by Lieutenant Colonel James E. Rudder, who scaled, seized, and secured the 100-foot cliff against determined German counterattacks. It consists of a simple granite pylon atop a concrete bunker with inscriptions in French and English on tablets at its base. Turned over to the American government in 1979 for care and maintenance in perpetuity, this thirty-acre battle-scarred area remains much as it was on 8 June 1944.

Jedburgh Memorial, Peterborough Cathedral, England

On 21 May 1996, the Dean The Very Reverend Michael Bunker dedicated a memorial to the OSS Jedburghs with these words: "We meet today to give thanks for the work and witness of the Jedburghs during the Second World War, in word and music to recall the gifts of friendship and comradeship; to commend to God's loving mercy all those who gave their lives and whose names are recorded on the memorial tablet in the Sprite Chapel in this Cathedral Church. . . . The small band of three hundred volunteers recruited from the armed forces of Britain, America, and France with a small contingent from the Netherlands, Belgium, and Canada bear their own witness to a call to every person to work for peace and justice."

The Kachin Cultural Center, Mytikyina, Burma

In 1990, members of the OSS Detachment 101 (Det 101) Association determined that they not only wanted to preserve their history here in the United States, they also wanted to do something in Burma as a tribute to the indigenous tribesmen that were invaluable to them against the Japanese in World War II. After donating their memorabilia to the JFK Special Warfare Museum, they focused on developing projects in support of the Kachin culture. First, they reprinted and distributed Kachin and Jingpaw translations of books dealing with agriculture, health, and education basics to the tribes; but this only whetted their appetite to do more. The result is a living memorial known as the Kachin Cultural Center. The two-story building of local and natural materials overlooks the Irrawaddy River housing a library, museum, school, and playground. Det 101 has provided monies to build the center, hire teachers, and buy equipment. Two statues of a U.S. soldier and a Kachin Ranger stand watch, surveying the jungles for

Members of OSS Detachment 101 work with Kachin militia, indigenous Burmese tribesmen, training them in guerilla techniques and American weaponry to fight the Japanese during World War II. (JFK Special Warfare Museum)

the Japanese, in front of the center as a testimony of the bond the two groups forged during World War II. Plaques commemorating the MARS Task Force, Merrill's Marauders, and the 10th U.S. Air Force, all participants in the China-Burma-India Theater and all forebearers of modern Special Operations units, encircle the statues.

101—Project Old Soldier (Crop Substitution Project)

Independent of the Kachin Cultural Center, but sponsored also by the OSS Veterans (not the Association), Project Old Soldier is another way for the veterans to pay back what they felt was unparalleled loyalty by Burma's indigenous populations. The project is a cooperative farming venture to convince local farmers to grow crops other than poppies used in the drug trade. Project Old Soldier provides monies for the field agents, stock, seeds, fertilizer, herbicide, and equipment needed to implement this program.

Foreign Museums

Canadian Airborne Museum, Petawawa CFB, Canada

The Canadian Force Base (CFB) Petawawa is home of the Canadian Airborne Museum, established in 1985. The museum serves as the base museum as well as that for the Canadian Airborne Forces. The collections of several Canadian units and that of the First Special Service Force are prominently displayed, their history illustrated by oversized photographs and full-scale dioramas. A vehicle park containing twenty-five various ground and air combat/transportation vehicles and equipment is located adjacent to the museum.

Carpetbagger Aviation Museum, Harrington, Northamptonshire, Great Britain

The Carpetbagger Aviation Museum was formed in 1993 for the fiftieth anniversary reunion of the U.S. Air Force's 801st/492d Bomb Group ("The Carpetbaggers"). Harrington served as the Office of Strategic Services (OSS) and Special Operations Executive (SOE) staging area from which to insert agents and supplies behind enemy lines in World War II Europe. Displays and exhibits depict the history of the airfield and vividly show the little-known role of the World War II special operations support.

First Special Service Force Memorial Ceremony in Artena, Italy 1991. One of five memorials placed in Italy, the plaque is mounted on the wall facing the upper piazza near Borghese palace. (Photograph courtesy of BG Edward Thomas, USAR (Ret))

Operation Iraqi Freedom

Operation Iraqi Freedom

Colonel John T. Carney, Jr., USAF (Ret)

Special Operations Forces, as seen through a night-vision lens, examine a .50-caliber machine gun as it is unloaded at an airfield in Northern Iraq. (U.S. Defense Department)

The war against Iraq in 2003 marked a transforming role for American Special Operations Forces. More than 10,000 SOF troops participated in Operation Iraqi Freedom. A few teams had infiltrated into and out of the country months before the war began, but most Special Operations teams entered Iraq on 19 March, two days before the ground offensive was launched.

Before the war, a senior Pentagon officer had likened Special Operations Command's highly-trained forces to a "Ferrari that's never been taken out of the garage," but Defense Secretary Donald R. Rumsfeld and Central Command's General Tommy Franks decided that SOCOM's units would play unprecedented roles in Iraqi Freedom, a full-up SOF road test equivalent to the Le Mans of modern warfare.

A disproportionate number of Special Operations troops were called to active duty for Iraqi Freedom from the Ready Reserves. Twenty-five percent of all 864,000 military personnel serving in all National Guard and Ready Reserve units were called up, but almost forty-two percent of Special Operations reservists—more than 7,000 of about 17,000 personnel from Army, Navy, and Air Force SOF Guard and Reserve units—were activated. The disproportionate SOF call-ups were understandable. Unlike conventional forces, SOCOM's units were engaged worldwide in the war on terrorism.

It took only about half as many U.S. forces to liberate Iraq in 2003, three U.S. divisions and an independent brigade organized in two corps forces plus one British division, as it did to free Kuwait in 1991, since Saddam Hussein's forces had been decimated in the first Gulf War. But Special Operations Forces took on more than twice as much of the burden in 2003 relative to the total coalition forces engaged in Iraq itself, roughly 154,000 troops. Special Operations Forces became responsible for almost three-fourths of the entire Iraqi theater of operations, an area roughly the size of California. They quickly seized airfields in southern, southwestern,

Above: *An Air Force Special Operations Command MH-53 Pave Low helicopter, assigned to the 352nd Special Operations Group, hovers at a strategic airfield located in the Kurd-controlled city of Mosul, Iraq. (U.S. Defense Department)*

Pages 312–313: *An Army Special Forces team trains at a staging base near Iraq under urban combat conditions in preparation for Operation Iraqi Freedom. On 10 April, Iraq's 5th Army Corps commander signed a cease-fire agreement with a coalition Special Operations commander and surrendered his forces to U.S. and Kurdish forces outside the town of Mosul, Iraq's third largest city. President Bush referred to the day as "a historic moment," but cautioned that the war was not over. (U.S. Defense Department)*

Above: *A special operations soldier mans a Mark 19 grenade launcher atop a Humvee as he and his team conduct a mounted patrol through the town of An Najaf, Iraq. (U.S. Defense Department)*

Above: *Over 300 Iraqi mortar rounds of Jordanian origin are disposed of in a large explosion by U.S. Army Special Forces and 26th Marine Expeditionary Unit personnel on the hillsides near Mosul, on 16 April 2003. (U.S. Defense Department)*

Above: *A special operations soldier sits on the bed of a Toyota Defender, or non-traditional tactical vehicle, near Mosul, in Northern Iraq. Similar vehicles were airlifted into Iraq during the pre-war operational deployment of Special Operations Forces. (Ruth Fremson, The New York Times)*

western, central, and northern Iraq, combed the deserts of western Iraq for Scud missile launch sites and to seal off Iraq's borders with Syria and Jordan, and operated throughout northern Iraq to help Kurdish freedom fighters liberate their homelands, seal the borders with Turkey, and decimate Iraqi forces in the north, where Saddam Hussein had positioned eleven of his seventeen divisions because he was expecting a major attack through Turkey and Iraqi Kurdistan.

Special Operations casualties were remarkably low, both in absolute and relative terms, considering their level of involvement in Operation Iraqi Freedom. Six Special Operations men were killed in action out of about 150 such fatalities overall, a fortuitous turning point in SOF fortunes. In the previous seven major military operations following the ill-fated Desert One rescue attempt in Iran in 1980, SOF, less than three percent of all military manpower, had accounted for 40 percent of everyone killed in action, more than thirteen times the casualty rate of conventional forces.

The Three-Week War

Operation Iraqi Freedom began on 19 March 2003 with two surprise attacks. One was a precise "decapitation attack" by cruise missiles and two F-117 stealth fighter bombers on a bunkered complex known as Dora

Farm on the southern edge of Baghdad, targeted as the probable location of Saddam Hussein and his two sons, Uday and Quasai. After the strike, an American operative on the ground there was reported to have said he observed what may have been the badly wounded Iraqi leader being loaded into an ambulance. The second attack was an operation by Navy SEALs and special boat teams to secure the FAW peninsula leading into the Persian Gulf.

As Defense Secretary Donald Rumsfeld later told American troops in a "town hall" meeting that he and Central Command's General Tommy Franks held with American troops in Doha, Qatar on 28 April, "While the Iraqi regime was waiting for General Franks to launch the air war, hundreds of Special Operations forces poured into all regions of the country, securing airfields, attacking terrorist facilities and regime targets, taking out the regime's capability to launch missiles and attack neighboring countries."

The campaign's ground offensive was launched at 6:00 a.m. on 21 March as the U.S. 3rd Infantry Division (Mechanized) and the 1st Marine Expeditionary Force rolled into southern Iraq from Kuwait while British forces attacked to seize and protect Iraq's southern oil fields and begin

Top, left: *Special Forces Lieutenant Colonel Kenneth Tovo, Commander of the Forward Operating Base 103, talks with ABC News reporter, Jim Scuitto. Marine General Peter Pace, Vice Chairman of the Joint Chiefs of Staff, paid special tribute to SOF's role in the war's success on ABC's 6 April "This Week," noting that "During this war, the Special Forces have done amazing feats of bravery." (U.S. Defense Department)*

Above: *Special Operations troops from Forward Operating Base 103 stand outside of a suspected chemical weapons facility in Iraq. (U.S. Defense Department)*

Above: *Special Forces soldiers prepare to fire mortars from Observation Point Red in support of Kurdish forces. Joint U.S.-Kurd operations were successful in preventing Iraqi troops in northern Iraq from moving towards Baghdad. (U.S. Defense Department)*

Left: *A local Iraqi woman thanks a civil affairs soldier as he distributes fliers on mine awareness in the neighborhoods of Kirkuk, Saddam Hussein's home town, in early April 2003. (U.S. Defense Department)*

Above: *Special Operations Forces soldiers stand at an observation point near Halabjah, Iraq. The Iraqi areas of operation held much terrain similar to that experienced in Operation Enduring Freedom in Afghanistan. (U.S. Defense Department)*

Above: *Special forces soldiers conduct reconnaissance with Kurdish leaders near Kirkuk, Iraq. Due to the actions of SOF teams and Kurdish soldiers, the hostile resistance in Hussein's home town was much less than anticipated. (U.S. Defense Department)*

their march on Basra, Iraq's second largest city. Sprung without the six-and-a-half-week-long preliminary bombing campaign that marked the early weeks of Operation Desert Storm to liberate Kuwait in early 1991, the audacious ground offensive caught Iraq's military off guard.

Within twenty-four hours, the U.S. 3rd Infantry had advanced almost 100 miles into Iraq on its 350 mile march to Baghdad, while Navy SEALs and coalition special forces teams seized Iraq's major gas and oil terminals near Rumalia in the northern Persian Gulf. British Royal Marines from 3 Commando Brigade worked with a fifty-six-man Polish special operations team to seize the key port city of Uum Qsar, an objective that was vital for delivering humanitarian aid to beleaguered Iraqis in Basra, Iraq's second largest city. The elite Polish unit, known as GROM (which stands for "thunder" and in Polish means Operational Mobile Response Group) was named after its commander in the first Gulf War, who had led a Polish unit into western Iraq to rescue a group of CIA operatives.

Meanwhile, Navy SEALs and a special boat team seized three oil terminals used for export through the Persian Gulf to make sure that Saddam could not repeat the ecological disaster that marked Operation Desert Storm when he opened a Kuwaiti oil spigot, polluted the gulf, and then set hundreds of oil wells ablaze in Kuwait. Only nine oil wells were torched in Iraqi Freedom, and all of those fires were extinguished by the end of April.

By day four, Special Operations troops quickly seized Tallil air base outside Nasiriyah and turned it into a refueling station for A-10 close air support planes, giving them at least one extra hour to cover advancing ground forces. By day five, General Tommy Franks said, "U.K., Australian, and U.S. Special Operations Forces [were] conducting direct action and strategic reconnaissance operations across the country. They're operating in small teams, very very mobile, going about their business from left to right and top to bottom [from West to East and from northern to southern Iraq]; and they're doing for us exactly what we want them to do. And they have accomplished some wonderful things out there."

While these operations were underway, on 25 March Army Rangers and other Special Operations Forces parachuted with troops from the 82nd Airborne Division onto the airfield known as H-2 in northwestern Iraq, giving coalition forces an immediate western front. Special Operations units were then able to comb the western desert for Scud missile launchers to preclude a repeat of Iraq's terrorist missile strikes against Israel in the early weeks of Desert Storm. H-2 also became a staging base for "direct action" missions against regime forces in Qa'im along the Syrian border, from where the largest number of Scud missiles had been launched against Israel in 1991.

On the night of 26 March, soldiers of the 173rd Airborne Brigade made a night drop onto Bashur airstrip in northern Iraq to open a second front with Special Operations Forces that had already been inserted into Kurdish-held territory. It was the first combat parachute assault ever made from wide-body C-17 transports, over 900 troops parachuting from fifteen C-17s escorted not by F-15 or F-16 fighter-bombers, but by side-firing AC-130 Special Operations gun ships. At the same time, Army Special Forces troops in northern Iraq joined Kurdish rebels in a successful attack

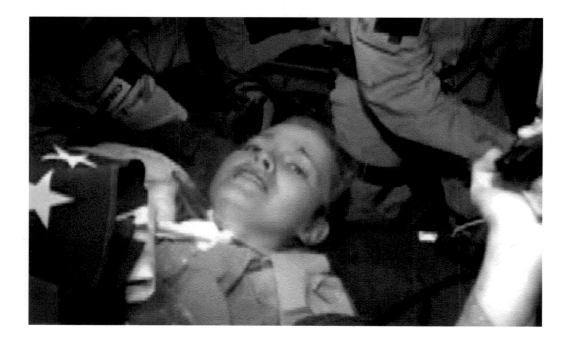

on a massive terrorist camp. By then, American Special Operations forces had seized five airfields in Iraq and, according to CENTCOM's deputy director of operations, were operating in "northern, southern, western, and central Iraq." Two weeks earlier, a small special operations team flew into An-Nasiriyah to destroy two paramilitary headquarters after another team had called in air strikes to destroy Ba'ath Party headquarters in As Samawa.

By 2 April, the 3rd Infantry Division had crossed the Euphrates River and closed to within thirty miles of Baghdad. U.S. Marines moved on the town of Kut and closed toward Baghdad from the southeast after crossing a canal and the Tigris River, while American Special Operations Forces mounted a raid by helicopter on the Tharthar Palace fifty-six miles outside Baghdad, a residence known to have been used by Saddam and his sons, while Special Forces teams worked with Kurdish militiamen to capture the northern town of Bardarash.

Above: *A special operations soldier keeps a watchful eye while on security detail with his M-4 rifle in An Najaf, Iraq, 18 April 2003. (U.S. Defense Department)*

By 4 April, SOF troops had prepared the way for lead elements of the 3rd Infantry to take over the entire Baghdad international airport and encircle the city. Three U.S. Special Operations troops were killed when a car bomb exploded near the Hadithah Dam on the Euphrates River, which they had begun securing to prevent flooding operations downstream near Karbala, while British troops clashed with irregular forces during a raid in Basra.

Special Operations teams soon undertook direct action missions to raid an Iraqi training camp near Haditha, and work with Kurdish forces to prevent movement of Iraqi forces from northern Iraq to Tikrit and Baghdad, and defeat an armored counter attack by tanks and armored personnel carriers. Over 900 of the 940 oil wells in the fields south of Baghad were now under coalition control, well over half all the 1,500 wells in Iraq.

All coherent resistance in Baghdad collapsed by April 9, only twenty days after coalition forces had entered Iraq; Saddam Hussein's control of Iraq was shattered as residents toppled icons of his Ba'ath Party and turned out in the streets.

On 11 April, SOF troops stopped a bus at a checkpoint in western Iraq with fifty-nine Iraqis carrying 630,000 U.S. dollars in $100 bills and letters offering rewards for killing American soldiers. That day, Central

Above: *Special Forces Lieutenant Colonel Kenneth Tovo, Commander, Forward Operating Base 103, conducts reconnaissance in Kirkuk, Iraq. (U.S. Defense Department)*

319

Top, left: *Special Operations Forces from Operations Detachment Alpha 083 pose for a group photo on 8 April 2003 in Iraq. Their specially modified Toyota Defender vehicle is visible at left. (U.S. Defense Department)*

Top, right: *Day One at the airport in Mosul, Army Special Forces Lieutenant Colonel Robert Waltemeyer, Commander of the Forward Operating Base 102 walks through the facility with Kurds and Arabs. (Ruth Fremson, The New York Times)*

Above, left: *Special Operations Forces soldiers guard an Iraqi prisoner in a makeshift prison at the Mosul airfield. (U.S. Defense Department)*

Above, right: *An Army Special Forces soldier directs local forces during a firefight outside a hospital in Mosul, Iraq. The support and training by Special Forces teams enabled the ready and willing of Kurdish troops the chance for victory against their Iraqi foes. (Ruth Fremson, The New York Times)*

Command issued its troops decks with fifty-five cards bearing photos and the names and positions of key Iraqi leaders who were wanted dead or alive. By 28 May, twenty-seven of them had surrendered or been taken into custody. The same day, SOF troops seized the Al Asad Airfield and found fifteen undamaged fighter planes hidden under camouflage.

President George W. Bush waited until 1 May to declare that "Major combat operations in Iraq have ended." Bush noted that in the nineteen months since the September 11, 2001 terrorist attacks on New York and Washington, "nearly one-half of al-Qaeda's senior operatives had been captured or killed"; but he cautioned that "we also have dangerous work to complete," noting that "As I speak, a Special Operations task force . . . is on the trail of the terrorists and those who seek to undermine the free government of Afghanistan."

Unique SOF Responsibilities

From the onset of Operation Iraqi Freedom, Special Operations Forces operated through four task forces or chains of command under U.S. Central Command's General Tommy Franks—Special Operations Command Central Command; Combined Joint Task Force West; Combined Joint Task Force North; and a Naval Special Warfare Task Group. All wielded

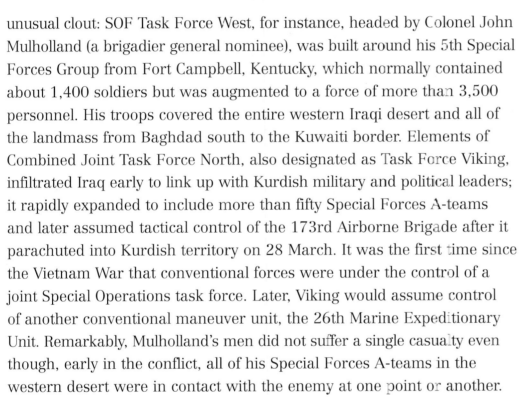

unusual clout: SOF Task Force West, for instance, headed by Colonel John Mulholland (a brigadier general nominee), was built around his 5th Special Forces Group from Fort Campbell, Kentucky, which normally contained about 1,400 soldiers but was augmented to a force of more than 3,500 personnel. His troops covered the entire western Iraqi desert and all of the landmass from Baghdad south to the Kuwaiti border. Elements of Combined Joint Task Force North, also designated as Task Force Viking, infiltrated Iraq early to link up with Kurdish military and political leaders; it rapidly expanded to include more than fifty Special Forces A-teams and later assumed tactical control of the 173rd Airborne Brigade after it parachuted into Kurdish territory on 28 March. It was the first time since the Vietnam War that conventional forces were under the control of a joint Special Operations task force. Later, Viking would assume control of another conventional maneuver unit, the 26th Marine Expeditionary Unit. Remarkably, Mulholland's men did not suffer a single casualty even though, early in the conflict, all of his Special Forces A-teams in the western desert were in contact with the enemy at one point or another.

Special Operations work was "more extensive in this campaign than in any I have seen," according to Army Major General Stanley McChrystal, deputy director of operations for the Joint Staff and the Pentagon's military spokesman for the war. "It's probably the most effective and widest use of Special Operations Forces in recent history, clearly. Probably, as a percentage of the effort, they are unprecedented for a war that also has a conventional part to it."

As an example of how fully U.S. Special Operations troops were committed in Iraq Freedom, Air Force Special Operations Command deployed seventy-three aircraft, according to Air Force Lieutenant General T. Michael "Buzz" Moseley, CENTCOM's combined air forces component commander. That represented almost fifty-seven percent of AFSOC's entire force at a time when the command's "low-density, high-demand" assets were widely engaged elsewhere throughout the world. AFSOC's Iraqi Freedom component included twenty-six MC-130 Combat Talons,

Above, left: *Iraqi citizens gather for a town meeting in center of Mosul with Commander, Forward Operating Base 102, supported by members of the 26th Marine Expeditionary Unit. (U.S. Defense Department)*

Above: *Two children from Kirkuk examine fliers they received from the soldiers of the 96th Civil Affairs Battalion and the 9th Psyop Battalion, 20 April 2003. Sporadic fighting continued near Mosul and Kirkuk as part of the 173rd Airborne Brigade moved into Kirkuk, northern Iraq's oil rich city, after its Kurdish population took over and began looting the city. Much of their anger turned on a soda factory owned by Saddam's son, Uday. (U.S. Defense Department)*

Above: *Soldiers assigned to the 96th Civil Affairs Battalion and the 9th Psyop Battalion talk with local Iraqi children on 20 April 2003, as they distribute fliers on mine awareness in the neighborhoods of Kirkuk in support of Operation Iraqi Freedom. (U.S. Defense Department)*

Mansour Alkhareji, an Arabic interpreter from Kuwait and U.S. Army Major Katherine Womble speak with an An Nasariyah power plant manager about restoring power to the city on 11 April 2003. Major Womble, a civil affairs team leader with the 358th Civil Affairs Brigade (Army Reserve), is working with the plant manager to restore power back to the city of An Nasariyah. (U.S. Defense Department)

eight AC-130H/U gun ships, eight EC-130E Commando Solo broadcasting aircraft (only two of them, according to U.S. Special Operations Command) eight HC-130O Combat Shadow refueling tankers, and thirty-one MH-53J/M Pave Lowhelicopters. When Secretary Rumsfeld flew into Baghdad on 30 April, he used an MC-130E from the 919th Special Operations Wing of the Air Force Reserve at Duke Field, Florida.

AFSOC planes flew 3,711 unconventional warfare sorties in Iraqi Freedom, over fifteen percent of all 24,196 Air Force sorties flown. AFSOC EC-130Es from the 193rd Special Operations Wing of the Pennsylvania National Guard broadcast 306 radio and 304 television hours. Moseley's planes had dropped about 30-million psychological operations leaflets urging Iraqi soldiers to lay down their arms and surrender and civilians to stay in their homes to avoid collateral damage. The largest Joint Search and Rescue Center in history used fifty-eight Air Force Special Operations and rescue helicopters, including sixteen HH-60 dedicated Night Hawk rescue aircraft, and also used fourteen British Special Operations and rescue helicopters, to fly 191 sorties and fifty-five rescue missions, saving seventy-three lives. The Army's 160th Special Operations Aviation Regiment also sent eight AH-6 and seven MH-6 Little Birds, eighteen MH-60 Black Hawks, and fourteen MH-47s, to complement CENTCOM's air assets.

Special Operations Central Command

Special Operations Forces working on their own and in direct support of Operation Iraqi Freedom's conventional maneuver forces were commanded two general officers. One was Army Brigadier General Gary Harrell, Commander of Special Operations Command U.S. Central Command (SOCCENT). Harrell's Army Special Operations teams and Navy SEALs operated in and out of Baghdad, trying to pinpoint locations of Saddam Hussein's Ba'ath Party leadership before, during, and after the 3rd Infantry Division moved into the city from the south and the west and Marines entered from the southeast.

Harrell's command center in Doha, Qatar, was dubbed "the Ghetto." At one point, according to *Newsweek*, Harrell was watching a plasma screen where a blue icon (one of his Special Forces teams in northern Iraq advising some Kurdish forces) was surrounded by numerous red icons, signifying several Iraqi brigades about to attack. An aide asked Harrell if he realized the red dots represented thousands of Iraqi troops with tanks. Harrell shrugged calmly, "Yeah, I know" and said of his men, "They're doing OK." One of the Special Forces sergeants took out three Iraqi tanks with Javelin shoulder-fired missiles and his team finished off the attackers with shotguns.

Special Operations task forces deployed in Operation Iraqi Freedom were given responsibility for three fronts of the four-front war, operating with none of the embedded reporters assigned to the conventional Army and Marine units launched by U.S. Central Command toward Basra and Baghdad on 21 March. Inserted before the ground war was launched, on what CENTCOM commander General Tommy L. Franks later referred to as

Iraqi electronic surveillance vehicles disguised as a recreational vehicle and an ambulance seized near the Mosul airfield by special operations forces. (U.S. Defense Department)

"S Day," for Special Operations Day, they conducted clandestine and largely unheralded missions throughout the western desert between Jordan and Baghdad and in the northern plains and mountains bordering Syria and Turkey. They scoured the desert looking for mobile Scud missile launchers and Saddam's elusive weapons of mass destruction, while screening Iraq's 134-kilometer border with Jordan. Early on in the three-week war, Special Operations Forces had seized three airfields in the western and northern deserts, known as H-1, H-2, and H-3. Special Forces teams also patrolled the 605-kilometer border with Syria as well as the rolling plains and mountains along Iraq's 331-kilometer border with Turkey, keeping long-running animosities between Turks and Kurds from complicating the war. Early in the war, fewer than 100 Special Forces men worked with about 10,000 Kurd Peshmerga fighters to route Iraqi troops throughout northern Iraq.

Special Forces Lieutenant Colonel Paul Gallo (center) is surrounded by his Tiger Team, consisting of members of Special Operations civil affairs and psychological operations teams in Mosul. (U.S. Defense Department)

SOCOM's Lead War on Terrorism

Well before Operation Iraqi Freedom began, President Bush had signed an executive order that designated U.S. Special Operations Command as America's lead agency for the entire war on terrorism. Representative Porter J. Goss, the Florida Congressman who chairs the House Select Intelligence Committee, said on ABC's "This Week" on 19 May that the command's broad new charter clearly included sanctions for preemptive strikes. Thus, SOCOM's operational tempo mushroomed in 2003: in mid-May, for instance, it had more forces deployed overseas than at any time in the command's history. By that time, less than halfway through the year, SOCOM had deployed forces to 132 countries, compared to 150 countries in all of 2002. To equip it for those new responsibilities, Congress appropriated $25.5-million to build the command a new "war fighting center" next to its MacDill Air Force Base headquarters in Tampa, Florida.

An Army Special Forces warrant officer draws a battlefield sketch for reporters. As with other combat units, embedded journalists were deployed with Special Operations Forces. (U.S. Defense Department)

*To U.S. Special Operations Forces, past, present, and future.
They normally serve this great Nation as "Quiet Professionals" in peacetime
as well as war, but lay their lives on the line without question when
crucial missions require. Hard-bitten SOF General "Barbwire Bob" Kingston,
who made military history as a second lieutenant in 1950 when he took a
tiny task force to the Yalu River, wept after he read heroic deeds
depicted in these pages, then asked with wonderment,
"Where do we find men like these?"*

Authors and Editors

BENJAMIN SCHEMMER, a West Point, Ranger, and Airborne graduate, was an infantry officer in Germany, on the V Corps staff, and in the 5th Infantry Division. He commanded a California National Guard tank company; became Chief of Customer Liaison for Boeing's Military Aircraft Systems Division; Manager of Advanced Systems Planning for Boeing-Vertol; a consultant to Department of the Army; Director of Land Force Weapons Systems in the Office, Secretary of Defense; editor of *Armed Forces Journal International*; and editor-in-chief of *Strategic Review*. He wrote *The Raid* and coauthored (with retired USAF Colonel John T. Carney) *No Room For Error*.

JOHN T. CARNEY, Jr., (Colonel, U.S. Air Foce, Retired) a leader in the special operations community since the mid-1970s, commanded both Air Force and joint-service Special Operations units assigned to the Joint Special Operations Command, the Air Force Special Operations Command, and the United States Special Operations Command. Carney has been in the forefront of planning and tactical execution of special operations missions, including the Iranian hostage rescue mission in 1980 and operations in Grenada, Panama, Iraq, and Kuwait. He coauthored (with Benjamin Schemmer) *No Room For Error*. Carney is the President/CEO of the Special Operations Warrior Foundation, a non-profit organization that provides college scholarship grants to children surviving fallen special operations troops.

PETER J. SCHOOMAKER, (General, U.S. Army, Retired) commanded the United States Special Operations Command from 1997 to 2000. As Commander-in-Chief, he was responsible for all special operations forces of the Army, Navy, and Air Force special operations units, active, guard, and reserve. General Schoomaker retired in December 2000 with more than thirty years of service. He commanded special operations units and organizations at every rank from captain to general and participated in numerous combat operations including the 1980 Iranian hostage rescue attempt known as Desert One, Urgent Fury in Grenada, Just Cause in Panama, Desert Shield, and Desert Storm in Southwest Asia, Uphold Democracy in Haiti, and other special operations throughout Central and South America, Africa, the Middle East, Europe, and Asia. General Schoomaker is a Director of the Special Operations Warrior Foundation and the Chairman of the Special Operations Memorial Foundation.

JOHN M. COLLINS (Colonel, U.S. Army, Retired) began his 30-year military career as a private in 1942, labored the next 24 years as Senior Specialist in National Defense with the Congressional Research Service, and has been one of National Defense University's Distinguished Visiting Research Fellows since 1996. Colonel Collins' long-standing connections with topflight profes-

sionals throughout the U.S. Special Operations community helped him trace SOF trends from the 17th century to modern times on land, at sea, and in the air. He has authored twelve books and many magazine articles that cover a broad spectrum of military topics, including Special Ops.

JOHN GARGUS (Colonel, U.S. Air Force, Retired) was born in Czechoslovakia from where he escaped at the age of fifteen. Commissioned through AFROTC, he served as a navigator in the Military Airlift Command and in various Special Operations units. He flew in the Son Tay POW rescue attempt and participated in air operations planning for that mission. His non-flying assignments included Deputy Base Command at Zaragoza Air Base in Spain and at Hurlburt Field in Florida and a tour as Assistant Commandant of the Defense Language Institute. He retired in 1983 after serving as the Chief of USAF,s Mission to Colombia. Father of four, he has been married to Anita since 1958.

GEORGE R. WORTHINGTON (Rear Admiral ,U.S. Navy, Retired) was born in Louisville, Kentucky, and was commissioned from the U.S. Naval Academy in June 1961. His initial tour of duty was in destroyers with an early staff tour as Aide-de-Camp and Flag Lieutenant for a Flotilla Commander. He applied for Underwater Demolition Team training and graduated with Class 36 in December 1965. Following graduation he served as operations and executive officer in Underwater Demolition Team ELEVEN, completing two combat deployments to Vietnam. Worthington served command tours commensurate with rank with SEAL Team ONE, Inshore Undersea Warfare Group ONE (operating the Navy marine mammal program) and Naval Special Warfare Group ONE, responsible for west coast SEAL Teams and Special Boat Squadrons. He served as Naval Attaché in the American Embassy in Phnom Penh during the last days of the *Khmer Republic.* Staff tours included assignments with the Chief of Naval Operations as program sponsor for Naval Special Warfare, Chief of Staff for the Special Operations Command (Europe), in Stuttgart, Germany, and, as a Flag Officer, the Secretary of Defense as Deputy Assistant Secretary of Defense (Special Operations and Counter-terrorism). He commanded the Naval Special Warfare Command as his last active tour.

ROXANNE M. MERRITT is a true product of the US Army. Born in an Army dispensary in Baumholder, Germany, in 1952, she cost her mother Marie and her father, then Captain Robert L. Merritt a grand total of S13.25. During the next fifteen years, she followed her parents to different duty stations around the world. Vacations were spent visiting museums, castles,

historic places, and shrines of all faiths. Roxanne graduated from New Mexico State University, in 1974 with a degree in history and a minor in Art History. Four years later, she graduated from Texas Tech University with her master's in Museum Science. During the interim, she garnered experience working for the University of Texas at El Paso Centennial Museum; the U.S. Army Air Defense Artillery Museum, Fort Bliss, Texas; the North Truro Historical Society, North Truro, Massachusets; the Ranching Heritage Center, Lubbock, Texas; and Tennessee Valley Authority Land Between the Lakes, Golden Pond, Kentucky. A month after graduation at Texas Tech, Roxanne rejoined the U.S. Army family as a civil servant as Director of the U.S. Army 2d Armored Division Museum, the unit she had been born into a scant twenty-six years earlier. Her next assignment was with the U.S. Army Ordnance Museum at Aberdeen Proving Ground, Maryland, as weapons curator. She was blessed to have been chosen as Curator of the JFK Special Warfare Museum in early 1981. Knowing a good thing when she had it, she has remained. She lives with her father and her Australian Cattle Dog Belle in Fayetteville, North Carolina.

Index